HORROR

A Thematic History in Fiction and Film

DARRYL JONES

School of English, Trinity College Dublin

A member of the Hodder Headline Group
LONDON
Distributed in the United States of America by
Oxford University Press Inc., New York

For Margaret Robson and
Miss Morgan Elizabeth Hannah Jones, age 6, with love

First published in Great Britain in 2002 by
Arnold, a member of the Hodder Headline Group,
338 Euston Road, London NW1 3BH

http://www.arnoldpublishers.com

Distributed in the United States of America by
Oxford University Press Inc.,
198 Madison Avenue, New York, NY10016

British Library Cataloguing in Publication Data
A catalogue record for this book is available from the British Library

Library of Congress Cataloging-in-Publication Data
A catalog record for this book is available from the Library of Congress

ISBN 0 340 76252 7 (hb)
ISBN 0 340 76253 5 (pb)

2 3 4 5 6 7 8 9 10

Typeset in 10/12pt Sabon by Phoenix Photosetting, Chatham, Kent
Printed and bound in Great Britain by MPG Books, Bodmin, Cornwall

What do you think about this book? Or any other Arnold title?
Please send your comments to feedback.arnold@hodder.co.uk

Contents

Acknowledgements

Like most books on horror, I suspect, this one is the product of the best part of a lifetime's interest in the subject – decades of unsystematic research finally given a semblance of order. I should therefore like to begin by thanking my parents, Yvonne and Dewi Jones, and especially, for the reasons given in the Introduction, my mother. Thanks, Mam!

More recently, particular debts of gratitude are owed to my friend and colleague Nick Daly, for innumerable discussions and much good advice over several years; to John Exshaw, who knows more about Italian cinema than anyone, and without whom I would never have seen any cannibal movies; to Liz McCarthy for giving me such generous access to her superb collection of videos; and to Jenny McDonnell, my partner in crime in innumerable visits to watch sleazy films.

At Arnold, I should like to thank my editors, Elena Seymenliyska, for her consistent enthusiasm for the project, and Eva Martinez, for bringing it home with patience, tolerance and good humour.

Thanks also, big and small, to the following: Graham Allen, Terence Brown, Steve Cadman, Peter Cosgrove, Nick Curwin, Aileen Douglas, Pauline Gallagher, Nicholas Grene, Kate Hebblethwaite, Ernest Hebert, Rachel Heffernan, Bob Jones, Jarlath Killeen, Ed King, Oisín and Fionn McNeill, Stephen Matterson, Frances Namba, John Nash, Helen O'Connell, Jan Palmer, Maria Parsons, Amanda Piesse, Marie Mulvey Roberts, Ian Campbell Ross, John Scattergood, Jim Simpson, Kate Thomas, Grant Williams, and, collectively, to my students, past and present, who have taught me at least as much as I taught them.

My greatest debts of love and gratitude are acknowledged in the dedication of this book, to my wife Margaret, and to my daughter Morgan – who bravely watched *The Curse of Frankenstein* (from behind the sofa) and *Dracula – Prince of Darkness* (from underneath a cushion).

Introduction

Ban this sick filth!

In 1979, when I was 12 years old, we got our first video recorder. The local video store was a few hastily cleared shelves in Hurley's record shop, run by two middle-aged men, Archie and Cliff, who knew what the public wanted: a complete set of Clint Eastwood movies and an impressive array of modern horror films. Something in my mother had a great desire to watch these horrors, but she would not do so alone. My father had no intention of watching them – which left me. And so it was that over a number of rainy afternoons my idea of 'Watch with Mother' was redefined to include *The Exorcist*, *Halloween*, *The Hills Have Eyes*, *The Texas Chain Saw Massacre*, and *Zombie Flesh Eaters*. It was to prove an inspired piece of parenting, one for which I am eternally grateful, and without which this book could never have been written.

Many of these films were subsequently banned, victims of the Video Recordings Act of 1984. These were the notorious 'video nasties', films so noxious, so powerful, that the smallest glimpse of them could pervert, deprave, and corrupt the mind. In the early years of the Thatcher government, a Britain riven by social and economic divisions, by the deliberate and barbaric dismantling, in half a decade, of an industrial working-class culture dating back two centuries, a Britain which, it sometimes seemed, was perpetually on the brink of meltdown, riot and class warfare, was further perturbed – or distracted – by dire warnings about a society of murderers and rapists driven into a frenzy by viewing video nasties. 'I got the ideas for the rapes from a so-called video nasty,' young, unemployed rapist Martin Austin, convicted in June 1983 on two counts of rape and seven of burglary, is reported to have told the police: he had been watching *I Spit on Your Grave*. 'These films have helped destroy my son's life,' said his mother. 'They must be banned before another boy's mind is infected by them.' 'Fury Over The Video Rapist', ran the headline in the *Daily Mail*, which asked 'How many more women will be savaged and defiled by youths weaned on a diet of rape videos ... ', and worried that 'our children can continue to buy sadism from the video-pusher as easily – and as cheaply – as they can buy fruit gums from the sweetie-shop' (Kerekes and Slater 2000: 37–8). What was going on here? These were films I had watched with my mother! The kindly old gents who provided them, and who were also busy furnishing me with the beginnings of my beloved record collection – were they 'pushers', peddling depraved filth to the nation's youth? I was confused.

The video nasties controversy was a modern manifestation of an ongoing historical debate focusing on what might best be called the ethics of representation: what can or cannot be shown, and to what extent government should legislate to restrict the availability and dissemination, or even the production, of violent or otherwise transgressive documents. It is what we would now call the debate over violence in the media, and it is a debate in which the horror genre has long played an important and controversial part, going back, as we shall see, at least as far as the publication of Matthew Lewis's *The Monk* in 1796. Reviewing that novel the year after its publication, Samuel Taylor Coleridge believed it to be 'a romance, which if a parent saw in the hands of a son or daughter, he might reasonably turn pale' (Coleridge 1797: 197) (see Chapter 1 for more on this). Somewhere around this time, Jane Austen was beginning to write *Northanger Abbey*, a novel submitted (but not accepted) for publication in 1803, revised for publication shortly before her death in 1817, and finally published posthumously, with *Persuasion*, in 1818. In her 'Advertisement by the Authoress' to this revised edition, Austen wrote: 'The public are entreated to bear in mind that thirteen years have passed since it was finished, many more since it was begun, and that during that period, places, manners, books, and opinions have undergone considerable changes' (1972: 35). That is to say, by the time it was published in 1818, *Northanger Abbey*, set around 1798, was already an *historical* novel, beneath whose surface was detectable the upheavals of that very turbulent decade, the 1790s, when England was at war with France (a war which finally ended at Waterloo in 1815 – a recent memory for Austen in 1817), living under constant fear of French invasion, with rioting on the streets of London and other cities, and a full-blown political uprising in Ireland. As I shall argue, the Romantic Gothic novel of the 1790s is a direct product of this instability; but it is also, *Northanger Abbey* suggests, a literary form directly addressing an implied (and, historically, an actual) audience of adolescent girls, the novels which Catherine Morland and Isabella Thorpe devour to enliven, but also to interpret, their own lives. When Isabella recites to Catherine the list of Gothic novels she has collated for her to read – including *The Mysterious Warning*, *The Necromancer*, and *Horrid Mysteries*[1] – Catherine excitedly articulates her criterion for a good read: 'but are they all horrid, are you sure they are all horrid?' Yes, says Isabella, they are all horrid, rest assured (or ill-at-ease): she knows this because her 'particular friend … a Miss Andrews, a sweet girl, one of the sweetest creatures in the world, has read every one of them' (Austen 1972: 61). What kinds of books are these, with their abductions, rapes, incest, imprisonments, and putrefying corpses, for the sweetest girls in the world to read? Modern studies of the audience for horror fiction and, especially, film, have all concluded that this audience is predominantly adolescent, and comprised of both sexes in more-or-less equal numbers (see, for example, Twitchell 1985; Dika 1987; Clover 1992). James B. Twitchell, for example, has posited something like an arterial connection between horror and adolescence:

> Anthropologists, sociologists and psychologists all agree [that] the primary concern of early adolescence is the transition from individual and isolated sexuality to pairing and reproductive sexuality. It is a concern fraught with unarticulated anxiety and thus ripe for horror. And so it is here, with the audience, with *this* audience, not with the myth, that any study of horror should begin. ... For the first time in life the early adolescent has the biological capacity to reproduce; now all that is needed is knowledge. There is nothing more frightening that power without knowledge, unless it be knowledge without control. ... Horror monsters may frighten, but that is partly because they are acting out the desires that we fear. When they do come out at nighttime, as monsters always do, they must move around using a body so full of power and yet lacking in control.
>
> (1985: 68–9)

Indeed, as Chapter 5 will argue, the career of the most successful horror-writer of all, Stephen King, would be unthinkable without this connection between horror and adolescence.

One of the unexpectedly beneficial effects of legislation such as the Video Recordings Act was that it has forced those of us on what might be termed the 'liberal' side of the debate – the anti-censorship lobby, fans of the genre, some (but by no means all) academics working in the humanities and social sciences – to formalize and clarify our own thinking and arguments on the subject. It seems, for example, intuitively obvious to me that blame, where it is to be apportioned in cases such as that of Martin Austin, might just as plausibly be laid at the feet of a government which had created a climate of unemployment, alienation, disenfranchisement and hopelessness, as at the makers, distributors or sellers of *I Spit on Your Grave*, however repellent I may find that film. At the very least, one should recognize that patterns of cause and effect are complex, and thus require complex responses, where necessary, of legislation and blame, and are certainly not well served by media frenzies or witch hunts.

But media frenzies and witch hunts were what we got in 1983–4, and then again a decade later with the Jamie Bulger murder case and the controversy over what role, if any, the film *Child's Play 3* might have had in his death. This case, of a three year old led away from a shopping centre and murdered by two ten year olds, was appalling, tragic, and terrifying, and should have been handled with the utmost sensitivity. It was not. The culpability in law of the killers, Jon Venables and Robert Thompson, hinged on whether or not they were considered, as minors, to have been aware of the implications of their actions: whether or not, as it was expressed, they could properly distinguish between 'good' and 'evil'. For what it's worth, my own feeling is that that the boys probably *could* have made such a distinction, and *were* aware of the implications of their action, though not, I suspect, its full enormity. But my own feelings are irrelevant here: what matters is that there was and remains some real measure of doubt on this issue, and thus over the boys' culpability. However, their daily appearances in court were accompanied by what can only be described as a lynch mob. 'Baying for blood' is the usual, melodramatic description for the behaviour of such a mob, and in this instance it is not entirely inappropriate. This is an issue of extreme delicacy and emotiveness, but here I only want to note that there are, sad to say, a great many *adult* killers of children, whose culpability in law is unambiguous, not open to *any* doubt; they are not, usually, the focus for such a mob, and certainly not with the degree of relentlessness shown here. What happened, it seems, is that onto the tragic but cloudy story of Venables and Thompson was mapped an *a priori* interpretive model which then governed responses. This model was the trope of the Demon Child: the killers were Evil Incarnate.

Produced in the wake of the Bulger case, the Newson Report of April 1994 contributed directly to the amendment of the Criminal Justice Bill in June of that year, making provision for much tougher censorship of videos. Martin Barker, one of the most consistent critics of simplistic or sensationalist accounts of 'media violence', has offered a powerful critique of the ways in which legitimate concerns about the relationship between representations of violence and violence itself are almost invariably mishandled by the press, the police, the courts, and the legislature:

> The aftermath of the murder of James Bulger in Liverpool gave a huge fillip to the prosecution case against TV, film and video. At the trial, the judge speculated on what might have prompted the killing. He wondered if there wasn't a connection with violent videos. He didn't mention any particular films, but the press had been primed, and one film, *Child's Play 3*, became their target. However, it soon became clear that, despite police efforts, there was not a scrap of evidence that the boys had watched the film. Did this failure produce retractions of the claim? Did any of the newspapers, or [David] Alton, or the other campaigners, admit they had been wrong? Not one. So urgent is the wish to find such a link, it seems, that when an exemplar like this falls apart the response is simply to carry on.
> (Barker 2001b: 28)

Alas, it is, and *Child's Play 3* was banned anyway. This seems to me to be a clear case of scapegoating: it is easier, quicker, and cheaper to 'blame' such a tragedy on an 'evil' film, or on an 'evil' genre, than it is to reform social services, welfare, or education legislation. This may sound like a classic liberal's lament – Society Is To Blame – and I acknowledge, again, that these are complex issues in which individual responsibility must, like social and political responsibility, play some part. I said earlier that it seemed to me 'intuitively obvious' that government policy was more likely to have an adverse effect on the individual psyche than horror movies. This is a hunch, and probably unproveable: what *has* been demonstrated, again and again, by studies in the field is that there is *no* conclusive evidence of a direct causal link between 'media violence' and real acts of violence. Rather, audiences respond to representations of violence in complex and often sophisticated ways (Barker 2001a). That is to say, responses to screen violence are not simply Pavlovian, in the way that pro-censorship campaigners and legislators implicitly assume, but are conditioned, even in children, by an awareness of *genre*. Though one cannot, then, definitively say that governments are to blame for the violent behaviour of citizens, one *can* say, with absolute certainty, that legislation on the censorship of 'video nasties' was based entirely on unexamined *a priori* assumptions and prejudices.

One of the implicit assumptions which underlies much thinking on 'media violence' is based on a class prejudice which, if stated directly, would be considered unacceptable and offensive. As Julian Petley has demonstrated, what often motivates the thinking of censors and pro-censorship campaigners is the belief that while 'we' (the middle classes) are sufficiently educated, secure, cultured and intelligent to interpret and contextualize what we see or read, 'they' (the working class) are not, and should not therefore be exposed to such extreme or transgressive documents, *especially* given their extant propensity to violence. A high-ranking official of the British Board of Film Classification famously remarked to *The Guardian*'s film critic Derek Malcolm that 'it is all very well for sophisticated, educated people like you to go to the ICA cinema and see Warhol's *Trash*. But think of its effect on your average factory worker in Manchester.' The BBFC's deputy director, Ken Penry, said of Abel Ferrara's *Driller Killer*:

> now and again you get clever dicks who say, 'Ah, this is art. This is bigger than it seems.' But I think of Joe Bloggs who's going to the Odeon on Saturday night who's not on that wavelength. He's going along seeing it literally and I always keep that in mind. Joe Bloggs is the majority and film censorship is for the majority.
>
> (Petley 2001: 175, 177)

Implicit in this kind of thinking is an insidious modern version of the social Darwinism we will see several times during the course of this study: the working class need to be prevented from viewing certain films because they are insufficiently educated and civilized to view them 'properly'; such films will bring out their inherent propensity for violence; this is because they are essentially bestial, 'less evolved' and therefore less fully human than we are. No one will admit to holding such views, of course, and yet so pervasive are these kinds of assumptions that they are even there, beneath the surface, in some of the research whose methods and conclusions Barker quotes with approval, such as the findings of Philip Schlesinger that:

men's perceptions and judgements of violent media were based
on *the rules and standards of the groups and communities to
which they belonged.* So, the street-fighting was judged
'ordinary' and in fact exciting by those men whose lives
included the kinds of relationships and risks that fairly easily
lead to such fights.

(Barker 2001a: 5)

Not, that is to say, middle-class academics. By the same token, Nicole Ward
Jouve's *'The Streetcleaner': The Yorkshire Ripper Case on Trial*, a generally
admirable and sometimes brilliant attempt by a feminist academic to
contextualize and understand the Yorkshire Ripper murders and the
repeated failure of the police to catch the murderer Peter Sutcliffe, was
perhaps fatally flawed by its author's almost total inability to understand or
sympathize with working-class masculinity, which came very close to
arguing that being a working-class man by definition made you want to go
out and murder women (Jouve 1986).

In part, this is a modern version of an ongoing suspicion among
intellectuals regarding what Louis James (1963) called 'fiction for the
working man', a term which I would want to recast as the more inclusive
'working-class culture', or 'popular culture'. Richard Hoggart's *The Uses of
Literacy* (1958), one of the great foundational texts of modern cultural
studies by an archetypal English working-class intellectual, warns of the
damaging effects of exposure to the wrong kinds of popular fiction:

> Since nothing is demanded of the reader, nothing can be given
> by the reader. We are in the pallid half-light of the emotions
> where nothing shocks or startles or sets on edge, and nothing
> challenges, or gives joy, or evokes sorrow; neither splendour
> nor misery: only the constant trickle of tinned milk-and-water
> which staves off a positive hunger and denies the satisfactions
> of a solidly-filling meal.

(Hoggart 1958: 237)

Hoggart's thinking here is in part a reflection of the influence of the previous
generation of thinkers on popular culture, particularly F.R. Leavis's *Mass
Civilization and Minority Culture* (1930) and Q.D. Leavis's *Fiction and the
Reading Public* (1932). These in turn were influenced by the great cultural
arbiter of the early twentieth century, T.S. Eliot, who did more than any
other individual to promote the idea of a canon of great literature as the
central plank of culture. There was another side to Eliot, however, who
wrote approvingly on Victorian and Edwardian popular culture, on the
music hall artiste Marie Lloyd, and on the decidedly populist Charles
Dickens. A generation earlier, in the last years of the nineteenth century, the
distinctions between 'high' and 'popular' culture blur further still, as

Nicholas Daly (1999) has argued, presenting a cultural landscape in which writers as ostensibly different from one another as Bram Stoker, H.G. Wells, Robert Louis Stevenson, Henry James, Joseph Conrad, and H. Rider Haggard coexisted (and sometimes collaborated) relatively happily.

Besides, the imperatives of institutions of power and authority which seek to regulate cultural production can themselves often be complex and contradictory. The making and reception of *The Exorcist* provides a good example of this. William Friedkin's film shocked and horrified many viewers when it was first released in 1973. The Reverend Billy Graham condemned it, declaring that 'there was an evil embodied in the very celluloid of the film' (Kermode 1998: 45). The film was banned in the UK and Ireland in the wake of the video nasties scandal of the early 1980s, and not subsequently given a video release until the late 1990s. *The Exorcist* was also banned elsewhere, including Tunisia, where it was seen as 'unjustified propaganda in favour of Christianity' (Kermode 1998: 87). If anything, the Tunisian government's response seems more rational than that of its British counterpart. This notorious film was made with the full blessing and connivance of the Catholic Church, and featured a number of Jesuit priests as actors, one of whom, Father Thomas Bermingham, SJ, was also the film's technical advisor on matters of religion. The film had audiences, those very audiences whom it so disturbed and terrified, dashing out of cinemas and into the nearest church, convinced of the literal existence of the Devil and therefore with a newly rejuvenated faith in Christianity. The increase in applications for the priesthood in the mid-1970s is directly attributable to *The Exorcist*: it was, in the words of Mark Kermode, 'the greatest advert for Catholicism that the world has ever seen'. Looking back on the making of the film in 1998, Father William O'Malley, SJ, who played Father Dyer, could even justify the film's most notorious image, that of young Regan MacNeil masturbating with a crucifix: 'It *was* merited. ... It served a purpose.'[2]

Given this history of unexamined prejudices and contradictions, the conclusion that suggests itself to me here is that the impulse to ban films such as *The Exorcist* was ultimately not predicated on moral or ideological grounds, since these grounds did not exist; rather, these films were banned for aesthetic reasons. That is, political decisions were made on *matters of taste*, based on the conservative aesthetic belief that it is the function and purpose of art to reinforce and reassure, to comfort and to confirm what we already know, rather than to question our assumptions, to shock, to confront, or to overturn. But taboos are there to be transgressed, so let's see what we can do about these beliefs ...

Notes

1. Austen here provides a list of genuine Gothic novels, all published in the 1790s, see Sadleir (1927).
2. Both quotations from *The Fear of God: 25 Years of the Exorcist* (BBC TV 1998).

|1|

Hating others

Religion, nationhood and identity

The Monk, Romantic Gothic, and Britishness

Modern Britain was conceived in horror. The development of the Gothic novel, and thus of modern horror fiction, in English, in the second half of the eighteenth century, coincides with (is both a component and a by-product of) the period of the formation of a British national identity.[1] Modern nations can be understood, to use Benedict Anderson's famous phrase, as 'imagined communities', potentially disparate political, cultural and ethnic groupings willed into unity by acts of imagination, articulated through narrative, myth and symbol (Anderson 1991). National identities are often formed oppositionally, that is in a Self—Other relationship to a (usually neighbouring) rival nation, which is made to embody all that is venal, reprehensible, archaic, or otherwise rejected. For Britain, this vilified Other was France. Over the course of a 'long eighteenth century', from 1689 to 1815, Britain and France were at war on seven different occasions and for a total of some fifty-two years – though, as Linda Colley has noted, it is perfectly possible to view these as one extended war, 'less a series of separate and conventional wars, than one peculiarly pervasive and long-drawn out conflict which rarely had time to become a cold war in the twentieth-century sense' (Colley 1992: 3).

Colley further suggests that the major identifying feature of British national identity at the time was *Protestantism*.[2] Certainly the Gothic novel is collusive in this enterprise, shoring up the British, Protestant identity of its readers chauvinistically, through its presentation of a catalogue of caricatured untrustworthy foreigners. These were usually Catholic Europeans, either actually French, like the Marquis de Montalt in Ann Radcliffe's *The Romance of the Forest* (1791) (this trope is still going strong even as late as 1864 in the person of the grotesque French governess,

Madame de la Rougierre, in Sheridan Le Fanu's *Uncle Silas*), or else Italians like Manfred in Horace Walpole's *The Castle of Otranto* (1765) and Schedoni in Ann Radcliffe's *The Italian* (1797), or Spaniards like Ambrosio in Matthew Lewis's *The Monk* (1796), who had the status, as it were, of metaphorical Frenchmen. (One of the reasons the British could afford to be so hawkishly antagonistic towards their European neighbours is because, as an island nation, and one which furthermore was not invaded during the period, their main defence was naval; thus, not requiring a conscripted army to fight its eighteenth-century wars, Britain could indulge in militaristic behaviour without risking the mass slaughter of its citizens.) Furthermore, the 1790s, the great decade both of political unrest in England and also (and consequently) of the great flowering of the Romantic Gothic novel in Radcliffe and Lewis, was also a decade of great agitation for Catholic emancipation, perceived by many as yet another threat to a Protestant British identity.

The Marquis de Sade's famous description of the Gothic novel (writing in 1800, he was thinking particularly of Lewis's *The Monk*) as 'the necessary fruit of the revolutionary tremors felt by the whole of Europe' (Sade 1990: 49) seems to me to be doubly significant in this context, as not only is Sade referring to what has become a traditional conception of the Gothic novel as an ideologically and aesthetically radical or revolutionary form in which societal taboos are examined and violated (that is certainly what Sade himself was about, and – if his aim was not simply to make money through sensation and exploitation – may have been what Lewis was doing too), but also to the ways in which the systems, not only of thought and identity but ultimately of power and government, which were to shape late eighteenth-century political history insinuate themselves into Gothic novels. Furthermore, there is a sense in which the non-mimetic, non-realist modes of the fantastic, the Gothic, and the grotesque, working through symbolic acts of inversion and indirection, were the *only* aesthetic media with which to represent or respond to current events. Thus, by imaging forth the European Other as Catholic, superstitious, barbarous, irrational, chaotic, rooted in the past, the Gothic novel allowed a British audience conversely to identify itself as Protestant, rational, ordered, stable, and modern: Continental Europe is the domain of fantastic unreality, whereas England is rooted in contemporary realism. Symbolically, the further one gets from a stable centre-point, the further back in time (and into a barbarous past) one moves. A century after de Sade and Lewis, in Bram Stoker's *Dracula* (1897), Jonathan Harker, travelling across Europe by train to meet the Count in Transylvania, famously records the breakdown of modern technology on his journey:

> I had to hurry breakfast, for the train started a little before eight, or rather it ought to have done so, for after rushing to the station at 7.30 I had to sit in the carriage for more than an

hour before we began to move. It seems to me that the further
East you go, the more unpunctual are the trains. What ought
they to be in China?

(Stoker 1997: 10–11)

Thus, in Jane Austen's *Northanger Abbey* (1818, but first written, and
set, around 1798), Henry is able to admonish Catherine's Gothic
'fantasizing' – that Northanger is a Gothic castle; that General Tilney is a
Radcliffean villain who has murdered his wife – by emphasizing that such
things simply do not happen here and now, in modern England:

> Dear Miss Morland, consider the dreadful nature of the
> suspicions you have entertained. What have you been judging
> from? Remember the country and the age in which we live.
> Remember that we are English, that we are Christians. Consult
> your own understanding, your own sense of the probable, your
> own observation of what is passing around you – Does our
> education prepare us for such atrocities? Do our laws connive
> at them. Could they be perpetrated without being known, in a
> country like this, where social and literary intercourse is on
> such a footing; where every man is surrounded by a
> neighbourhood of voluntary spies, and where roads and news-
> papers lay every thing open? Dearest Miss Morland, what
> ideas have you been admitting?
>
> (Austen 1972: 199–200)

What Henry is insisting on here is England as a stable, modern, lawful
'imagined community', though admittedly this view is not presented
unproblematically by the novel (which, as a product of its time, alludes to
the national paranoia of the 1790s, fears not only of an invasion from
without, by France, but of insurrection from within, and of riots on the
streets of London). Chastened, Catherine acknowledges that 'Her visions of
romance were over', and realizes that her mistake has been in judging
English (for reasons I shall examine below, *Northanger Abbey* does not
admit of a Britishness) behaviour by the notoriously questionable standards
of Europeans:

> Charming as were all of Mrs Radcliffe's works, and charming
> even as were the works of all her imitators, it was not in them
> perhaps that human nature, at least in the midland counties of
> England, was to be looked for. Of the Alps and Pyrenees, with
> their pine forests and their vices, they might give a faithful
> delineation; and Italy, Switzerland and the South of France
> might be as fruitful in horrors as they were represented.
>
> (Austen 1972: 201–2)

A howlingly hysterical novel by almost any standards, Matthew Lewis's *The Monk* moves from taboo to taboo in a narrative dynamic of pure excess – part of the interest of the novel is in seeing the ways in which Lewis manages to top the extraordinarily lurid scene he has just presented with another even more extraordinarily lurid scene. Heaping excess on excess, there is a real sense in which the novel cannot end other than it does, by having Satan himself intercede to close the proceedings by tearing the protagonist limb from limb. The novel allows its readers vicariously to indulge in what must be called an Anglican's wet-dream (if Anglicans have wet-dreams) of Catholicism: homoeroticism, blasphemy, nuns, transvestitism, Satanism, rape, murder, incest, and necrophilia – these are apparently the things that Catholics (and foreigners!) do.

The Monk, then, lays the blame for the crimes and perversions it so gleefully presents squarely at the door of the Catholic church. Unambiguously, it is stated that, while Amrosio's talents and energies have made him an excellent man of the world, they have made him a lousy man of the cloth: 'Had his Youth been passed in the world, He would have shown himself possessed of many brilliant and manly qualities ... He would have been an ornament to his Country'; he is, however, orphaned and placed in the care of the church, where 'His Instructors carefully repressed those virtues, whose grandeur and disinterestedness were ill-suited to the cloister. Instead of universal benevolence He adopted a selfish partiality for his own particular establishment: He was taught to consider compassion for the errors of Others as a crime of the blackest dye' (Lewis 1973: 236–7). Ambrosio succumbs to a fatal combination of Mariolatry and enforced celibacy, becoming strangely drawn simultaneously to a portrait of the Madonna which he has been given, and which he treats as fetish or erotic icon, and to a young novice monk, Rosario. Rosario turns out not to be a monk but a woman, Matilda; furthermore, Matilda was the original for the portrait of the Madonna, painted specifically to attract Ambrosio's attention. I think we can say with absolute certainty that Matthew Lewis was no Mary Wollstonecraft, and *The Monk*'s view of women is pretty far from being an enlightened one, though this is only to say that it offers a traditionally Christian, dualist view of women as pure soul and corrupt body – proverbially as virgin and whore, with virginity as the symbolic dividing line. Following a scene, again deeply symbolic, in which Matilda miraculously survives the deadly bite of a serpent (the 'Cientipedoro'), Ambrosio succumbs to his carnal desires, but, in accordance with the old dialectic of desire and repulsion, is thereafter quickly revolted by Matilda, who is revealed at the novel's close not to have been a woman at all, but a limb of Satan (such are sexualized women in this novel), a demon placed with the explicit purpose of seducing Ambrosio. Having once succumbed to temptation, there is no stopping Ambrosio, whose next target is Antonia, desirable precisely because of her chastity, representative of course of 'purity' and 'innocence'. He makes a Satanic pact that he may gratify his desire for her; drugged and imprisoned in a tomb, Ambrosio rapes Antonia, and immediately afterwards rhetorically images her in terms both of sorcery and, even more strikingly, of dead female flesh, rotten meat:

> Wretched Girl, you must stay here with me! Here amidst these lonely Tombs, these images of Death, these rotting loathsome corrupted bodies! ... What seduced me into crimes, whose bare remembrance makes me shudder? Fatal Witch! was it not thy beauty? Have you not plunged my soul into infamy? Have you not made me a perjured Hypocrite, a Ravisher, an Assassin!
> (Lewis 1973: 385)

This linking of the unchaste woman and decaying flesh is reiterated at the novel's close, with the climax of the narrative of Agnes, the seduced nun who gives birth in a dungeon and is discovered clutching her baby's decomposing corpse.

The Monk opens by charging the entire population of Madrid with ungodliness, presenting their religion as mere outward show (to be contrasted with the private, inward virtue with which Protestants liked to associate themselves). Ambrosio, like Dracula, Svengali and a host of other untrustworthy foreigners, exercises a sinister, mesmerizing control over his audience: 'All found their attention irresistibly attracted while He spoke' (Lewis 1973: 18). The entire long opening scene presents a grotesque version of Catholic oratory and worship, based on rhetoric, ritual, and the force of authority: religion as performance rather than substance (the reader is given only the vaguest account of what Ambrosio actually *says*, which doesn't matter anyway as the audience pays no attention to his words, but rather is captivated by his presence). The sinister, manipulative monk is of course the staple figure of Protestant anti-monastic literature of the period. Even more strikingly than Ambrosio, it is Schedoni, the villainous monk of Ann Radcliffe's *The Italian* (1797) – which was written as a direct response to Lewis's novel – who best embodies this, and is represented as pure, malevolent charisma: 'his eyes were so piercing that they seemed to penetrate, at a single glance, into the hearts of men, and to read their most secret thoughts; few persons could support their scrutiny, or even endure to meet them twice'.

Schedoni is, in fact, a perfect embodiment of British anti-Catholic thinking:

> The elder brothers of the convent said that he had talents, but denied him learning; they applauded him for the profound subtlety which he occasionally discovered in argument, but observed that he seldom perceived the truth when it lay on the surface; he could follow it through all the labyrinths of disquisition, but overlooked it, when it was undisguised before

him. In fact he cared not for truth, nor sought it by any bold
and broad argument, but loved to exert the wily cunning of his
nature in hunting it through artificial perplexities. At length,
from a habit of intricacy and suspicion, his vitiated mind could
receive nothing for truth, which was simple and easily
comprehended.

(Radcliffe 1968: 35, 34)

Schedoni here represents a Catholic theology of 'subtlety', 'wily cunning',
'artificial perplexities', and 'labyrinths of disquisition': devious rhetoric as
opposed to the 'simple and easily comprehended' revealed 'truth' of
Protestantism. Of course, as the phrase 'labyrinths of disquisition' suggests,
what Radcliffe primarily does through Schedoni is to introduce a version of
that most powerful Catholic bogeyman of the Protestant imagination, the
Inquisitor, demonically twisting the truth in the name of a sadistic dogma
masquerading as piety.

Though they presented the Spanish Inquisition as an institution rooted in
a barbaric past from which enlightened Protestant Europe had thankfully
escaped, writers of anti-Catholic Gothic such as Lewis and Radcliffe knew
also that it was still in operation, and still empowered to execute heretics.
The Inquisition was not formally abolished until 1834, and their last
execution (of a schoolteacher named Cayetano Ripoll, for deism) was
performed as late as 1826.[3] In Charles Maturin's ferociously anti-Catholic
Melmoth the Wanderer, the Spaniard Monçada, forced against his will into
a monastic life and finally imprisoned in the dungeons of the Inquisition,
notes a history of ongoing atrocities: 'Examination followed examination
with a rapidity unexampled in the annals of the Inquisition. Alas! That they
should be *annals*, – that they should be more than records of *one day* of
abuse, falsehood, and torture' (Maturin 1968: 234). Both Ambrosio and
Schedoni end up as victims of the institution which has been the source of
their power throughout the novels. Like several of Radcliffe's novels, *The
Italian* closes with a trial scene, in which the truth finally triumphs over
falsehood and casuistry. Schedoni poisons himself and drops dead in the
middle of the courtroom. At the close of *The Monk*, Ambrosio, who is
tortured by Inquisitors 'Determined to make him confess not only the
crimes which He had committed, but also those of which He was innocent',
is left with 'dislocated limbs, the nails torn from his hands and feet, and his
fingers mashed and broken by the pressure of screws' (Lewis 1973: 424,
425).

Lewis is of course pandering to British chauvinism in *The Monk*, a
pandering too disreputable and extreme for many. In *Northanger Abbey*,
that most telling account of the nature of readership at the end of the
eighteenth century, it is John Thorpe, the would-be rake and most
unseductive seducer of women, who reads *The Monk*, and he clearly reads
it as a form of pornography. A notable contemporary cartoon, James

Gillray's 'Tales of Wonder!' (1802), shows a group of over-weight, over-aged ladies reading two works by Lewis, *The Monk* and his collection *Tales of Wonder* (1801), with looks of horrified pleasure on their faces. Certainly, *The Monk* was not polite reading material. Attacks on the novel by contemporary critics and commentators, however, tended to focus not on sex but on religion (though the novel invariably conflates these) in viewing the novel as blasphemous.

What's most interesting about this is that the most celebrated criticism of the novel's blasphemous content was by Samuel Taylor Coleridge, writing from a perspective of Anglican orthodoxy. For Lewis's contemporaries, *The Monk*'s most controversial passage was this, on the possibility of interpreting the Bible in immoral ways:

> [Elvira], while She admired the beauties of the sacred writings, was convinced, that unrestricted no reading more improper could be permitted a young Woman. Many of the narratives can only tend to excite ideas the worst calculated for a female breast: Every thing is called plainly and roundly by its name; and the annals of a Brothel would scarcely furnish a greater choice of indecent expressions. Yet this is the Book, which young Women are recommended to study; which is put into the hands of Children, able to comprehend little more than those passages of which they had better remain ignorant; and which but too frequently inculcates the first rudiments of vice, and gives the first alarm to the still sleeping passions. ... She had in consequence made two resolutions respecting the Bible. The first was, that Antonia should not read it, till She was of an age to feel its beauties, and profit by its morality: The second, that it should be copied out with her own hand, all improper passages either altered or omitted. She had adhered to this determination, and such was the Bible which Antonia was reading: It had been lately delivered to her, and She perused it with an avidity, with a delight that was inexpressible. Ambrosio perceived his mistake, and replaced the Book upon the Table.
>
> (Lewis 1973: 259–60)[4]

Two things need to be said about this passage. Firstly, this is unmistakably the voice of Protestantism, which had from its outset focused on the Bible as a site of intellectual and ideological struggle. Indeed, the early history of Protestantism (and particularly its prehistory in Lollardy) can fairly be viewed as a movement for the translation of the Bible from Latin into the vernacular, thus placing it in the hands not of a select few priests to give the Official Line from the pulpit, but theoretically putting knowledge in the hands of all who could read, thus enabling the word of God to reach individuals (and their consciences) unmediated by the interpretations of priests, who operated in the interests of traditional hierarchies and power-structures. *Melmoth the Wanderer* goes even further than *The Monk* in this respect, suggesting that Catholics are kept in total ignorance even of the *existence* of the Bible. The once-haughty Juan di Monçada, in a letter smuggled to his brother Alonzo, forced into monastic life and effectively imprisoned in a convent (the letter is subsequently eaten), describes the ways in which the Catholic church has assumed control of his family, an experience which has turned him into a *de facto* Protestant:

> Must there not be something very wrong in the religion which thus substitutes external severities for internal amendment? I feel I am of an inquiring spirit, and if I could obtain a book they call the Bible (which, though they say it contains the words of Jesus Christ, they never permit us to see) I think – but no matter.
>
> (Maturin 1968: 129)

Furthermore, it is entirely in keeping with *The Monk*'s position in a tradition of anti-monastic literature (or propaganda) that Ambrosio, the embodiment of the Catholic hierarchy, should so pervert the meaning of the Bible that it becomes, in his imagination, an immoral text; and also that the virtuous Antonia, whose very virtue makes her one of several characters in the novel who are themselves, like *Melmoth*'s Monçada brothers, *de facto* Protestants, should be so keen to read the Bible for herself. This is a self-defeating element in the literature of extreme anti-Catholicism which we will see again in *Melmoth the Wanderer*.

Second, the reference to excising a perceived immorality from classic texts should remind us that this was the great period of bowdlerizing, in which seemingly the entire canon was scoured for filth. Dr Thomas Bowdler's own great work, *The Family Shakespeare* (1818), was subtitled 'in which nothing is added to the original text; but those words and expressions are omitted which cannot with propriety be read aloud in a family'. And Bowdler was not alone: James Plumtre's *The English Drama Purified* had already appeared in 1812, and he had also produced a 'revised and corrected' version of the great self-improving Protestant classic, *Robinson Crusoe*. From as early as 1798, bowdlerized, abridged and altered editions of *The Monk* had begun to appear.[5] This should remind us, as the Introduction noted, that moral panics surrounding the reception of horror are not only a contemporary phenomenon – but nor are these panics limited to horror.

In general, *The Monk*, Coleridge believed, 'is a romance, which if a parent saw in the hands of a son or daughter, he might reasonably turn pale' (Coleridge 1797: 197). This seems a fair enough point given the novel's concerns, though it's worth noting that, as *Northanger Abbey* acknowledged, the target audience for horror, then as now, is precisely those 'sons and daughters' whose parents would be shocked if they knew what they were reading, or watching – isn't that the point? He goes on to comment specifically on the passage quoted above:

> The impiety of this falsehood can be equalled only by its impudence. ... If it be possible that the author of these blasphemies be a Christian, should he not have reflected that the only passage in the scriptures, which could give a shadow of plausibility to the *weakest* of these expressions, is represented as spoken by the Almighty himself? ... We believe it not only absolutely impossible that a mind may be so deeply depraved by the habit of reading lewd and voluptuous tales, as to use even the Bible in conjuring up the spirit of uncleanness.
>
> (Coleridge 1797: 198)

What Coleridge had intended as a moral and aesthetic criticism soon became a political one, since, as André Parreaux notes, 'The introduction of the word *blasphemy* had far reaching consequences, of which Coleridge, it seems, was not fully aware when he used it.' Blasphemy was a crime, 'punishable at common law by fine and imprisonment, or other infamous corporal punishment: for Christianity is part of the laws of England', according to Sir William Blackstone's definitive *Commentaries on the Laws of England* (1765–9) (Parreaux 1960: 94, 112). If Coleridge was unaware of the legal implications of blasphemy, T.J. Mathias was not.[6] Mathias, a minor poet who had gained a measure of infamy with his satirical *The Pursuits of Literature*, suggested in his notes to that poem, 'I believe this 7th Chap. of Vol. 2 [of *The Monk*] *is* actionable at Common Law' (this chapter contains the notorious 'Bible' passage), and called in verse for the Attorney General to take action:

> Why sleep the ministers of truth and law?
> Has the State no controul, no decent awe,
> While each with each in madd'ning orgies vie,
> Pandars to lust and licensed blasphemy?
> Can Senates hear without a kindred rage?
>
> (Parreaux 1960: 109, 111)

A case against Lewis was drawn up, but never prosecuted, as Lewis immediately agreed to oversee a bowdlerized edition of the novel, *Ambrosio, or The Monk*, published in February 1798, in which not only was the offending 'Bible' section removed, but also virtually all the references to sexuality were cut (which wouldn't really have left much of a novel, except that Lewis also made 'considerable Additions' to his 1796 text). According to Parreaux, Lewis so freely altered his own novel as he feared that a court-case for blasphemy might also lay open to legal scrutiny his own homosexuality – and 'Sodomy was a still a capital offence' (Parreaux 1960: 119).

As noted earlier, there is a strong sense in which the heady ideological and theological concerns in some of the more extreme instances of Romantic anti-monastic literature, in *The Monk* and *Melmoth the Wanderer*, for example, take their animus so far that it becomes self-defeating, potentially opening these novels up to accusations of vindicating what they set out to condemn. Part of *The Monk*'s critique of Catholicism lies in the ways in which it equates with superstition, with irrational, pre-Enlightenment forms of thinking. However, unlike Radcliffe's much-criticized device of the 'explained supernatural', closing her novels in *Scooby Doo* fashion by providing a rational, secular explanation for what had seemed to be supernatural events, it seems that the characters of Lewis's novel are perfectly *right* to be superstitious, since their belief in the supernatural, and in its malign influence on human life, is vindicated at every turn – such is the price of Lewis's sensationalism. In *Melmoth*, the Spaniard Monçada is turned by his experience of Catholic institutions into Maturin's idea of a Protestant *manqué*: 'let every one of us answer for ourselves – that is the dictate of reason', he says to the Superior of the convent, who unsurprisingly replies: 'Of reason, my deluded child, – when had reason any thing to do with religion?' (Maturin 1968: 97)

However, Melmoth himself, the novel's Satanic tempter, also becomes, in his role as a mouthpiece for the author's own anti-Catholicism, an unlikely advocate for Protestantism. On an idyllic island in the Indian Ocean, he attempts (with the aid of a surprisingly powerful telescope) to demonstrate to the *ingénue* Immalee the follies and cruelties of the world's religions. After showing some Hindus crushing themselves under the Juggernaut of Vishnu, Melmoth suggests a parallel with Catholicism and its veneration of martyred saints. However, he manages to find one exception to this pageant of absurdity:

> However it was, he felt himself compelled to tell her it was a new religion, the religion of Christ, whose rites and worshippers she beheld. .... 'But why is there no splendour or magnificence in their worship; nothing grand or attractive?' – 'Because they know that God cannot be acceptably worshipped but by pure hearts and crimeless hands; and though their religion gives every hope to the penitent guilty, it flatters none with false promises of external devotion supplying the homage of the heart; or artificial and picturesque religion standing in the place of that single devotion to God, before whose throne, though the proudest temples erected in his honour crumble into dust, the heart burns at the altar still, an inextinguishable and acceptable victim.'
>
> (Maturin 1968: 296–7)

Although we are told that Melmoth is not really in control of his own words here, but is being spoken through by a higher power, and although this *does* succeed in converting Immalee to Christianity, the implication here is obvious, and obviously contradictory: Satan is a Protestant!

'Celtic Gothic'?

Melmoth the Wanderer is one of a series of nineteenth-century fictions – others include James Hogg's *The Private Memoirs and Confessions of a Justified Sinner* (1824) Sheridan Le Fanu's 'Carmilla' (1872), Robert Louis Stevenson's *The Strange Case of Dr Jekyll and Mr Hyde* (1886), Oscar Wilde's *The Picture of Dorian Gray* (1891), and Bram Stoker's *Dracula* (1897) – sometimes referred to as 'Celtic Gothic'. This is a highly problematic category, which needs treating with great caution, but it reflects a general suspicion that what is still sometimes called 'the Celtic fringe' (an objectionable phrase because of its cultural-imperialist underpinnings: Scotland, Ireland, and Wales are not on the 'fringe' of – that is, marginal to – anywhere, though they *surround* England on two sides, with Celtic Brittany providing a third) provide cultural locales conducive to the production of Gothic, or of melodrama. More generally, this has led to a belief that Gothic, horror, and melodrama are literary forms belonging to the cultural margins, the disenfranchised, the voiceless, or even the culturally 'backward': Victor Sage goes so far as to suggest that 'the paradigm of the horror plot [is] the journey from the capital to the provinces' (1988: 8). This is certainly the paradigm of what I would want to call 'regional Gothic', and thus in the ideological rhetoric of horror, Catholics, Welshmen, hillbillies and cannibals are all pretty much the same. Why this should be so, and if indeed it *is* so, is a tricky question, but one I shall attempt to answer here.

What is certain is that historically, this kind of thinking was fairly commonplace. Indeed, as Joep Leerssen has noted, the construction of a 'Celtic' identity, both as a term of disparagement and as a mark of belonging, is roughly historically congruent with the forging of a British identity, which in many ways it opposes (as do Frenchness and Catholicism). Furthermore, Celticism functioned as a form of counter-Enlightenment:

> the term 'Celtic' carries with it the indelible connotation of 'Otherness', regardless of whether it be used in the third or in the first person. ... The construction of the Celt in itself documents the revolt against rationalism and against the Enlightenment, and the attributes stereotypically ascribed to 'the Celt' have a profile to match.
>
> (Leerssen 1996: 4, 5)

In this, Celticism exactly parallels and closely resembles the Gothic. In *Northanger Abbey*, Catherine Morland's suspicion, noted earlier, that 'Italy, Switzerland and the South of France might be as fruitful in horrors as they were represented' in Ann Radcliffe's novels is followed by a further telling suggestion:

> Catherine dared not doubt beyond her own country, and even of that, if hard pressed, would have yielded the northern and western extremities. But in the central part of England there was surely some security for the existence even of a wife not beloved, in the laws of the land, and the manners of the age. Murder was surely not tolerated. Servants were not slaves, and neither poison nor sleeping potions to be procured, like rhubarb, from every druggist. Among the Alps and Pyrenees, perhaps, there were no mixed characters. There, such as were not as spotless as an angel, might have the dispositions of a fiend. But in England it was not so; among the English, she believed, in their hearts and habits, there was a general though unequal mixture of good and bad.
>
> (Austen 1972: 202)

This is clearly parodic (and contains the delicious suggestion that where Europeans and Celts deal in poisons, the English need laxatives), but nevertheless, the carefully-constructed eighteenth-century 'British' identity has fractured here, and Catherine's thinking aligns the dangerous, lawless inhabitants of 'the northern and western extremities' of these islands (Scotland, Wales, Ireland) with their murderous European counterparts, all governed by passions and set in explicit opposition to a stable, lawful, moderate Englishness. In Ireland, the novelist Maria Edgeworth (whose work Jane Austen, as *Northanger Abbey* acknowledges, admired enormously) surveyed the political scene of the 1830s, dominated by the figure of Daniel O'Connell:

> It is impossible to draw Ireland as she is now in a book of fiction – realities are too strong, party passions too violent to bear to see, or care to look at their faces in a looking-glass. The people would only break the glass, and curse the fool who held up the mirror to nature – distorted nature in a fever.
>
> (Hare 1894: 202)

Ireland here is figured as non-representable in realist terms – the mimetic 'mirror up to nature' is broken.[7] This kind of thinking has become a critical commonplace in theories about the relationship between fiction and ideology in Ireland (and, it has to be said, in Wales and Scotland), powerfully articulated in the 1990s by Terry Eagleton in his influential essay, 'Form and Ideology in the Anglo-Irish Novel':

There may, however, be rather more particular reasons why
the realist novel thrived less robustly in Ireland than in Britain.
For literary realism requires certain cultural conditions, few of
which were available in Ireland. The realist novel is the form
par excellence of settlement and stability, gathering individual
lives into an integrated whole; and social conditions in Ireland
hardly lent themselves to any such sanguine resolution. What
resolutions the Irish novel does bring off have a notably
factitious ring to them, fabular inventions or schematic devices
which cut against the grain of the fiction itself.
                                          (Eagleton 1995: 146–7)[8]

Similar, and equally celebrated, though even more problematic, is Declan
Kiberd's controversial assertion in *Inventing Ireland* that Ireland is (or has
historically been figured as) 'England's unconscious' (Kiberd 1995: 27–63).
     The most celebrated and influential nineteenth-century exponent of this
view of the relationship between some kind of intrinsic 'Celtic' character
and the writing produced by the Welsh, Scottish and Irish was Matthew
Arnold. In 'On the Study of Celtic Literature' (1866), his attempt to outline
the role of national identity in cultural production, Arnold articulates what
seems a staggeringly casual theory of the aesthetics of 'Celticism':

Balance, measure and patience, these are the eternal
conditions, even supposing the happiest temperament to start
with, of high success; and balance, measure and patience are
just what the Celt has never had. Even in the world of spiritual
creation, he has never, in spite of his admirable gifts of quick
perception and warm emotion, succeeded perfectly, because he
never has had steadiness, patience, sanity enough to comply
with the conditions under which alone can expression be
perfectly given to the finest perceptions and emotions.
                                          (Arnold 1972: 118)

What this obviously does is to infantilize the Celtic nations – and, as with
Austen's account of Catherine's thinking in *Northanger Abbey*, to articulate
a belief that they are in some ways 'backwards', uncivilized, immoderate,
incapable of reason (and insane!): Romantic, perhaps, but certainly not
belonging to modernity. What's strangest about this, though, is that Arnold
believed himself to be, and was believed by many of his contemporaries to
be, a defender of Celticism as a desirable alternative to the Philistinism of
the English middle class.
     The background to Arnold's thinking on Celticism comes from his
reading of the great Breton scholar Ernest Renan's *La poésie des races
celtiques* (1860): Renan believed that 'the Celtic race, especially with regard
to its Cymric or Breton branch, is an essentially feminine race' (Renan 1970: 8)

– that is, irrational, potentially hysterical, capable of delicacy but not of measured public or political judgement. It was reading Renan which confirmed Arnold's suspicion that 'I have long felt we owed more, spiritually and artistically, to the Celtic races than the somewhat coarse Germanic intelligence readily perceived, and been increasingly satisfied at our own semi-Celtic origin, which, as I fancy, gives us the power, if we will use it, of comprehending the nature of both races' (Murray 1996: 170). Though his remarks about the desirability of eliminating the Welsh language have proved understandably controversial, Arnold himself was quite passionate about Wales and Welsh culture, and was an occasional visitor to, and speaker at, the National Eisteddfod, the Welsh-language cultural festival: declining one invitation to attend the Chester Eisteddfod in 1866, Arnold wrote to the organizer hoping that the Welsh would take the opportunity 'for renewing the famous feat of the Greeks, and conquering their conquerors' (Edwards 1996: 19). He did attend, however, the inauguration of the first Chair of Celtic Studies at the University of Edinburgh in 1875, an acknowledgement, in the words of his biographer Nicholas Murray, of 'his role as a begetter of the Celtic Revival' (Murray 1996: 278). Certainly, compared to many of his contemporaries, Arnold's view of Celtic culture was a model of enlightened tolerance – this, for example, is from John Stuart Mill's 'Considerations on Representative Government' (1861):

> Experience proves, that it is possible for one nationality to merge and be absorbed in another: and when it was originally an inferior and more backward portion of the human race, the absorption is greatly to its advantage. Nobody can suppose that it is not more beneficial to a Breton, or a Basque of French Navarre, to be brought into the current of the ideas and feelings of a highly civilized and cultivated people ... than to sulk on his own rocks, the half-savage relic of past times, revolving in his own mental orbit, without participation or interest in the general movement of the world. The same remark applies to the Welshman or the Scottish Highlander, as members of the British nation.
>
> (Edwards 1996: 19)

Broadly Arnoldian ideas of Celticism were to have a profound effect on writers and cultural theorists at the end of the nineteenth century and into the twentieth century. The Irish Revival was predicated to no small extent on such Celticism, and Welsh writing saw a resurgence of interest in Arthurianism, and neo-Medievalism more generally. The most celebrated figure influenced by this kind of thinking was W.B. Yeats, drawn by a simultaneous and on occasion indistinguishable interest in Irish nationalist politics and in the occult to connections with the 'Oriental' mysticism of the

Theosophist movement and then to the arcane secret society of the Order of the Golden Dawn. The occult, as Terence Brown notes, 'was ... a controlling, energizing obsession throughout his life', and this precisely, Yeats thought, because of his Irish identity: 'The folklore of the Irish countryside ... with its hauntings, revenants and changelings, its Hallowe'en games to placate the walking spirits of the dead, was an integral part of everyday awareness, even in the middle-class world of Yeats's childhood' (Brown 1999: 33, 38).

Born in Leamington, Warwickshire, in 1875, but claiming Celtic ancestry, Aleister Crowley, the notorious wizard, Satanist, and self-proclaimed 'Great Beast' was, like Yeats, a devotee of the Order of the Golden Dawn. Crowley based a good deal of his occult persona on the head of the Order, Samuel Liddell Mathers, himself a kind of Celticist, who styled himself MacGregor Mathers, Comte de Glenstae (in spite of the fact that he was an Englishman who had never set foot in Scotland at the time), and then, after moving to Paris, the Chevalier Mathers MacGregor (Symons 1973: 34). Yeats went to Paris in 1896, to meet with the 'Chevalier MacGregor', 'to discuss the Celtic mysteries with him' (Brown 1999: 93). Meanwhile, in Wales, the celebrated surgeon, freethinker and vegetarian Dr William Price (1800–93) declared himself Archdruid, and took to wearing ceremonial robes decorated with cosmological symbols. In his 80s he fathered a son, whom he named Iesu Grist (Jesus Christ), and who died in infancy; a pioneer of cremation, Price was arrested in 1884 for attempting to cremate his son's corpse, though the resulting law-case (unsurprisingly, one of many faced by Price) led directly to the Cremation Act of 1902.[9]

Arnoldian Celticism is still prevalent, not only in Kiberd's assertion that Ireland is 'England's unconscious' (though Kiberd is well aware of the implications of his pronouncement), but also in thinking, for example, about the contents of anthologies of fantastic literature – Peter Haining, the editor of collections of supernatural stories from Ireland and from Wales, writes in the Introduction to *Great Welsh Fantasy Stories* of the 'two words which for me most accurately summarize Wales and the Welsh – "legendary" and "magical"' (Haining 2000: 14).[10] As we shall see, this is a version of Celticism which fiction has been happy to propagate.

James Hogg's *The Private Memoirs and Confessions of a Justified Sinner* is rightly acknowledged to be one of the great psychological tales of the double in English (and will be given full attention as such in Chapter 4). The double here, though, is more than a purely psychological device: it also embodies a split national identity within the political union of Britain, both English and not-English – a pulling two ways. This motif of the divided self as *nationally* divided resurfaces throughout the history of 'Celtic Gothic'. Often, in the case of the texts I am discussing at the moment, this is a tension between a 'Celtic' (or, troublingly, an 'authentic'), indigenous identity, and an imposed, powerful, centralizing English one: that is to say, between difference and conformity, represented in terms of violence and respectability: this seems to be precisely the complex of thinking worked through in the most celebrated of all double stories, *Dr Jekyll and Mr Hyde*, and closely to resemble the position of the other great fin-de-siècle double story, Oscar Wilde's *The Picture of Dorian Gray*, a novel which acts as a kind of parable of Wilde's own divided identity (both married and gay; both Irish and English). Hogg's ambiguous tale of Robert Wringhim and Gil-Martin, who is *both* Satan and a projection of Wringhim's own madness, is itself a doubled narrative, a twice-told tale, and it is in this twice-telling that the novel's national concerns articulate themselves.

The narrative of the ultra-Calvinist 'Justified Sinner', Wringhim, whose extreme Antinomian faith (that is, 'against the law' – the moral law of this world, carried out by a belief in justification through good works; Antinomian sects and churches adhered to a rigid belief in justification by faith alone, as indicative of a higher order)[11] leads him to believe that, as one of the elect, there is simply nothing he can do which will lead to his damnation, and thus he can do anything, because God has willed it so, is itself framed by the 'Editor's Narrative', the narrative of an unnamed editor (probably John Gibson Lockhart) from *Blackwood's Edinburgh Magazine*, which closes with the discovery of Wringhim's manuscript in the grave of his exhumed corpse. Founded in 1817, *Blackwood's Edinburgh Magazine* was, in the words of Robert Morrison and Chris Baldick, 'an exciting blend of raucous humour, penetrating intelligence, arrogant ultra-Toryism, and Gothic terror. ... Politically speaking, *Blackwood's* was on the extreme right, espousing a narrow version of High Church Tory bigotry that truculently opposed all forms of Whiggery and any faint-heartedness in the Tory ranks' (Morrison and Baldick 1995: vii, ix). The Editor, then, is far from a neutral reporter. Indeed, the early part of the 'Editor's Narrative', recounting events which took place around 1703–4 – that is, in the years leading up to the union of Scotland with England and Wales in 1707 – is heavily concerned with the politics of Scottish identity, coloured by the Editor's own High Tory principles. The hypocritical Calvinist, the Rev. Wringhim (Robert's probable father), is naturally a Whig; the good-hearted Laird of Dalcastle, as a result of his dealings with the Rev. Wringhim, 'join[ed] with the cavalier party of that day in all their proceedings' (Hogg 1981: 19). This early section of the novel leads up to a riot, inflamed by Robert Wringhim, which culminates in a running street-battle of Whigs against Cavaliers, which itself climaxes in Whigs inadvertently attacking Whigs: 'Finally, it turned out, that a few gentlemen, two-thirds of whom were strenuous Whigs themselves, had joined in mauling the whole Whig population of Edinburgh. The investigation disclosed nothing the effect of which was not ludicrous' (Hogg 1981: 31).

It is against this political background that this 'strange tale of Diablerie and Theology', as the *Westminster Review* of 1824 called *Justified Sinner*, plays itself out (Hogg 1981: 256). Throughout the eighteenth century, Edinburgh was the major centre for Enlightenment thinking in these islands, home to David Hume, Adam Smith, and many others.[12] *Justified Sinner* clearly describes a pre-Union, pre-Enlightenment Scotland, characterized by superstition and folklore: the novel's opening words are 'It appears from tradition' (Hogg 1981: 1). This is complex, though, as it appears that the novel's joke may be at the expense of the Enlightened Edinburgh Editor, a metropolitan man of letters who turns out to be lost in an older, oral culture. On the trail of a story, literally and metaphorically trying to dig up the past, the Editor seeks out a shepherd, called 'James Hogg', who had submitted a letter to *Blackwood's*, reprinted in the novel, describing the exhumation of the mummified corpse of a suicide (the actual Hogg, himself a shepherd, *had* submitted such a letter to *Blackwood's* – it had been published a year before *Justified Sinner*, in 1823). The Editor passes himself off to Hogg as 'a great wool-stapler, come to raise the price of that article', but gets short shrift: 'he eyed me with distrust, and turning his back on us, answered, "I hae sell'd mine"' (Hogg 1981: 246–7). When he does speak to the Editor, Hogg mystifies him in Scots:

> 'Od bless ye, lad! I hae ither matters to mind. I hae a' thae
> paulies to sell, an' a' yon Highland stotts down on the green
> every ane; an' then I hae ten scores o' yowes to buy after, a' if
> I canna first sell my ain stock, I canna buy nae ither body's. I
> hae mair ado than I can mange the day, foreby ganging to
> houk up hunder-year-auld banes.
>
> (ibid.: 247)

Not for the last time in this kind of Gothic, we find language used and understood (or *not* understood) as a mark of difference and of hostility by a minority culture to an imperial or metropolitan incomer. 'We could make nothing of him,' the Editor says, and having read Wringhim's exhumed manuscript, he is baffled, too, by that: 'I do not understand it ... I confess that I do not comprehend the writer's drift.' Which is, he also confesses, precisely what he expects from James Hogg: 'But, God knows! Hogg has imposed as ingenious lies on the public ere now' (ibid.: 247, 253–4, 246).

Old dark houses

In his story of 'Mr Justice Harbottle', the Dublin writer Sheridan Le Fanu presents a skewed image of a grotesque English legal system through its embodiment, a monstrous, Hogarthian hanging judge: 'He had a great, mulberry-coloured face, a big, carbuncled nose, fierce eyes, and a grim and brutal mouth. ... This old gentleman had the reputation of being about the wickedest man in England' (Le Fanu 1993: 88). Harbottle is the dispenser of an English system of justice which is as monstrous as he is: 'That sarcastic and ferocious administrator of the criminal code of England, at that time rather a Pharasaical, bloody, and heinous system of justice.' The judge gets wind of a plan to indict him by the Court of Appeal, which he describes as 'A Jacobite plot ... this business smells pretty strong of blood and treason', and is captured by constables who are the ghosts of his previous victims. The supernatural Court of Appeal, dispensing in its rough justice what amounts to forms of subaltern revenge, is presided over by Harbottle's terrifying double, Chief-Justice Twofold, 'a dilated effigy of himself; an image of Mr Justice Harbottle, at least double his size, and with all his fierce colouring, and his ferocity of eye and visage, enhanced awfully' (Le Fanu 1993: 95, 92–3, 108).

For his collections of short stories, Le Fanu tended to use framing narratives to unite otherwise potentially disparate material. The volume which contains 'Mr Justice Harbottle', for example, *In a Glass Darkly*, presents itself as the papers of the doctor and supernatural researcher Martin Hesselius, who provides one of the sources for that most celebrated (and problematic) of all experts in that most celebrated (and problematic) of all Irish Gothic novels, Dr Van Helsing (even the name is an echo) in Bram Stoker's *Dracula*. *The Purcell Papers*, published serially in the *Dublin Magazine* between 1838 and 1840, and collected posthumously (and given their current title) by Arthur Graves in 1880, are offered as manuscripts from the collection of an Irish Catholic priest, Father Francis Purcell:

> To such as may think the composing of such productions as these inconsistent with the character and habits of a country priest, it is necessary to observe that there did exist a race of priests – those of the old school, a race now nearly extinct – whose education tended to produce in them tastes more literary than have yet been evinced by the *alumni* of Maynooth.
>
> (Le Fanu 1880: 1: 2)

It is important to note the care with which Le Fanu establishes the provenance of these tales. As an Anglo-Irish Protestant, Le Fanu is himself pulled in two ways with respect to his supernatural material, which he clearly wants associated with Ireland's Catholic population, superstitious and pre-modern. Nevertheless, as a writer of supernatural fiction, he is also engaged with his subject, which he wishes to present as effectively, forcefully and plausibly as possible. Purcell, then, paradoxically is simultaneously for Le Fanu a distancing device and a guarantor of the veracity of a troublesome subject, which simultaneously draws and repulses *him*, reflective of the divided nature of the Protestant Anglo-Irish as internal colonizers, both Irish and not-Irish. Purcell is a Catholic priest, and thus pre-modern, implicated in the superstitious narratives he collects, yet he is also a cultured Catholic priest with a properly civilized antiquarian hobby. Thus Purcell is not a *modern* Irish Catholic priest: St Patrick's College,

Maynooth, established in 1795 for the education of Irish Catholic priests in an attempt at a *rapprochement* with that decade's movement for Catholic emancipation, was viewed with suspicion by the Anglo-Irish ascendancy caste, as a threat to their power-base. Importantly, then, Purcell is pre-Maynooth (Maynooth priests are caricatured here as uncivilized or peasant-like), one of an earlier generation probably educated at St Omar's seminary in France. Purcell, then, is himself an embodiment of Anglo-Irish cultural division – a Catholic priest, and thus a figure of suspicion, but not *entirely* an *Irish* Catholic priest, and thus given a measure of credence.[13]

Unsurprisingly, given this kind of outlook, paranoia is particularly prevalent in Irish Gothic, and Le Fanu's most celebrated novel, *Uncle Silas*, provides a classic example of this. For the Anglo-Irish protestant ascendancy caste, seeing all around them an indigenous population whom they tended to caricature as backward, superstitious, and with a propensity for violence, but who also outnumbered them greatly, the image of the 'Big House' simultaneously as fortress against outside oppression and as a prison from which escape was difficult, was a natural one. In Le Fanu's famous vampire-story, 'Carmilla' (originally collected by Dr Hesselius in *In a Glass Darkly*), the remote Styrian *Schlosses* of the aristocracy are walled fortresses against the plague which rages outside, the *oupire*, which takes the life of many peasants, and of which the vampire herself is an embodiment and metaphor (an identical image, of aristocrats walling themselves in their castle against the plague, famously animates Poe's 'The Masque of the Red Death'); they are also far-flung islands of civilization – to visit them is a difficult, time-consuming affair, and communication between them is practically impossible. In *Uncle Silas*, the young heiress Maud Ruthyn is transported after her father's death from one great house, Knowl, to another, Bartram-Haugh, the home of her mysterious Uncle Silas, a reclusive Swedenborgian mystic with a shady past. Swedenborgianism is described early in the novel in supernatural terms resembling the Order of the Golden Dawn: 'In my hazy notions of these sectaries there was mingled a suspicion of necromancy, and a weird freemasonry, that inspired something of awe and antipathy' (Le Fanu 2000: 11). Old Silas himself is consistently imaged in supernatural terms:

> And so it was like the yelling of phantom hounds and hunters, and the thunder of their coursers in the air – a furious, grand, and supernatural music, which in my fancy made a suitable accompaniment to the discussion of that enigmatical person – martyr – angel – demon – Uncle Silas – with whom my fate was so strangely linked, and whom I had begun to fear.
>
> (ibid.: 155)

Seeing him for the first time in many years, Silas's cousin, Lady Monica Knollys, tells Maud: 'I could hardly believe my eyes – such white hair – such a white face – such mad eyes – such a death-like smile … such a spectre. I asked myself is it necromancy, or is it delirium tremens that has reduced him to this?' (ibid.: 250). His house, Bartram-Haugh, is similarly decayed, similarly supernatural, 'bleached and phantasmal … [an] enchanted castle'. As Lady Knollys notes, Silas and Bartram-Haugh are, in fact, one and the same, doubles of each other:

> We forget how well it is that our present bodies are not to last always. They are constructed for a time and place of trouble – plainly mere temporary machines that wear out, constantly exhibiting failure and decay, and with such tremendous capacity for pain. The body lies alone, and so it ought, for it is plainly its good Creator's will; it is only the tabernacle, not the person, who is clothed upon after death, Saint Paul says, 'with a house which is from heaven.' So Maud, darling, although the thought will trouble us again and again, there is nothing in it; and the poor mortal body is only the cold ruin of a habitation which *they* have forsaken before we do. So this great wind, you say, is blowing toward us from the wood there. If so, Maud, it is blowing from Bartram-Haugh, too, over the trees and chimneys of that old place, and the mysterious old man, who is quite right in thinking I don't like him; and I can fancy him an old enchanter in his castle, waving his familiar spirits on the wind to fetch and carry tidings of our occupation here.
>
> (ibid.: 193, 155–6)

In its paranoid depictions of the struggles of a young girl imprisoned in a mysterious, labyrinthine house, what *Uncle Silas* most resembles is the novels of Ann Radcliffe. Indeed, so labyrinthine is Bartram-Haugh that, towards the end of the novel, when Maud is abducted by the horrific French governess, Madame de la Rougierre, whom she believes wants to take her to a French boarding-school (it is part of a plot by Silas, who is after Maud's inheritance), she thinks that she is in a hotel in Dover, when in fact she has simply been returned to imprisonment in an obscure part of the house. Also like Radcliffe's novels, it is important to realize the extent to which the narrative is mediated through the perceptions of the ingenuous and highly sensitive heroine: as Sage notes, 'she is often wrong in her judgements: intransigently orthodox in her beliefs, she suspects "superstition" all round her' (Le Fanu 2000: xxi). This is certainly true, but it should also be noted that, as in Radcliffe, and as *Northanger Abbey* also suggests, there is a strong sense in which the rhetoric of Gothicism and the supernatural is the only means by which these young heroines, linguistically circumscribed by decorum, can represent material threats, to their chastity, their life, or both.

Though Bartram-Haugh is in Derbyshire, it is also (and more authentically) in County Cork. That is to say, *Uncle Silas* was originally an

Irish tale, 'Passage in the Secret History of an Irish Countess', later collected amongst the *Purcell Papers*. The story is narrated by 'Lady Margaret', and the Uncle Silas character is 'Sir ArthurT-n', of Carrickleigh, County Cork. The story is a 'locked room' mystery – Sir Arthur lives in exile, suspected of killing Hugh Tisdall, to whom he has amassed heavy gambling debts. It also contains a nameless proto-Madame de la Rougierre, a servant employed by Sir Arthur: 'a tall, raw-boned, ill-looking elderly Frenchwoman' (Le Fanu 1880: 2: 57). Like Bartram-Haugh, Carrickleigh – which really *is* a crumbling Ascendancy fortress – is in ruins, falling to pieces with neglect, a house of stagnant fishponds, broken avenues and walls, and 'a general air of dilapidation': 'I shall not soon forget the impression of sadness and gloom which all that I saw produced upon my mind', Lady Margaret says on entering it (ibid.: 2: 27, 26).

Old dark houses, unsurprisingly, figure large in James Whale's *The Old Dark House* (1932), this time with a Welsh setting, and based on J.B. Priestley's novel *Benighted* (1927). The film opens with Mr and Mrs Waverton (Raymond Massey and Gloria Stuart) and Penderel (Melvyn Douglas) travelling by car 'somewhere in the Welsh mountains', on the way to Shrewsbury, caught in a torrential storm which is soon to cause the landslide which will trap them in the house. Lost in Wales, they are trying to get across the border to England, though the cynical Penderel notes that, if nothing else, their current situation is not dull, and as such is preferable to the security offered on the other side of the border:

> As a matter of fact, taking one thing with another, I'm not particularly sure that I want to go to Shrewsbury. As far as that goes, I don't particularly want to go anywhere. Something might happen here, but nothing ever happens in Shrewsbury.

It becomes apparent that they are indeed nowhere – that their location doesn't exist at all in any normal cartographic sense:

> MARGARET: Well, now, for heaven's sake, stop. Let's look at a map or something.
> PENDEREL: My own view is we're not on a map.
> MARGARET: *(holding a sodden map)* Oh, you look, Philip. I can't see anything! It's all a stupid puddle!
> WAVERTON: Seems to represent this country very well. Everything here *is* underwater.
> PENDEREL: Oh, just drive on. We'll arrive somewhere sometime.

Immediately after this, there's the landslide, and they arrive at the house. That the house is 'not on a map', in some non-existent or at least uncharted place in Wales, is reiterated throughout the film. Virtually the first words in

The Old Dark House are a dialogue between Margaret and Waverton: 'Do you happen to have any idea where we are?' 'I haven't the least idea in the world.' Waverton later talks of 'driving along roads that aren't there'. When his knocking on the door gets no reply, Penderel says: 'I should've thought that was loud enough to wake the dead. That's an idea. ... Wouldn't it be dramatic – supposing all the people inside were dead, all stretched out with the lights quietly burning about them.' It is not, however, precisely one of the dead who appears at the door, but one of the Welsh, the scarred face of Morgan (Boris Karloff), the mute butler, who mutters and groans at them: 'Even Welsh ought not to sound like that,' Penderel quips. As with the incomprehensibility of Hogg's Scots being interpreted as a mark of hostility by the metropolitan Editor of *Justified Sinner*, here Morgan's threatening growls are mistaken for a native language by the travellers who want to be in England. (Sir William, the good-hearted Northern industrialist, later attempts to sing 'The Roast Beef of Old England'!) Having established that Morgan's is the nearest to an authentically Welsh identity that the film allows, the men of the Anglo-Welsh Femm family, who live in the house, express their fear of his potential for violence in ways which should, I hope, be familiar. Horace Femm (the astounding Ernest Thesiger) says, 'I'm afraid I'm rather nervous. I am rather a nervous man. But the fact is, Morgan is an uncivilized brute. Sometimes he drinks heavily. A night like this would set him going, and once he's drunk, he's rather dangerous.' The bed-ridden 102-year-old patriarch Sir Roderick Femm also tells the Wavertons: 'Morgan is a savage, but we must keep him.'

The Old Dark House is brilliantly perverse, a clear reflection of the sensibilities of its director, the cultured, gay Englishman James Whale, and particularly for his fondness for smuggling homosexual allusions into his films in a kind of visual polari. In Ernest Thesiger (like Charles Laughton a married gay man) Whale found a memorably camp interpreter. Famously, as Dr Pretorius in *The Bride of Frankenstein*, Thesiger enters Henry Frankenstein's bedroom, dismisses his bride, sits on the bed with Henry and discusses alternative ways of creating life, 'a new world of gods and monsters!' (*Gods and Monsters*, of course, was the title of a film biography of James Whale, concentrating on his last days, and particularly on his relationship with a young gardener played by Brendan Fraser; Whale himself was played by the cultured, gay English actor Ian McKellen.) Thesiger here is Horace Femm, and one has to wonder to what extent this name is a deliberate pun on 'femme' – all the more so since, most disconcertingly, the aged patriarch Sir Roderick Femm is played by a woman (Elspeth Dudgeon, but actually credited as 'John Dudgeon').[14] Horace Femm admits that he is effectively imprisoned in the house (as his maniac brother Saul Femm is literally imprisoned) – 'Can you conceive of anybody living in a house like this if they didn't have to?' – as he is wanted by the police for an unspecified crime (homosexuality?).

The truth which the film teasingly suggests about the house and its inhabitants is also bound up in a narrative strongly suggestive of sexual perversion. Sir Roderick tells the Wavertons: 'This is an unlucky house. Two of my children died when they were twenty. And then other things happened. Madness came. We are all touched with it a little. Except me. At least, I don't think I am.' Rebecca Femm (Eva Moore), a stern Calvinist who rebukes her atheist brother Horace for mocking the Lord, tells Margaret the story of her sister Rachel, whom men pursued. Rachel falls off a horse, damages her spine, and spends what remains of her life bed-ridden, and in great pain. Rebecca's narrative is strongly suggestive of incest as the cause of the Femms' madness:

> They were all Godless here. They used to bring their women here – brazen, lolling creatures in silks and satins. They filled the house with laughter and sin, laughter and sin. And if I ever went down among them, my own father and brothers, they would tell *me* to go away and pray. They wouldn't tell Rachel to go away and pray. And I prayed, and left them with their lustful red and white women.

Rebecca delivers this speech with her face largely reflected in a distorting mirror. Afterwards, she tells Margaret, who is in her underwear, that she, too, will rot, however young and beautiful she is now, and then, very oddly, carefully checks her hair in the mirror before leaving the room. Margaret then looks in the mirror, which reflects back two images of her face, both hideously distorted; this is cross-cut with shots of Rebecca reflected in the mirror, and with Morgan's scarred face looking in at the door. Later, Margaret, throwing shadows on the wall, is attacked in shadow by Rebecca; she runs screaming into Morgan's room, where he drunkenly assaults her. The distorted features and relations of incest are a common trope of regional Gothic (perhaps most famously in *Deliverance*; in a specifically Welsh context, the incestuous family also features in the film adaptation of Ed Thomas's *House of America*), with families far from centres of civilization seemingly turning in on themselves, and grotesquely redoubling themselves. Are Morgan's scarred face and mute speech the signs that he is the product of an incestuous relationship? When Sir Roderick says, 'Morgan is a savage, but we must keep him', is this because Morgan is his own son? When the psychopathic Saul Femm falls to his death at the end of the film, Morgan (very movingly) howls with grief and cradles him in his arms. Is *Saul* Morgan's father? Rebecca tells us that Rachel was not turned away from the 'laughter and sin' of her father and brothers, but is *Rebecca* in fact Morgan's mother? She is certainly the only one to whose word he pays heed; he is dumb where she, we are told on a number of occasions, is deaf; and her speech to Margaret inter-cuts images of her own face distorted in the mirror with that of Morgan at the door.

   The Old Dark House is not the only classic Universal horror film that uses Wales as its location. *The Wolf Man* features Lon Chaney Jr as the hapless Larry Talbot, returning to his home village in Wales, where he is bitten by the werewolf Bela (Bela Lugosi), transforms, undergoes agonies of remorse, self-doubt and frustration, and is finally shot dead by his own father, Sir John Talbot (Claude Rains, who looks a good deal younger than Lon Chaney Jr!).[15] While the Welsh location is never *named* in the film, it is assumed, and given credence by the names of a number of supporting characters (Dr Lloyd, Jenny Williams), and Denis Gifford, presumably working from Curt Siodmak's original script (which mentioned Wales many times as the setting), and making deductions from the first sequel, *Frankenstein Meets the Wolf Man*, which is far more clear about the Welsh location, identifies the unnamed village as 'Llanwelly', though in the original script Siodmak had set the film in the parodically nonsensical 'Llansileffraillerychmair'.[16] *The Wolf Man*, though, presents, if anything, an even more bizarre version of Wales than does *The Old Dark House*, offering a demented cultural geography where Englishmen (Sir John Talbot, conceivably Anglo-Welsh), Americans (Larry, who has been away, and Ralph Bellamy's Paul Montford, making no pretence at anything other than an American accent, in spite of the fact that it is stated that Montford has lived locally his whole life), and Eastern European gypsies (Bela and his mother Maleva, memorably played by Maria Ouspenskaya) unproblematically co-exist – Wales is literally nowhere here, other than a plausible locus of weirdness. As Sir John himself says, 'We are a backward people.' Even stranger is *Frankenstein Meets the Wolf Man*, which takes place in the *Mitteleuropean* state of Visaria, to which Maleva and the resurrected Larry Talbot travel from Wales in a horse and cart. Wales, that is, in the cultural imagination of Universal Studios, at least, is somewhere in the vicinity of Transylvania.

Beyond the fringe: *The Wicker Man* and *Candlenight*

Perhaps the most celebrated cinematic 'Celtic Gothic', though, is *The Wicker Man*. Anthony Schaffer's *Golden Bough*-inspired take on culture-clash and clashes of belief-systems played out on Summerisle, a balmy Hebridean island (protected by the Gulf Stream) famous for its apples, whose inhabitants have taken to (or rediscovered) paganism, was notoriously dogged by production and post-production difficulties, differences, and wrangles, and thus exists in a number of different forms, none of them entirely adequate.[17] Nevertheless, it remains a film of great power and originality – so much so, in fact, that Allan Brown in his authoritative account of the film's making seeks to deny that *The Wicker Man* is a horror film at all, working as he does within an evaluative system in which a horror film cannot be 'serious': 'No, it isn't a horror film' (Brown 2000: 72).[18] (Yes, it is.)

Sgt. Neil Howie (Edward Woodward), an Episcopalian policeman from the West Highland Constabulary, is called from the mainland to Summerisle after an anonymous letter reports the disappearance of a girl, Rowan Morrison. Summerisle has Mediterranean-style terraces and palm trees, and, familiarly, the harbourmaster's first words to Howie are 'Have you lost your bearings?' Though *The Wicker Man* playfully opens with a caption reading, 'The producers would like to thank The Lord Summerisle and the people of his island off the west coast of Scotland for this privileged insight into their religious practices and for their generous co-operation in the making of this film', once again we are not on any map. Pagan symbols abound: a sun-face on a flag (later revealed as the island's sun-god, Avenallau), an eye on the harbourmaster's boat. The island's pub is the Green Man, and, in classic fashion, when Howie enters, the place falls dead silent. At night, Howie walks out of the pub towards the graveyard, past groups of people seemingly having sex; there is a naked girl crying on a gravestone. All of this 'pagan' licentiousness is counterpointed with scenes of Howie praying at his bedside, and flashbacks of him reading the lesson in church and receiving communion. These scenes of Howie are in turn inter-cut with the notorious scenes of Willow MacGregor's (Britt Ekland) seductive song and dance, which begins with her lying naked in bed (while Howie, in the next room, wears brown pyjamas!), and ends with her writhing against the wall and slapping herself, while Howie sweats on the other side. The next morning, Willow brings him a cup of tea, and says, 'I expect you'll be going back today. You wouldn't want to be around here on May Day – not the way *you* feel.' The film cuts to a shot of a maypole, with boys dancing around it.[19]

The film's ideological clash is effectively articulated across three dialogues, two between Howie and the schoolteacher Miss Rose (Diane Cilento), and between them a long scene with Howie and Lord Summerisle (Christopher Lee, in a fantastic wig). The first comes when Howie visits the school, interrupting Miss Rose's lesson on magical stones, and finds Rowan Morrison's name in the register (the islanders, including her mother, sister and schoolfriends had previously denied her existence):

> MISS ROSE: Here we do not use the word [dead]. We believe that when the human life is over, the soul returns to trees, to air, to fire, to water, to animals. So that Rowan Morrison has simply returned to the life-forces in another form.
> HOWIE: You mean to say that you ... you teach the children this stuff?
> MISS ROSE: I tell you – it is what we believe.
> HOWIE: You never learn anything of Christianity?
> MISS ROSE: Only as a comparative religion. The children find it far easier to picture reincarnation than resurrection. Those rotting bodies – they're a great stumbling-block for the childish imagination.

At the end of the film, with Howie about to be sacrificed to the gods by burning in the wicker man, he and Miss Rose continue their dispute:

> MISS ROSE: You will undergo death and rebirth – resurrection, if you like. The rebirth sadly will not be yours, but that of our crops.
> HOWIE: I am a Christian, and as a Christian I hope for resurrection. And even if you kill me now, it is I who will live again, not your damned apples.

The film's studious balance between the opposing belief-systems is maintained up to the very last shots, with Howie, immolated in the wicker man, singing 'The Lord's My Shepherd', while around him the islanders dance and sing 'Sumer is icumen in'. The island's crops have failed, which is why the islanders need Howie, their virgin sacrifice – and why Howie is served horrible tinned broad beans at the Green Man, followed by tinned peaches, which are something of a feature of this film – the nymphomaniac librarian (the great Ingrid Pitt – tragically under-used in all extant versions) also eats them while Howie interrogates her. As a propitiatory symbol of fertility and fecundity, in a derelict church Howie finds a breastfeeding woman with an egg in her hand (later, he sees pregnant women caressing the apple-blossom); there are apples on the altar – Howie sweeps them off and replaces them with a makeshift cross. Summerisle's chemist sells foreskins, snake-oil embrocation, brains, and hearts, as well as animal foetuses preserved in jars. Past some amazing phallic topiary on the way to Lord Summerisle's castle, Howie sees naked schoolgirls dancing and leaping over a fire in a stone circle. They are learning, says Lord Summerisle, parthenogenesis, 'reproduction without sexual union'.

   Anthony Schaffer suggests that *The Wicker Man* is 'an archetypal film. It's about perhaps the deepest, most meaningful question man can ask himself: what do I believe and why do I believe it?' (Brown 2000: 187). The discussion which follows, between Lord Summerisle and Howie, really is the key to the film, exposing both of the protagonists' rival belief-systems as equally valid *social* constructs rooted in supernaturalism:

> HOWIE: What's all this? You've got fake biology, fake religion. Sir, have these children never heard of Jesus?
> LORD SUMMERISLE: Himself the son of a virgin impregnated, I believe, by a ghost. ... It's most important that each new generation on Summerisle be made aware that here the old gods aren't dead.
> HOWIE: And what of the true God, to whose glory churches and monasteries have been built on these islands for generations past? Now, sir, what of Him?
> LORD SUMMERISLE: Well, he's dead. He can't complain – he had his chance and, in modern parlance, blew it.

During the course of the discussion, Lord Summerisle acknowledges to Howie that 'the old gods' were forcibly reintroduced to Summerisle as an experiment by his grandfather, who was working at perfecting a new strain of apple (the 'Summerisle Famous'), as a way of encouraging a more willing agricultural workforce. Thus, what appears to be a relic of a system of belief surviving precisely because of its geographical and cultural marginality is in fact revealed as purely material, an imposition of nineteenth-century agrarian capitalism and, strangely, a product of science. The film itself is equally materialist: if it has a position, it would appear to be atheistical – certainly, it is unwilling to endorse either belief-system. Schaffer's original screenplay, much cut in any surviving version, is even more revealing here. For one thing, Lord Summerisle admits that the Summerisles are a recently ennobled family, and not immemorial landowners: his grandfather, 'a distinguished Victorian scientist, agronomist and freethinker – the T.H. Huxley of the Trossachs you might call him', actually bought the island in 1868 as a location for his experiments. Furthermore, he appears to have been influenced in his choice by Arnoldian Celticism:

> The tradition of the arcane and the mysterious cleaves to the people of this island with a tenacity which makes it seem an inherent and inalienable possession. And as even you must be aware Sergeant, there's no race which cultivates a keener sense of spiritual vision than the Celtic. ... These islanders needed little urging. My grandfather simply told them about the Stones – how they in fact formed an ancient temple, and that he, The Lord of the Manor, would make a sacrifice there every day to their old Gods and Goddesses, particularly those of Fertility and Fruitfulness, and that as a result of this worship (*Preacher's voice*) the barren island would burgeon and bring forth fruit in great abundance. (*normal voice*) For an atheist, grandfather had a singularly biblical turn of phrase, don't you think?
>
>   (Brown 2000: 217–19)[20]

Like his father, however, and like the islanders, Summerisle professes a sincere belief in his adopted family religion: he describes himself to Howie as 'A heathen, conceivably, but not, I hope, an unenlightened one' (ibid.: 222). (A version of this remark survives in the film.)

When asked about the disappearance of Rowan Morrison, Lord Summerisle tells Howie, 'We don't commit murder up here. We're a deeply religious people.' Rowan's exhumed grave, with her navel-string dangling above it, turns out to contain a hare, the hare which her sister Myrtle had drawn Howie as a representation of Rowan earlier in the film, and which Lord Summerisle and Miss Rose consider as vindication of their belief in metempsychosis. Howie tells them, 'I think Rowan Morrison was murdered under circumstances of pagan barbarity which I can scarcely bring myself to believe as taking place in the twentieth century.' On reading in the library about pagan rites and human sacrifice, Howie exclaims: 'Dear God! Even *these* people can't be *that* mad!' But there are at least two hundred years of thinking which suggest that, from a 'mainland' perspective, they certainly are.

Unjustly, the release of *The Wicker Man* drew suspicion upon the activities of the 'New Age' Findhorn community in the north-east of Scotland (who themselves grew, and continue to grow, prize-winning cabbages!) (Brown 2000: 64). While the inhabitants of Summerisle are certainly pagans and separatists, the film makes no real suggestion that they are *nationalists* as such, though the overtones are difficult to avoid, especially given that the 1970s was a period of powerful nationalist activism across these islands. As I noted earlier, for W.B. Yeats the connection of nationalism and the occult was an inescapable one. The final stanza of his 1938 poem 'The Statues' presents the Irish nationalist leader Padriag Pearse as a shaman or necromancer, calling up the shade of the Irish hero Cuchulain to aid the cause for independence in 1916:

> When Pearse summoned Cuchulain to his side,
> What stalked through the Post Office? What intellect,
> What calculation, number, measurement, replied?
> We Irish, born into that ancient sect
> But thrown upon this filthy modern tide
> And by its formless spawning fury wrecked,
> Climb to our proper dark, that we may trace
> The lineaments of a plummet-measured face.
>
> (Yeats 1982: 375–6)

As Terence Brown has noted, this is a direct allusion to the Welsh leader Owen Glendower's famous remark in Shakespeare's *Henry IV, Part 1*, 'I can call spirits from the vasty deep', to which Hotspur responds 'But will they come when you do call for them?' (III, I, 53, 55): 'Yeats believed they had for him, and for Pearse' (Brown 1996: 222).

But it is Glendower's next remark – or Owain Glyn Dŵr, as we should more properly call him – which most interests me here, as its spirit animates one of the most interesting of all recent works of 'Celtic Gothic', Phil Rickman's novel *Candlenight* (1991): 'I can teach you, cousin, to command / The devil' (III, I, 56–7). R.R. Davies, in his study of Glyn Dŵr, suggests that Wales, more than any other part of these islands, was ripe for the mythological interpretation of its history:

> The very absence of indigenous native political institutions and
> of a ruling, governmental elite around whom a more practical
> and present oriented political culture might develop, as in
> England and Scotland, endowed the mythical and prophetic

ideology of the poets and their associates in Wales with arguably a much greater resilience than elsewhere. After all, it was the sole vernacular ideology in Wales.

(Davies 1997: 159)

Glyn Dŵr himself was simultaneously a learned Renaissance statesman and a mage who 'consulted masters of prophecy as if they were political pundits and ... larded his political correspondence with historical and prophetic lore'; he was 'both a historical and a mythic figure' (ibid.: 169, 325).

Candlenight provides a Gothicized rationale for the activities of the ultra-nationalist Welsh secret society, Meibion Glyn Dŵr (the Sons of Glyn Dŵr), popularly credited with forms of direct action such as the burning of English-owned holiday cottages in rural Wales (English or metropolitan 'incomers', by pricing out locals in buying houses, were artificially inflating property prices to the detriment of rural Welsh communities, many of whose inhabitants could no longer afford to live locally). Rickman originally worked as a journalist for Radio Wales, and *Candlenight* has its origins in a radio documentary, *Aliens*, examining the often fraught relationship between these English incomers and their Welsh neighbours. As Rickman subsequently explained:

> *Aliens* related to a period in the mid-eighties when a lot of people in England were buying up land very quickly in certain parts of Wales. The land was cheap and it was assumed that you could make a killing. But ... [the thing] which inspired the documentary and then the book, was not all of these English people were *welcomed* by the Welsh. There was a strong feeling of invasion, of being invaded. And the English felt unaccepted, unwanted. Unloved, I suppose. An odd statistic I uncovered at the time was that 60% of the calls the Samaritans were receiving were from English people in Wales who simply couldn't handle it any more.
>
> (Mathew n.d.)

In *Candlenight*, Dai Death the undertaker comments on this economic climate from a Welsh perspective, with an account of depopulated indigenous (agricultural) communities:

> 'Local boy wants a home of his own, priced out of the market before he starts.' ... It was, he thought, only a matter of time. They were bound to discover this place, the English. Some young stockbroker-type would cruise out here in his Porsche and spot a derelict barn, ripe for conversion, and make the farmer an offer he'd be a fool to refuse. And another farmer would hear about it and he'd sell *two* of his buildings. Then

some poor widow would be staggered at how much she could get for her cottage. And in no time at all, there'd be a little colony of English, enough to hold a bridge party with After Eight mints.

(Rickman 1993: 35, 37)

Rickman's idyllic Welsh village, Y Groes (The Cross) – which, like Summerisle, has its own microclimate – proves irresistible to all who come under its spell, though it remains a thoroughgoing Welsh-language community in which superstition, the occult and pre-Christian religion (or certainly pre-Nonconformist Christianity, the dominant religion of Wales but 'a passing phase' in Y Groes) (Rickman 1993: 179) all play a major part. The mysterious deaths of several English incomers and visitors are revealed to be a consequence of the village's occult nationalism: the village was founded by the bearers of Glyn Dŵr 's body, which lies entombed in the local church, casting its protective spell and requiring blood sacrifice, the sacrifice of English incomers. (Adam of Usk's contemporary account of Glyn Dŵr's burial is mysterious, and opens the door to mystical interpretations of his death: 'he was buried at night by his followers. But his burial was detected by his opponents; so he was re-buried. But where his body lies is unknown.') (Davies 1997: 327) The first victim, the antiquarian Professor Ingley, is conducting 'scholarly probings into a society still obsessed with its own mythology' (Rickman 1993: 29). Berry Morelli, an American journalist covering a local by-election, describes Wales as 'just about the most obscure country in Western Europe'; Winstone Thorpe, Morelli's ancient colleague, describes Wales to him as 'A hard and bitter land, old boy. Don't have our sensibilities, never been able to afford them. We go there in our innocence, the English, and we're degraded and often destroyed. ... We're really not meant to be there, you know, the English' (Rickman 1993: 288, 54). In the by-election, the nationalist Plaid Cymru candidate, Guto Evans, is a modern language-activist who has no truck with mystical Celticism. An academic historian, he is author of a study of Glyndŵr:

> There had been claims, Guto wrote, that Glyndŵr had been trained in Druidic magic and could alter the weather – a couple of his victories were put down to this ability. All crap, Guto said, the English view of the Welsh as wildmen from the mountains who, having no military sophistication, needed to put their faith in magic.
>
> None the less, Guto conceded, all this stuff added to Glyndŵr's charisma, and put him alongside King Arthur as the great Celtic hero who had never really died and one day would return to free his people from oppression.
>
> Prophecies. Signs and portents and prophecies.
>
> (Rickman 1993: 295)

What *Candlenight* ultimately does is to expose the occult or mystical origins behind traditional nationalist thinking. The spiritual leader of Y Groes is the druidic Reverend Elias ap Siencyn, a fictionalized version of the ultra-nationalist poet R.S. Thomas ('Loony Welsh Nationalist vicar?' 'Lots of them about, my dear. Never read R.S. Thomas?' as one exchange has it, just in case we missed the allusion), who seems magically able to transmute into an ancient tree, or glade of trees, just as the village itself 'seemed somehow organic, like wild mushrooms in a circle' (Rickman 1993: 319, 89). Here, certainly, as for Yeats, there is no necessary discrimination to be made between occultism and nationalism.

Cannibals: eating others

Melmoth the Wanderer's Monçada recounts the tale of a pair of young lovers caught together in a convent, who are, as punishment, walled up together in a dungeon and left to die of starvation (the tale is told to him by their jailer). In desperation, they resort to cannibalism:

> It was on the fourth night that I heard the shriek of the wretched female, – her lover, in the agony of hunger, had fastened his teeth in her shoulder; – that bosom on which he had so often luxuriated, became a meal to him now.
>
> (Maturin 1968: 212–13)

For a Protestant with Maturin's Calvinist leanings, the connection between Catholicism and cannibalism was an irresistible one, based as it was on a hostile understanding of the Catholic doctrine of transubstantiation, a literal interpretation of Christ's words at the Last Supper: 'And as they were eating, Jesus took bread, and blessed *it*, and brake *it*, and gave *it* to the disciples, and said, Take, eat, this is my body.'[21] The doctrine of transubstantiation, then, holds that, in the ceremony of the mass, the host is literally transformed into the body of Christ, which is then consumed by the worshippers in what is interpretable (by the likes of Maturin) as an act of real physical cannibalism.

As a violation of one of the most powerful and pervasive taboos, cannibalism has traditionally also provided a powerful cultural anathema, with cannibals clearly beyond the pale of civilized human society. Taboos concerning what may or may not be eaten are famously of great anthropological importance since, in the words of Mary Douglas's essay 'Deciphering a Meal', 'Food categories ... encode social events' (Douglas 1999: 231). In her landmark study of pollution and taboo, *Purity and Danger*, Douglas discusses the most celebrated of all dietary regulations, the Biblical abominations of *Leviticus*, which forbid the eating of cloven-hoofed animals which do not chew their cud (swine), birds of prey or carrion birds, swarming animals, animals which go upon their belly, and several other apparently arbitrary categories. Douglas suggests that in approaching this apparent arbitrariness, 'The only sound approach is to forget hygiene, aesthetics, morals and instinctive revulsion', and to concentrate instead on 'the principles of power and danger', the ways in which the eatings of abominable foods is a form of unholiness, that which is incomplete and thus rejected by God (Douglas 1984: 49). Gustave Flaubert's novel of decadence and cruelty during the Carthaginian wars, *Salammbô* (1862), which itself contains episodes of cannibalism, of corpses 'hung up in bits in butcher's shops', is also more generally revealing on the subject of the violation of food-taboos: outside the walls of Carthage are the mysterious, savage 'Unclean-Eaters', who live in 'huts, of seaweed and slime, ... without rulers or religion, all mixed together, completely naked, both sickly and wild, execrated by the people for centuries because of their disgusting diet' (Flaubert 1977: 49, 61).

One notable way, then, of defining subordinate or colonized peoples as savage and thus in need of colonizing (bringing a civilizing influence for their own good) was to brand them as cannibals. The first contact of European explorers and colonizers with Amerindian cannibals in Brazil in the sixteenth century led to a series of disquisitions on the relationship between 'barbaric' cannibals and their 'civilized' (would-be) conquerors. The most celebrated of these was by the great French essayist Michel de Montaigne in his essay 'On Cannibals' (1580). Montaigne begins by establishing a connection (a familiar one to us by now) between savagery and cartography – cannibals dwell in marginal lands, not on any map – 'We need topographers to give us exact descriptions of the places where they have been' (Montaigne 1958: 108) – and thus effectively *imaginary*: that is, populated as vividly by the European imagination as by the natives. Like several of his contemporaries, Montaigne takes what we might call a culturally relativistic approach, choosing not to use the cannibals in order to underwrite and define European civilization, but rather as a way of highlighting European savagery:

> I do not believe, from what I have been told about these people, that there is anything barbarous about them, except that we call barbarous anything that is contrary to our own habits. ... We are justified therefore in calling these people barbarians with reference to the laws of reason, but not in comparison with ourselves, who surpass them in every kind of barbarity
>
> (Montaigne 1958: 108–14)

Is it not better, Montaigne asks, to treat prisoners courteously and well, and then ritualistically to eat them, rather than torture them slowly to death? The massacres of Protestant Huguenots in France from the 1570s through to the 1590s, which saw instances of cannibalism at the sieges of Paris and Saucerre, and especially the sale and public consumption of butchered Huguenot corpses after the St Bartholomew's Day massacres of 1572, added credence to Montaigne's position: Protestant commentators noted, as Maturin was later to note, that the transubstantiated mass predisposed Catholics to cannibalism (Rawson 1992).

It did not take long for the English to start imagining their Celtic neighbours in cannibalistic terms: 'We have Indians in Cornwall, Indians in Wales, Indians in Ireland', one commentator noted in 1652 (Rawson 1992: 346). Fynes Moryson, an Elizabethan colonial administrator in Ireland, records in his *Itinerary* (1617) his suppression of a rebellion in Tyrone, and also of the famine which went along with it, forcing the Irish to eat grass (Moryson records the sight of Irish people lying dead on the roadsides, their mouths stained green). As Claude Rawson notes, the symbolic connotations of this are obvious and powerful: the Irish are like cattle, and should be treated accordingly, and more generally Moryson's remark tars the Irish with 'the ethnic slur of unclean eating' (1992: 336–44).

In this 'unclean eating', Moryson's Irish resemble (or anticipate) the atavistic Yahoos from Jonathan Swift's *Gulliver's Travels* (1726), savages (though not actually cannibals) who violate food-taboos and live in their own excrement. (This, however, is complex, as Montaigne's cannibals, living in a state of prelapsarian purity, resemble Swift's saintly Houyhnhms, not least in their inability to tell lies. Furthermore, the Yahoos, however savage, are clearly human, whereas the Houyhnhms are not – they are horses: Gulliver, who sides with the Houyhnhms against the Yahoos, and who sails away from their island in a Yahoo-skin boat, would seem to be guilty of savage atrocities, if not actual cannibalism.) It was Swift, an Anglo-Irish Protestant clergyman, who wrote the most celebrated of all texts on cannibalism and the Irish, 'A Modest Proposal' (1729). Here, Swift famously suggests that as a response to widespread famine and poverty in Ireland, children should be bred as livestock, thus simultaneously providing a source of food and income. 'A Modest Proposal' is a satire, but it is difficult to gauge precisely the degree, or the target, of Swift's satirical intent here. After all, it is quite explicitly Irish *Catholics* whom Swift proposes be eaten: 'it would greatly lessen the number of Papists, with whom we are yearly over-run, being the principal breeders of the nation, as well as our most dangerous enemies' (Swift 1976: 443). Although Swift's 'Proposal' does include a brief recognition that cannibalism is an appropriate metaphor for England's relationship with Ireland – '*perhaps I could name a country which would be glad to eat up our whole nation*' – its real target does seem to be the Catholic Irish, who are indeed regarded here as livestock, likened to 'sheep, black cattle, or swine', and who are referred to as 'our savages' (Swift 1976: 445, 441).

There were Scottish cannibals too. The notorious fifteenth-century Scottish highwayman and cannibal, Sawney Bean, lived in a cave near Ballantrae in the south-west of Scotland, reputedly fathering an incestuous family of forty-seven children, and was allegedly responsible for over a thousand murders over the course of twenty-five years.[22] Bean's exploits became the stuff of legend, especially through the eighteenth and nineteenth centuries. S.R. Crockett's rattling Scottish adventure novel, *The Grey Man* (1896), has its narrator Launcelot Kennedy and his companions trapped in Bean's cave:

> But that which took my eye amid the smoke were certain vague shapes, as it had been of the limbs of human beings, shrunk and blackened, which hung in rows from either side of the cave. At first it seemed that my eyes must certainly deceive me, for the reek drifted hither and thither, and made the rheum flow from them with its bitterness. But after a little study of these adornments, I could make nothing else of it, than that these poor relics, which hung in rows from the roof of the cave like hams and black puddings set to dry in the smoke, were indeed no other than the parched arms and legs of men and women who had once walked the upper earth – but who by misfortune had fallen into the power of this hideous, inconceivable gang of monstrous man-eaters.
>
> (Crockett 1896: 272)

(They also discover various body-parts in pickle-barrels.) Bean himself enters, stepping on a naked 'lad of six or seven': 'The imp squirmed round like a serpent and bit Sawny [sic] Bean on the leg, whereat he stooped, and catching the lad by the feet, he dashed his head with a dull crash against the wall, and threw him quivering like a dead rabbit in the corner.' The boy's mother attacks Bean with a knife, which he takes from her, cutting her throat: 'I saw a great part of the crew swarm thick as flies – fetching, carrying, and working like bees upon spilled honey about the cornet where had lain the bodies of the lad and the woman' (ibid.: 275–6, 277). Their dismembered corpses are placed in a cauldron.

Our heroes are saved when Kennedy's companion, Dominie Mure, frightens the cannibals off by playing loudly on the bagpipes! Relative to what has come before, this seems rather bathetic, though it does contain the appealing idea that cannibals, as subjects of colonialism, can be defeated by the pipes, nationalist symbols of identity. Mure himself eventually kills Bean, stabbing him repeatedly through the heart in an act of personal vengeance – Bean has previously eaten his beloved Mary Torrance. Other accounts of Bean's death, though just as legendary, are more suitably gruesome: an early nineteenth-century chapbook account of Bean's life and crimes reports that 'The men first had their privy members cut off, and thrown into the fire before their faces; then their hands and legs were cut off, by which amputation they bled to death in a few hours after' (Anon. *c.*1810: 8). (This should stand as a warning to all would-be cannibals.)

Flaubert's *Salammbô* is far from alone as a nineteenth-century high-cultural flirtation with cannibalism. Géricault's great painting *The Raft of the Medusa* (1819) is a dramatic imaginative reconstruction of the fate of the 149 passengers of the frigate *Medusa* which foundered on the way to Senegal: the handful of survivors resorted to cannibalism. Géricault even talked to the ship's carpenter, who had made the raft, and who made a model of it for his studio; he also set up a studio near a hospital, the better to study the bodies of dying men (Clarke 1969: 309). It is the fate of the cabin-boy Richard Parker to be eaten by his hungry shipwrecked companions in Edgar Allan Poe's *The Narrative of Arthur Gordon Pym of Nantucket* (1838); Richard Parker was also the name of the cabin-boy of the shipwrecked *Alignonette*, killed and eaten by Captain Thomas Dudley and the other six survivors. Mikita Brottman notes in her study of 'Cannibal Culture':

> Known as the 'custom of the sea', cannibalism was considered legitimate as long as straws were drawn to determine who was going to be eaten. Nevertheless, it was usually the cabin boy who ended up on the menu; in fact, the captain would normally take the cabin boy on board his lifeboat when a ship was abandoned to ensure there would be adequate provisions.
>
> (1998: 14)

(With good reason: as Swift's 'Modest Proposal' notes, children are tenderer and tastier than adults.) In the twentieth century, Norman Mailer repeatedly draws on cannibalism and imagery in his work, in *An American Dream*, *The Barbary Shore*, and notably in *Cannibals and Christians*, an attempt to view twentieth-century politics through the lens of cannibalism; Monique Wittig's lesbian fiction graphically features cannibalism and dismemberment; while Thomas Harris's *Hannibal* is an (over-)ambitious attempt to draw connections between cannibalism and European civilization.

The raw and the cooked: cannibals onscreen

But it is in the cinema, of course, where cannibals have most flourished. *Dr X*, one of the great Mad Scientist movies, has its 'Full Moon Killer', the one-armed Professor Wells (Preston Foster), author of a study of cannibalism, creating a new limb and a mask from 'synthetic flesh', which he has created from 'the flesh of real people, the flesh that Africans eat'. Two of his colleagues, Professors Haines and Rowitz, were themselves shipwrecked on Tahiti for three weeks, along with a third scientist, who mysteriously disappeared without trace. Surveying these untrustworthy suspects, Dr Xavier himself (Lionel Atwill) declares that 'One of us in this room may be a cannibal'; he believes that one of then 'at some point in the past, was driven to cannibalism ... the memory of that act was driven like a nail into that man.'[23]

Unquestionably the greatest of all cannibal movies, *The Texas Chain Saw Massacre* is also, for my money, the greatest of all modern horror movies (as well as having what is undoubtedly the finest title of *any* film, ever, and featuring, in Marilyn Burns's performance as Sally Hardesty, the greatest example of sustained screaming since Fay Wray in *King Kong*). The anthropologist Claude Lévi-Strauss's (1970) fundamental category distinction between 'raw' and 'cooked' food as an index of civilization is generally borne out also in cannibal movies, with cultured European and American cannibals such as Hannibal Lecter or the 'Wendigo' cannibals of the Rocky Mountain army camp in *Ravenous* (Robert Carlyle, Guy Pearce and Jeffrey Jones) eating their victims deliciously cooked, while the Amazonian 'savages' of the Italian 'gut-muncher' cannibal movies of Ruggero Deodato, Umberto Lenzi and others prefer to chow down on the raw internal organs of their (preferably still living) victims.[24] The disenfranchised white trash of *The Texas Chain Saw Massacre* fall somewhere in between these two poles: their culinary method of choice is the barbecue.

Chain Saw is one of several film to be based, however loosely, on the hideous exploits of Ed Gein, the Wisconsin cannibal, necrophile, and serial-killer.[25] Gein started out disinterring corpses, moving on in the 1950s to the murder of a number of middle-aged women, using their bones, dismembered body-parts and flayed skins as ornaments, furniture and clothing. The terrible room into which Pam (Terri McMinn) stumbles in *Chain Saw*, a veritable museum of human artefacts (and, also very disturbingly, chicken-feathers), is clearly a reconstruction of Gein's den, and the film's opening sequence shows corpses being exhumed and displayed as though having sex, caught in the flashbulb of a camera, though its other claims to historical veracity ('one of the most bizarre crimes in the annals of American history', as the film's spoken introduction has it) are patently false.

The film begins with a group of young people – Sally Hardesty, her boyfriend Jerry, her wheelchair-bound brother Franklin, and their friends Kirk and Pam – driving to a cemetery in a van, to see whether the Hardestys' grandfather's grave has been violated. Interviewed to mark the British TV premiere, Tobe Hooper suggested that *Chain Saw* was actually about 'a bad day – it's about a cosmically bad day', and certainly the film heavily deploys apocalyptic imagery and symbols, tokens and portents: there are shots of solar flares, and of a dead armadillo in the road (the armadillo has had a special symbolic significance in the horror film since its memorable use in Tod Browning's *Dracula*); a drunken old man sitting in a tyre tells Franklin that 'Things happen hereabouts that they don't tell about. I see things'; they pick up a mad hitchhiker, who cuts into the palm of his hand with

Franklin's knife, photographs the young people and then ritualistically burns the photo (it is the Hitchhiker who has been digging up corpses – his is the flashbulb which illuminates the opening sequence), and then scrawls what looks like an occult symbol with his own blood on the side of the van.

Nevertheless, the film also offers a more prosaic, materialistic rationale for its events: economic disenfranchisement. The cannibal family all worked in a nearby slaughterhouse (as did the Hardestys' grandfather), but were made redundant as the slaughterhouse was mechanized for a faster turnover, and have since put their professional skills to a different use, providing meat for the barbecue sold at the father's garage and store (early on, the film juxtaposes images of the youngsters in their van with cattle lined up for slaughter; rather wonderful-looking gigantic sausages, presumably made from her companions, are later served to Sally Hardesty). Grandpa, once a champion slaughterman, is now so enfeebled that he is initially taken for a corpse himself (not least because he sits upstairs in a room with his wife's decomposed body and, most oddly, their dead dog). He is brought back to a semblance of life by sucking the blood from Sally's finger, and tries further to revive his old, powerful self by killing Sally in the old way, while the father, Old Man (the magnificent Jim Siedow), reassures her:

> It won't hurt none. Why, Grandpa's the best killer there ever was. Why, it never took more than one lick, they say. He did sixty in five minutes once – they say he could've done more if the hook and pull gang could've gotten the beefs out of the way faster.

Now too weak to lift the hammer, Grandpa repeatedly fails to kill Sally, who eventually manages to escape.

Chain Saw is one of a series of important American regional Gothic films from around the 1970s, all of which dramatize bruising encounters between modern, urban types and deranged backwoods (and backwards) folk: others include *Deliverance*, *Death Trap*, *The Hills Have Eyes*, and *Southern Comfort*. While not all cannibal movies, nor even necessarily all horror movies *per se*, they are all 'city slicker' narratives – the formal template here is *Wuthering Heights*, and more direct antecedents include the Southern Gothic writings of William Faulkner and, particularly, Flannery O'Connor. *Death Trap*, Tobe Hooper's flawed but fascinating sequel to *Chain Saw*, stars Neville Brand (the fourth most decorated soldier in World War II!) as Judd, a murderous Bayou hotelier who wields a scythe and keeps a Nile crocodile as a pet (the local gators aren't hungry enough, apparently), alongside a distinguished supporting cast which includes Stuart Whitman, a young Robert Englund (Freddy Krueger himself), Carolyn Jones (the original Morticia Addams, here as the local madame), and sleazy horror stalwart Mel Ferrer. Here, Hooper expands upon a technique which had proven particularly effective in *Chain Saw*, where the Old Man menaces

Sally in his store and barbecue to the sound of country and western music on the radio, thus juxtaposing a homely, comforting version of the American South with its terrifying underside. In *Death Trap*, virtually every scene is played out to such accompaniment.[26]

Like *Chain Saw*, Wes Craven's *The Hills Have Eyes* is an authentic cannibal movie. The Carter family, Californian suburbanites, accidentally drive into an air testing range while taking a vacation detour to look for a mysterious diamond mine (which is, typically, not on any map), crash, and find themselves menaced by a family of inbred mutant cannibal survivalists. As is often the case in Craven's films, the suburban family finally turn on their attackers and dispose of them. Having more to lose from the encounter in material terms, they are ultimately more dangerous, just as in *The Last House on the Left*, the affluent Collingwoods finally kill the psychotic escaped criminals holed up in their house, in *A Nightmare on Elm Street* the good folk of Elm Street initially form a mob to lynch and burn the child-murderer Freddy Krueger, and in *Scream* the masked slasher turns out to be both Billy and Stu, two middle-class kids out for kicks.

It is Italian cinema, however, which has provided the most complete vision of man-as-meat, with a series of notorious, long-banned cannibal movies made during the 1970s and 1980s, a list which includes *Cannibal Holocaust*, *Cannibal Ferox*, *Eaten Alive*, *Prisoner of the Cannibal God*, *Deep River Savages*, and a number of others. Together, these constitute the most extreme body of work in cinematic history, if not in aesthetic history *tout court*, offering a grim, relentlessly repellent vision of the human body and of human culture. Though the films do differ from one another in detail and intensity – one, *Prisoner of the Cannibal God*, even features actors you've heard of (Stacy Keach, Ursula Andress), and is fundamentally an exotic adventure narrative, a kind of Indiana-Jones-with-entrails – they all follow what is essentially the same plot. In these films, a group of modern, urban, Western adventurers, scientists, or film-makers, travels up the Amazon, encountering first nature in the raw, and then a tribe of Amerindian cannibals, invariably described as belonging to a culture fundamentally of the Stone or Iron Age. That is to say, the cannibals are figured as *less evolved* than their Western counterparts, and the films' dietary logic follows itself a kind of Darwinian principle, moving 'up the ladder' from depictions of animals eating each other, to animals eating humans (or anyway, attacking or killing them), to humans eating animals (real footage of the killing and eating of live animals is a regular feature in these films), to Amerindians eating each other, and culminating in scenes of the cannibals eating the Westerners. Like Montaigne's essay, however, the films do attempt some degree of relativism: the Westerners are usually untrustworthy types – capitalists out to secure uranium rites (*Prisoner of the Cannibal God*), exploitative film-makers (*Cannibal Holocaust*), drug-dealers on the run (*Cannibal Ferox*), Jim Jones-type cultists (*Eaten Alive*) – who do great damage to the Amazonian communities they effectively

invade, leading to an anthropophagous revenge. Typically, the films close by
asking who the 'real savages' were.

Ruggero Deodato's *Cannibal Holocaust* is by far the most noteworthy of
these films. Though unquestionably disgusting and quite possibly immoral,
the film is aesthetically and intellectually worthy at least of serious
consideration: Deodato himself is an extremely accomplished film-maker,
and the film has a number of potentially very intelligent points to make
about the relationship between ethics, aesthetics, and profit in film-making,
and about what should or should not be represented onscreen. The only
book-length study of Deodato's work suggests that '*Cannibal Holocaust* is
the bastard son of the mondo [exploitation] genre. It seeks to critique the
form and lambast the methods of its proponents' (Fenton *et al.* 1999: 65).
Deodato, however, blows any chance he gets of his film being viewed as a
serious statement *about* the exploitative nature of film-making, rather than
a work *of* exploitative film-making, since his own film is at every point
guilty of the excesses it supposedly condemns.

Cannibal Holocaust opens by juxtaposing images of the Amazon and its
rainforests with the 'urban jungle' of New York, where a TV presenter intones
a paean to Western modernity: 'Today we are on the threshold of conquering
our galaxy, and in the not-too-distant tomorrow we'll be considering the
universe. And yet man seems to ignore the fact that on this very planet there
are still people living in the stone age and practising cannibalism.' The film
has two main narrative strands, presented in reverse chronological order.
The first is the story of NYU anthropology professor Harold Monroe (played
by the unlikely figure of Italian porn-star Roberto Bolla, here credited as
Salvatore Basile), who goes up the Amazon on a search-and-rescue mission
for a group of missing film-makers and finds himself among cannibals, the
Yamamono or 'Tree People', a tribe so mythically ferocious that no white
person has ever seen them and lived to tell of it. Monroe finds their
decomposing bodies with cameras placed in their ribcages, which the
Yamamono girls seem to worship as idols, and also some miraculously
preserved cans of film. The second half of the film has Monroe viewing the
footage with a group of TV executives. It is here that we meet the film-makers,
documentarist Alan Yates, who made his name filming in Vietnam and Africa,
and his crew, Faye Daniels, Jack Anders, and Mark Tomazzo.

From its very opening shots, then, the film continually and explicitly
juxtaposes images of American modernity and Amazonian savagery, arguing
(mendaciously, I suggest) for a relativistic view of human barbarism. Monroe,
who himself takes part in Yamanono cannibal rites, is later interviewed in a
New York television studio, while monitors behind simultaneously show
both himself and a boxing match. Yates and his crew are revealed as a group
of entirely disreputable film-makers – manipulative and evil, willing to stage
atrocities in their desire for good material: 'Keep rolling! We're gonna get an
Oscar for this!' Mark says, while Alan says, 'This is gonna make us rich and
famous . . . This is gonna make us lots of money!' Back in New York, Monroe

is shown their previous film, *The Last Road to Hell*, a document of savagery and executions in a modern African state (Uganda?), which is described to Monroe as a 'put-on' (that is, staged for the camera), but which seems to consist of genuine atrocity footage. Everything in this section of the film is itself filmed, thus setting up a mock-debate on the ethics of film-making and representation, a debate to which, in a less obviously sleazy context, the inclusion of 'The Last Road to Hell' might have contributed meaningfully. When their guide Felipe is bitten by a poisonous snake, the film-makers needlessly amputate his leg and then film him bleeding to death: 'You still shooting?' they ask (as later, when a caiman gets into the river with Alan, he says, 'Forget about me! Film it! Film it!'). Mark shoots a pig, while Alan says to camera, 'Here we are at the edge of the world and human history. Things like this happen all the time in the jungle – it's survival of the fittest. In the jungle, it's the daily violence of the strong overcoming the weak.' To demonstrate this, Mark and Jack herd members of the peaceable Yacumo tribe into a hut which they then torch, wanting to pass it off as a massacre by the cannibal Yamamonos. This section of the film closes as the film-makers are attacked and eaten by the Yamamonos: they continue to film as Jack is graphically dismembered, disembowelled, and cannibalized, and as Faye is raped and beheaded: 'Think of the film!' Mark tells Alan. Finally, Alan turns the camera on himself, filming his own death. Back in New York, the TV executive finds the footage extraordinary, while Monroe is horrified: 'It is offensive, it is dishonest, and above all it is inhuman', he says, offering an inadvertently powerful critique of *Cannibal Holocaust* itself; 'It's a rough cut', she replies, unable to distinguish between the ethics and the aesthetics of film-making, and always thinking of profit. Where Monroe had earlier likened the cannibal tribes to 'civilized' modern powers, describing the Yamamono and their enemies the Shamatari as 'two superpowers ... perpetually at war with each other', the film closes with his asking, in a fashion typical of the genre, 'I wonder who the real cannibals are?' Discussing this closing comment, Deodato himself has suggested that 'We should have left no doubt in the minds of the spectators about the moral stance of the film. They make me laugh, some of the critiques against me, when they speak of the "gratuitous pleasure" of certain scenes' (Fenton *et al.* 1999: 19). The TV studio agrees to burn the film, but not before we have seen it ourselves.

Notes

1. As a Welshman, I have, like many in these islands, very serious problems with any notion of a contemporary 'British' identity, as I take it as an imperializing synonym for 'Englishness', and as expressive of an imposed unity which no longer obtains and has become damaging. However, as the (Welsh) historian Linda Colley has argued, it is entirely proper to describe the process of forming a national identity across the eighteenth century as 'British': 'we can plausibly regard Great Britain as an invented nation superimposed, if only for a while, onto much older alignments and loyalties' (Colley 1992: 1).

2. See Colley (1992: 11–54) for the role of Protestantism in forging a national identity. See Sage (1988) for a major study of the relationship between Gothic and Protestantism.
3. See Burman (1984). Deism was a form of rational Christianity, an attempt to reconcile traditional Christian thinking with the Enlightenment.
4. For a richly detailed account of the accusations of blasphemy made against the novel, upon which I draw heavily here, see Parreaux (1960: 79–143).
5. For Bowdler, Plumtre and *The Monk*, see Parreaux (1960: 97–8).
6. For Mathias, see Parreaux (1960: 103–11).
7. For an account of the role of the broken mirror in Irish writing (though it does not make reference to this remark of Edgeworth's), see Caraher (2000).
8. For accounts, some sceptical, of a 'Gothic' Wales or Scotland, see Sullivan (1987); Bianchi (1995); McMillan (1995).
9. For Price, see Bracegirdle (1997).
10. Peter Haining, Introduction to *Great Welsh Fantasy Stories* (Haining 2000: 14). See also Haining (1999).
11. For an account of Antinomianism and its relationship with religious dissent, see Thompson (1993: 3–21).
12. For a good introduction to this subject, see Broadie (1997).
13. Furthermore, as W.J. McCormack notes, 'Any further uneasiness about a Papist narrator is largely dissolved by placing the stories in the remote early decades of the previous century. The priest is now safely dead: his papers relate confessions and adventures relating from the first years of his ministry' (McCormack 1997: 55–6). See also Sage (1988: 40–8).
14. Whale's most recent biographer, James Curtis, is rather cagey on this subject: 'It is not known whether Whale took any private amusement in the sexual confusion of the role' (Curtis 1998: 181). The identity of 'John Dudgeon' was a mystery until 1975, when Whale's partner, David Lewis, finally explained things: 'Jimmy couldn't find a male actor who looked old enough to suit him … so he finally used an old stage actress he knew called Elspeth Dudgeon. She looked a thousand' (Curtis 1998: 180).
15. He wasn't. Rains was born in 1889; Chaney Jr was born Creighton Chaney in 1906 – so Rains could conceivably be his (very young) father.
16. See Gifford (1977). Most accounts of the film, indeed, identify its Welsh location: see, for example, Newman (1996: 343); Jones (1999: 416).
17. British viewers are most likely to have seen an 84-minute print (an edit overseen by Roger Corman), and American viewers a 102-minute print, which plays some scenes in a different order and does not contain material which *is* in the shorter version. Neither of these, however, can be reckoned 'complete', nor can the 96-minute American cinema version cut by Robin Hardy and Ron Weinberg in 1977. Christopher Lee, one of *The Wicker Man*'s stars, is on record as believing that the film should have run 'between two-and-a-half and three hours'. See Brown (2000: xix–xx, 148).
18. Brown seeks to compare *The Wicker Man* favourably to the contemporaneous and similarly powerful *The Exorcist*, which is reasonable, though he does so in the crassest of terms: 'In truth, *The Exorcist* attracts the serious attentions only of those who enjoy the sight of crucifixes violating teenage vaginas' (2000: 71).
19. This scene is controversial for a number of reasons, not all to do with eroticism. In the American print, this takes place on Howie's *second* night in Summerisle, not his first: the next scene, where Willow brings Howie a cup of tea the next morning, is cut from the American version, though it *does* feature in the shorter British cut (presumably for the sake of some kind of consistency, since in the American version's chronology, by the time Willow talks to Howie it already *is* May Day). There is also the question of who, precisely, is writhing naked in

Willow MacGregor's room: Britt Ekland was pregnant during filming, and consented only to show her breasts – Willow's bottom, however, belongs to a body double (a botty double!). Brown quotes Robin Hardy: 'we had to get a go-go dancer very quickly to play her backside' (Brown 2000: 90). The go-go dancer's name, unfortunately, is lost, though Ekland has subsequently complained that she had a 'huge arse'!

20. Brown's Appendix 6 reproduces a full transcript of Schaffer's original encounter between Howie and Lord Summerisle.
21. Matthew, 26:26. The version in Mark (14:22) is virtually identical, while in Luke (22:19), Christ exhorts his disciples: 'This is my body which is given for you: this do in remembrance of me.' All quotations are from the King James's version.
22. For an accessible account of Bean's career, though one which at no point attempts to distinguish between fact and fiction, see Haining (1994: 23–36).
23. For a reading of the cannibal elements of *Dr X*, see Brottman (1998: 161–3).
24. *Ravenous* was inspired by the case of Alferd Packer, who in 1874 led a group of gold prospectors into the Colorado Rockies. He was the only one to return. Later, the bones of his companions were discovered near Lake Fort Gunnison, stripped of flesh. Packer was imprisoned for 40 years, and remains the only American ever to have been convicted of cannibalism (Brottman 1998: 15). Nor is *Ravenous* the only film to have been based on the Packer case: in 1995, Trey Parker of *South Park* fame directed *Alferd Packer – The Musical* (aka *Cannibal – The Musical*). The 'wendigo', or 'windigo', is an evil spirit reputed by the Native Americans to take over the bodies of men, causing an insatiable compulsion for human flesh. *Ravenous*, like *Dr X*, assumes that cannibalism is instantly and powerfully addictive: once you pop, you can't stop.
25. Others include: *Psycho*; *Deranged: The Confessions of a Necrophile*, which features a brilliant performance from Western stalwart Roberts Blossom as Ezra Cobb, who digs up his beloved mother's corpse and takes it home with him, and takes to body-snatching and then serial-murder for corpses to keep her company; Jame Gumb ('Buffalo Bill') in *The Silence of the Lambs*, making an outfit from the flayed skins of his victims; and *Ed Gein*, a purportedly faithful biopic.
26. *Death Trap* was the film's UK title. It was also released as *Eaten Alive*, *Horror Hotel*, *Horror Hotel Massacre*, *Legend of the Bayou*, *Murder on the Bayou*, and *Starlight Slaughter*. This sheer number of titles attests to the difficulties and complexities in the making and distribution of this film, which in turn accounts for why it is so obscure and rarely seen. The film is loosely based on the activities of Joseph Ball, owner of the Sociable Inn on Highway 181 outside Elmsdorf, Texas, in the 1920s and 1930s, who was discovered to have killed some 25 women and fed their remains (along with horse meat and live dogs) to the five alligators he kept in a pool out back.

|2|

Mad science

Frankenstein and his monsters

> I was working in the lab late one night
> When my eyes beheld an eerie sight
> > (Bobby 'Boris' Picket and the Crypt-Kickers)[1]

'And you call yourself a scientist?'

The Naked Lunch, William Burroughs's notorious novel of junkiedom, contains the following snippet of dialogue between Dr Benway, unethical experimental psychologist and brain-surgeon, and his assistant Dr Schafer:

> SCHAFER: I tell you, I can't escape a feeling ... well, of *evil* about this.
> BENWAY: Balderdash, my boy ... We're scientists ... Pure scientists. Disinterested research, and damned be him who cries, 'Hold, *too much*!' Such people are no better than party poops.
> > (Burroughs 1986: 109)

This dialogue draws quite self-consciously upon a tradition rooted in Gothic fiction and then developed upon by the horror movie in the 1930s and 1940s, the tradition of the Mad Scientist. In his book *Monsters and Mad Scientists*, film theorist Andrew Tudor writes: 'The belief that science is dangerous is as central to the horror movie as is a belief in the malevolent inclinations of ghosts, ghouls, vampires and zombies' (1989: 133). Furthermore, Tudor notes that, during the period covered by his study, 1931–84, in just over a quarter of horror movies (264 of the 990 films given a UK cinema release) 'science is posited as a primary source of disorder, and in 169 of them that impulse is given flesh in the person of a "mad scientist"' (ibid.: 133). Cinema is itself a technological medium, and thus the workings of science have been the source of particular fascination to it. The great American inventor Thomas Edison was responsible for one of the first cinematic *Frankenstein*s in 1910 (that is to say, the Edison Manufacturing Company studios made the film; the director was J. Searle Dawney, and Charles Ogle played the Monster), as well as being himself the subject of several biopics. Recently, *Shadow of the Vampire* has John Malkovich playing the *Nosferatu* director F.W. Murnau as a classic mad scientist.

The twentieth century, in particular, provided ample reasons to fear science. The early century saw what the popular imagination understood as the 'dethroning' of humanity from the centre of creation as a consequence of Darwinist evolutionary theory, and many early horror movies reflect this, particularly in the wake of the Scopes 'monkey trial' of 1925, which saw a Tennessee schoolteacher prosecuted for teaching evolution. *King Kong* gave audiences man-as-monkey writ large – writ very large indeed! – while a number of films from the 1930s and 1940s are concerned with scientists seeking to interpose themselves into the scheme of evolution by creating humans from apes: *Murders in the Rue Morgue, The Island of Lost Souls, Dr Renault's Secret, The Ape Man, The Jungle Captive*. In the mid-century, nuclear fears fed a series of radiation-mutation horrors which I discuss below, while the nuclear scientists themselves heavily influenced cinematic mad science, particularly the figures of Edward Teller, the Hungarian-American cold warrior most influential in the development of the hydrogen bomb, and Wernher von Braun, the former Nazi V-2 rocket scientist who became a senior scientific figure in the American space administration, and who was himself immortalized by Curt Jurgens in a whitewashing biopic, *I Aim at the Stars* (the comedian Mort Sahl suggested that this should be retitled *I Aim at the Stars . . . But Sometimes I Hit London!*). Figures such as these combine in the creation of the mid-century's archetypal mad scientist, Dr Strangelove. More recently, fears over cloning and genetic engineering inform the *Jurassic Park* series of books and films.

Implicit in all of these fears is the image of the scientist 'playing God', an image which has accompanied horror-science from the beginning. While the theme of usurping the role of God through creating life is certainly present in Mary Shelley's original *Frankenstein* (1818), as its subtitle, *The Modern Prometheus*, implies, its thematic *centrality* to that text has been overstated (it is far more prevalent in the revised edition of 1831, which tones down the original's radicalism, offering a more acceptably conventional Christian morality). Nevertheless, this notion of playing God as the major transgression of scientists *has* become a central concern in cinematic mad science. 'It's alive! It's alive! Oh, in the name of God! Now I know how it feels to be God!' exclaims Henry Frankenstein (Colin Clive) in James Whale's *Frankenstein*, this last line considered so inflammatory that it was excised from the film, replaced by a thunderclap. In *The Island of Lost Souls*, Dr Moreau (Charles Laughton) asks Edward Parker (Richard Arlen) whether he knows 'what it feels like to be God' – the film was banned

outright in Britain for 25 years. Whale's *Frankenstein* includes a warning
prologue spoken by Edward Van Sloan – not directed by Whale and
prefixing the movie at the behest of producer Carl Laemmle – which offers
a thematic synopsis of the film: 'We are about to unfold the story of
Frankenstein, a man of science who sought to create a man after his own
image, without reckoning upon God.' Whale's great sequel, *The Bride of
Frankenstein*, has Frankenstein's associate Dr Pretorius offer a toast 'To a
new world of gods and monsters!' In *The Raven*, Jean Thatcher (Irene
Ware) tells the Poe-obsessed neurosurgeon Dr Vollin (Bela Lugosi), 'You're
almost not a man at all. You're more like –' 'A god?' Vollin says, finishing
her sentence, 'But a god tainted with human emotion'; while in *The Fly*
(1958), Helene (Patricia Owens), the wife of physicist André Delambre (Al
Hedison), says of his research: 'It's frightening. It's like playing God', to
which André replies 'God gives us intelligence to uncover the wonders of
nature. Without that gift, nothing is possible.' In *Jurassic Park*, Dr Ian
Malcolm (Jeff Goldblum) offers a critique of the billionaire industrialist
John Hammond's (Richard Attenborough) programme of genetic
engineering to recreate dinosaurs that is entirely based on Hammond's
having violated the natural order of things: the dinosaurs had their shot, he
says, but blew it – we should not tamper with evolution (the evolutionary
biologist Stephen Jay Gould describes Malcolm's critique here as 'vacuous
pap ... the oldest diatribe, the most hackneyed and predictable staple of
every Hollywood monster film since *Frankenstein*') (1997a: 229, 232).[2] Nor
are such hubristic statements confined to cinematic mad science: perhaps
influenced by this tradition, Stephen Hawking closes his *A Brief History of
Time* with the famous comment about science enabling us to 'know the
mind of God' (1988: 193), a comment which has since been taken up and
adapted by a number of other practising scientists to describe their work,
and which resonates profoundly with almost a century of similar
pronouncements from Hawking's dubious celluloid colleagues.[3]

We should not, however, assume that all horror-movie science is
necessarily *mad* science. Horror can result from fundamentally benign
scientific endeavour which goes awry. This is the basic position of André
Delambre and of Seth Brundle (Jeff Goldblum) in both versions of *The Fly*,
working on a matter-transfer device, who accidentally fuse their own genes
with those of a fly, in Brundle's case creating the monstrous 'Brundlefly'.
This is also the case with Professor Deemer (Leo G. Carroll) in *Tarantula*,
who, searching for a nutrition serum to end world hunger, inadvertently
creates a rampaging giant spider, and of the cancer researchers in *Island of
Terror*, who accidentally create a deadly bone-sucking, silicone-based
lifeform. This, too, is the situation of Dr Susan Tyler (Mira Sorvino), the
glamorous NYU entomologist in *Mimic* who, in order to stop the spread of
'Strickler's Disease', which only affects children and is wiping out the child
population of New York, and which is spread by cockroaches, introduces a
genetically engineered bug, 'the Judas Breed', into the roach population in

order to destroy them. This then mutates into a deadly race of super-evolved bug-men, living in a colony in the New York subway system, disguising themselves as the homeless tunnel-dwellers who are also their prey.

Or, horror can be the result of the unexpected consequences of technological advancement, in technophobic narratives in which science itself is seen as the threat, rather than the workings of individual scientists. Earlier technophobic films most commonly figured the threat in the form of transfiguring radiation, a common trope of 1950s' horror, overshrouded as it was by cold war terrors and particularly fears of nuclear annihilation. Radiation, most often through nuclear testing, produces giant mutations – ants in *Them!*; a lizard in the Toho Studios' *Godzilla*-cycle (given its recent history, a fire-breathing nuclear monster which lays waste to cities was particularly significant to Japan in the 1950s); crabs in *Attack of the Crab Monsters*. The spider in *Tarantula*, though not atomically mutated, also clearly belongs in this category. In *The Incredible Shrinking Man*, radiation produces the converse, with the increasingly tiny Scott Carey (Grant Williams) finally vanishing into nothingness – a memorable image of individual powerlessness in the face of modern technology. In films from the 1960s onwards, zombification tends to be the preferred outcome of exposure to forms of radiation, as in the astonishing *Night of the Living Dead*, or in *Nightmare City*, aka *Invasion by the Atomic Zombies*: often, these films are genuinely apocalyptic, raising the possibility of the total destruction of humanity (as such, they form a part of the tradition of invasion narratives to be discussed in Chapter 6). *Tarantula* is also a kind of forerunner to a series of films from the 1970s and 1980s concerned with mutation either through pollution or through chemical-biological research: *Night of the Lepus* (giant rabbits); *Bug* (pyromaniac cockroaches, released by an earthquake, experimented on by biologist Bradford Dillman); *Food of the Gods* (from a story by H.G. Wells, and featuring a rampaging giant chicken); *Piranha* (in which the eponymous nasties are developed as a biological weapon for use in Vietnam); *Alligator* (in which a sewer-dwelling reptile terrorizes Chicago, grown to giant size after eating laboratory animals used in hormone-experiments). From the same period, James Herbert's series of *Rats* novels (from 1974) also feature deadly mutated super-rats, here almost succeeding in overrunning London. Most recent, and most extreme of all technophobic narratives are those films which envisage a (near-) future in which humanity is destroyed or enslaved by machines, a genre which has its contemporary origins in *Demon Seed*, and its most celebrated examples in the *Terminator* movies, and in *The Matrix*.

Horror can also result from the total severing of scientific concerns from ethical concerns in a grotesque version of 'disinterested' scientific pursuit, 'for its own sake', without concern for the consequences. This is probably the most influential type of horror-science, as practised by the paradigmatic trio of mad scientists, Doctors Frankenstein, Jekyll, and Moreau, though all three of their original novels at least gesture towards the idea that their scientific advances are made in some way for the betterment of humanity. This 'classic' mad science will be the substance of the latter parts of this chapter.

Finally, at the extreme end of our spectrum, there are scientists whose aims are explicitly evil: Dr Ten Brinken inseminating a prostitute with the semen of a hanged man in the several cinematic versions of Hanns Heinz Ewers's novel *Alraune* (1911); Rottwang (Rudolf Klein-Rogge) creating an artificial woman to put down a workers rebellion in *Metropolis*; the sadistic Vollin in *The Raven* with his laboratory full of torture-devices ('Try to be sane, Vollin,' one of his victims implores); Dale Coba (Patrick O'Neal) replacing women with docile automata in *The Stepford Wives*; Dr Mengele (Gregory Peck) creating clones of Hitler in *The Boys From Brazil*; Dr Hannibal Lecter, the cannibalistic psychologist, in his various guises. And this is not to mention the host of mad scientists bent more generally on world domination.

In spite of this range of approaches, it has been fairly noted that science is generally given a bad press in the horror genre. For one thing, there is an uncomfortable conservatism in the portrayal of the scientist – not only a mistrust of the products of a science unchecked by ethical considerations (which would be reasonable), but also what amounts to a more general suspicion regarding intelligence, knowledge and learning. The astronomer Carl Sagan has written powerfully on this subject:

> The technological perils that science serves up, its implicit challenge to received wisdom, and its perceived difficulty, are all reasons for some people to mistrust and avoid it. There's a reason people are nervous about science and technology. And so the image of the mad scientist haunts our world – down to the white-coated loonies of Saturday morning children's TV and the plethora of Faustian bargains in popular culture, from the eponymous Dr Faustus himself to Dr Frankenstein, Dr Strangelove, and *Jurassic Park*.
> But we can't simply conclude that science puts too much power into the hands of morally feeble technologists or corrupt, power-crazed politicians and so decide to get rid of it.
>   (Sagan 1997: 14)

As the Introduction suggested, the horror genre has often been understood as an inherently radical one, dealing as it does in the violation of social taboos – but here again it is worth suggesting that the contrary may well be true, that horror works to enforce social norms, for example by reinforcing traditional Christian views of creation and the place of humanity – those who seek to question these views invariably meet a sticky end.

The mad scientist's 'moral enfeeblement' is often represented in terms of *physical* lack – most commonly, the missing hand acts as a synecdoche (shorthand!) for the mad scientist. In H.G. Wells's *The Invisible Man* (1897), Griffin, the scientist who has turned himself invisible and is now unable to rematerialize, is first 'seen', by Mr Hall, the landlord of the inn where he is holed up, as 'a handless arm waving towards him'; this is also how Griffin is first experienced by Dr Cuss, the local GP: 'No hand, just an empty sleeve. Lord, I thought, that's a deformity' (Wells 1995a: 14, 22). In *Metropolis*, Rotwang has an artificial hand, as does Inspector Krogh (Lionel Atwill) in *Son of Frankenstein* – Krogh is not himself a mad scientist, but he is a victim of mad science, having had his arm torn off by the Monster as a child: 'One does not easily forget, Herr Baron, an arm torn out at the roots,' he tells Wolf von Frankenstein (Basil Rathbone). Adding insult to injury, the Monster also tears off Krogh's artificial limb! In *Mad Love*, aka *The Hands of Orlac*, the greatest hand movie of them all, concert pianist Stephen Orlac (Colin Clive) has his hands crushed in a train accident; the brilliant, but mad (and severely sexually frustrated) surgeon Dr Gogol (Peter Lorre) grafts on a pair of replacement hands, taken from Rollo, the murderous knife-thrower. Gogol is in love with Orlac's wife Yvonne (Frances Drake), and tries to drive Orlac mad by convincing him that Rollo's hands are taking Orlac over, at one point memorably donning a pair of chrome hands to pass himself off as Rollo, telling Orlac: 'I have no hands. Your hands were mine. I am Rollo the knife-thrower. They cut off my head, but Gogol put it back!' (Culture just doesn't get any better than this.)[4] Dr Strangelove himself (Peter Sellers) has a prosthetic arm which uncontrollably gives Nazi salutes.

Hands also feature notably in Hammer Studios' *Frankenstein*-cycle. In *The Curse of Frankenstein*, Baron Frankenstein (Peter Cushing) wishes to create 'a man with a perfect physique, with the hands of an artist and with the matured brain of a genius'. The hands of the hanged man whose corpse makes the Monster are inadequate – 'Just look at these hands! Great clodhopping things! No wonder he was a robber. With hands like those he couldn't have been anything else – except perhaps a gorilla' – and so he goes off to Leipzig, returning with 'Bardello's hands – the hands of the world's finest sculptor'. *Frankenstein Created Woman* has the Baron (Cushing) with scarred hands perpetually covered by black gloves – presumably they were damaged in the fire that closes the previous entry in the cycle, *The Evil of Frankenstein* – and so cannot perform surgery, having to rely instead on the drunken surgeon Dr Hertz (Thorley Walters). This problem is revisited in *Frankenstein and the Monster From Hell*, where the Baron (Cushing again) complains that his damaged hands have 'lost all sensitivity': here, the hands certainly operate as a synecdoche for the Baron himself, since, as Jonathan Rigby notes, 'we know that the Baron himself lost that capacity years before' (2000: 208).

Away from Hammer, the radioactive zombies of *Night of the Living Dead* become, in Elliott Stein's phrase, 'a symphony of psychotic hands' (Stein 1970: 38–9), an endless display of seemingly disembodied hands, all reaching to grasp and kill the surviving people (this vision of a dehumanized mass as 'hands' – the only part of the body which has use-value in industrial capitalism – has its most famous expression in Charles Dickens's industrial novel *Hard Times*). Dr Polidori (James Mason) in *Frankenstein: The True Story* has a badly scarred, clawlike hand, which he also perpetually hides beneath a black glove. More recently, Brundlefly disgustingly vomits off Stathis Borans's (John Getz) hand with corrosive digestive fluid in Cronenberg's *The Fly*, and John Frankenheimer's troubled *The Island of Dr Moreau* goes out of its way to show Marlon Brando's absurd mad vivisectionist getting his hand gnawed off by one of his creatures. Hannibal Lecter's supernumary digit, excised by every film version of Thomas Harris's novels, is clearly a version of the deformed hand, and the controversial ending of Ridley Scott's *Hannibal*, where Lecter (Anthony Hopkins) cuts off his own hand to evade capture, makes perfect sense in the light of this tradition of handless doctors. Best of all, in *The Terminator* all that survives of Arnold Schwarzenegger's rampaging cyborg is a hand and forearm, preserved and experimented on by the boffins of *Terminator 2* who inadvertently bring about the destruction of humanity – a lasting symbol of the dangers of unchecked scientific research.

Amputated hands can signify forbidden knowledge – the removal of the organ of discovery. This has been frequently noted and interpreted – by Freud and by S.S. Prawer as a symbol of castration; by Skal as indicative of 'where the single-minded pursuit of a scientific obsession can result in a "lost grip" on reality'[5] – and certainly, it is symbolic of a more general sense of lack in the scientist: a lacking in moral or ethical sense, in human understanding, in social skills, in sexual relations. Scientists, horror books and films tell us, are just not normal.

'My hideous progeny'

The centrality of Mary Shelley's *Frankenstein* to a modern horror tradition has made the creation of life – raising the dead, reanimating dead tissue or inanimate matter – the major preoccupation of the classic mad scientist. *Re-Animator*, a loose adaptation of H.P. Lovecraft, has unhinged medical student Herbert West (Jeffrey Combs) discovering a brain-revivifying serum – accused at the very beginning of the movie of murdering his mentor Dr Gruber, West screams out 'I gave him *life*!' But *Frankenstein*'s scientific concerns themselves belong to an older tradition, and provide the modern mad scientist with a rich ancestry of enquiry and experimentation at the frontiers of human knowledge – alchemy.

In *Man Made Monster*, a film which features the reanimation of a dead man through electricity, mad scientist Dr Rigas (Lionel Atwill) is told that 'this theory of yours isn't science – it's black magic.' Working on the boundaries of science and mysticism, the alchemists typically strove for eternal life, untold wealth, or unlimited knowledge through the discovery of the philosopher's stone or the elixir of life, and gained a reputation as black magicians, particularly because of their connections with shady secret societies such as the Illuminati or Rosicrucians, reputedly possessed of arcane or even diabolical knowledge. In 1528, Dr Johannes Faustus was forced out of Ingolstadt (home of Victor Frankenstein's university, and birthplace in 1776 of the Illuminati, who were outlawed in 1785), accused of alchemy and quackery. In his study of Faustianism in literature, J.W. Smeed places the historical Faust 'somewhere between the travelling conjurers, hypnotists, and purveyors of "wonder cures" on the one hand, and a genuine student of natural sciences on the other' (Smeed 1975: 2). In 1540 or 1541, he is believed to have blown himself to pieces while preparing chemical potions in an inn at Staufen. The smell of the chemicals was taken for brimstone, a sure sign that Faust had been taken off by the devil himself.[6] By the publication of Johann Spies's *Historia von D. Iohann Fausten* in 1587, Faust had entered the realm of legend as the scientist who sells his soul to the Devil in exchange for forbidden knowledge: this is the version of Faust which Christopher Marlowe inherited for his great tragedy *Dr Faustus* (1604). Given Enlightenment beliefs in the self-evident benefits of knowledge, and in the desirability and inevitability of human progress, it is perhaps not surprising that eighteenth-century Fausts should be more sympathetic to the Doctor's aims, with Part I of Goethe's *Faust* (1773) the most likely source for Mary Shelley's knowledge of the legend.

Frankenstein is not Shelley's only foray into mad science and alchemy. In and around the 1820s, she wrote a series of works concerned in various ways with reanimated human beings, or more broadly with atemporal and anachronistic men. Her novel *The Last Man* (1826) chronicles the sole human survivor in a future world destroyed by plague (I shall discuss this more fully in Chapter 6). In 1819, she wrote 'Valerius: The Reanimated Roman' (an ancient Roman awakens in modern England), and in 1824 she may have published a story in *The New Monthly Magazine* entitled 'Rome in the First and Nineteenth Centuries', which is the opposite of 'Valerius' (the narrator falls asleep in contemporary Rome, only to awaken in ancient Rome).[7] 'The Mortal Immortal', a tale of an alchemist and disciple of Cornelius Agrippa, who discovers the elixir of life, opens:

> July 16, 1833. – This is a memorable anniversary for me; on it I complete my three hundred and twenty third year!
>
> The Wandering Jew? – certainly not. More than eighteen centuries have passed over his head. In comparison with him, I am a very young Immortal.
>
> (Shelley 1976: 219)

Most interesting of all, though, is her essay 'Roger Dodsworth: The Reanimated Englishman' (1826), in which she discusses a celebrated contemporary hoax. In 1826, an English physician, Dr James Hotham, crossing the French Alps on the return journey of a visit to Italy, discovered a frozen human body in a glacier, dressed in seventeenth-century clothing. The body was dug from the glacier, it thawed out, and in doing so miraculously came back to life. The thawed body announced himself to be Roger Dodsworth, an Englishman, 37 years old, who had been frozen while crossing the Alps in 1654. News of this event was first reported on 28 June 1826 in the *Journal du Commerce de Lyon*, and by July 9 the story had featured in at least six British newspapers. In the ensuing months, the miraculous case was widely discussed, by amongst others, Thomas Moore, William Cobbett, and Samuel Rogers – not to mention Roger Dodsworth himself, who notes that since defrosting, he's been catching up on his reading: 'atte present I am reading ye history of England, by one HUME, and it is prettye to read of men and things off which I had no knoledge' (Robinson 1975: 24). Dodsworth has also been reading, he says, *The Journal of the Plague Year*, *Robinson Crusoe*, and *Gulliver's Travels*. In her own essay on the Dodsworth case, written in the autumn of 1826, Shelley writes:

> Now we do not believe that any contradiction or impossibility is attached to the adventures of this youthful antique. Animation (I believe the physiologists agree) can as easily be suspended for an hundred or two years, as for as many seconds. A body hermetically sealed up by the frost, is of necessity preserved in its pristine entireness. . . . Mr Dodsworth did not sleep; his breast never heaved, his pulses were stopped; death had its finger pressed on his lips which no breath might pass. . . . His victim has cast from him the frosty spell, and arises as perfect a man as he had lain down an hundred and fifty years before.
>
> (1976: 43)

The freezing and reanimating of human tissue is a characteristic concern of subsequent mad science, and was to become the motivating principle of at least two subsequent *Frankenstein* movies, both from the Hammer stable: *Frankenstein Created Woman* and *Frankenstein Must Be Destroyed*.

On hearing the news about Roger Dodsworth, Shelley writes: 'Mr Godwin . . . suspended for the sake of such authentic information the history of the Commonwealth he had just begun' (1976: 43). This is not surprising, since Shelley's father William Godwin, as an Enlightenment rationalist, was fascinated by the problem of mystical knowledge – by alchemists, Illuminati, and Rosicrucians – the secret society possessed of mystical knowledge and the elixir of life, said to have been founded by Christian Rosencreutz, and whose members were said to have included the alchemists Paracelsus, Cornelius Agrippa, and John Dee. In her fascinating study of the role of Rosicrucianism in the Romantic novel, *Gothic Immortals*, Marie

Roberts describes Godwin's *St Leon* (1799), whose protagonist gains eternal life through the *elixir vitae*, as the 'seminal Rosicrucian novel', and notes that the Rosicrucians settle in the literary imagination as 'a species of magician scientists' (Roberts 1990: 5). Percy Shelley, an avowed disciple of Godwin, published the similarly themed novel *St. Irvyne: The Rosicrucian* anonymously (as 'a gentleman of the University of Oxford') in 1811. In 1834, Godwin published *The Lives of the Necromancers* (the publication was arranged and paid for by Mary Shelley). This was a sceptic's guide to mystics, containing chapters on (amongst others) Albertus Magnus, Raymond Lulli ('Doctor Illuminatus', the supposed discoverer of the elixir of life), Cornelius Agrippa, and John Dee (whose amanuensis, Edward Kelly, who had had both ears cut off as punishment for forgery, dug up freshly buried corpses, which then spoke to him), as well as a general chapter entitled 'Quacks, who in Cold Blood Undertook to Overreach Mankind'. Seven years later, in 1841, Charles Mackay published his monumental work of debunking, *Extraordinary Popular Delusions and the Madness of Crowds*, whose longest chapter by far is entitled 'The Alchymists', which deals with 'the erring philosophers or the wilful cheats, who have encouraged or preyed upon the credulity of mankind ... and all the motley trible of quacks, empirics, and charlatans' (Mackay 1932: 99). Mackay's final chapter is entitled 'Relics'.

Of Albertus Magnus, Godwin writes:

> It is related of Albertus, that he made an entire man of brass ... This man would answer all sorts of questions, and was even employed by its maker as a domestic. But what is more extraordinary, this machine is said to have become at length so garrulous, that Thomas Aquinas, being a pupil of Albertus, and finding himself perpetually disturbed in his abstrusest speculations by its uncontrollable loquacity, in a rage caught up a hammer, and beat it to pieces. According to other accounts the man of Albertus Magnus was composed, not of metal, but of flesh and bones like other men.
>
> (1834: 261)

Aquinas *was* famously bad-tempered; after his death, his decapitated body was boiled down to the bone, the better to procure relics. (Tristram 1976: 153). In the Preface to *Lives of the Necromancers*, Godwin writes again:

> But man lives in the past and the future. ... [He] contrives machines ... which may gradually add to the accommodations of all, and raise the species generally into a nobler and more honourable character ... Man looks through nature, and is able to reduce its parts into a great whole. ... He takes to pieces the substances that are, and combines their parts into

new arrangements. He peoples all the elements from the world
of his imagination.

(1834: vi–vii)

Which brings me to Mary Shelley's most famous novel ...

In 1691, Konrad Dippel, who was to become notable as an alchemist and
Rosicrucian, enrolled in the University of Giessen, signing himself 'Konrad
Dippel Frankensteiner'.[8] Though not himself a Frankenstein, Dippel was
born in Castle Frankenstein on Magnet Mountain, to the north of the Rhine
in Germany, in 1673. Leaving Giessen under a cloud after completing his
dissertation, De Nihilo (*On Nothing*), Dippel settled at the Imperial
University of Strasbourg, the university that had given Paracelsus an
honorary degree, to pursue his alchemical researches. Dippel became the
first person to distil prussic acid, little knowing that in 1821 Dr John
Polidori, who had been with Mary Shelley on the storytelling night at the
Villa Diodati, the night of the conception of *Frankenstein*, would commit
suicide by drinking prussic acid. In 1732, Dippel's experiments reached
their fruition, and he wrote to the local nobleman, Count Ernst Ludwig von
Hesse, offering to share his secret, on condition that Hesse grant Dippel
possession of Castle Frankenstein, with its attendant title, Baron
Frankenstein. Hesse refused, and the following year Dippel published a
pamphlet in which he predicted that, as a result of his experiments, he
himself would die in 1801, age 135 (Dippel exaggerated: in 1801 he would
only have been 128).

Victor Frankenstein is a student of Albertus Magnus, Paracelsus and
Cornelius Agrippa:

> It may appear very strange, that a disciple of Albertus Magnus
> should arise in the eighteenth century; but our family was not
> scientifical, and I had not attended any of the lectures given at
> the schools of Geneva. My dreams were therefore undisturbed
> by reality, and I entered with the greatest diligence into the
> search for the philosopher's stone and the elixir of life. But the
> latter soon obtained my undivided attention: wealth was an
> inferior object; but what glory would attend the discovery, if I
> could banish disease from the human frame, and render man
> invulnerable to any but a violent death!
>
> (Shelley 1996: 22)

Frankenstein is certainly 'a species of magician scientist', though he is
seldom read as an alchemist, let alone as the necromancer that he literally is:
he raises the dead. He practises diabolical black magic: 'The raising of
ghosts or devils was a promise liberally accorded by my favourite authors,
the fulfilment of which I eagerly sought'; Shelley's Introduction to the 1831
edition calls Victor 'the pale student of unhallowed arts' (ibid.: 22, 172).

While his scientific background, for obvious reasons is frequently commented on, it is Luigi Galvani and Erasmus Darwin whom commentators focus on, rarely mentioning the fact that, shortly previous to *Frankenstein*'s publication, Georg Frank von Frankenau (note the name) had been ennobled by the Emperor Leopold for his research on the transmutation of life from dead matter, or that Benjamin *Frank*lin had, in the eighteenth century, been conducting his own experiments with electricity.[9]

Of course, there is much more to *Frankenstein* than alchemy, otherwise Shelley's novel would not have had the profound cultural resonances it has. These resonances, the fact that *Frankenstein* means so much in so many contexts, and has attained a truly mythic status, are in part a consequence of the novel's riotously overdetermined nature. It is, as it were, a novel with 'too much' meaning, and this is largely because the Monster himself has proved an enormously flexible symbol, capable of a great number of applications and interpretations. When Shelley writes in the Preface to the 1831 edition, 'And now, once again, I bid my hideous progeny go forth and prosper' (ibid.: 173), she is describing both the book and its Monster. Indeed, as Fred Botting (1991) has noted, there is a sense in which *the book itself* is the monster, possessed of a life of its own and rampaging out of Shelley's authorial and interpretive control, consistently generating new identities and meanings. Indeed, by 1824, well before the publication of the revised edition, a stage-play, *Presumption; or, The Fate of Frankenstein*, had appeared, featuring T.P. Cooke as the Monster (Shelley herself admired his performance very much), and introducing a figure who was to become a staple, Fritz, the hunchbacked assistant. Throughout the nineteenth century, as Chris Baldick has shown, the Monster developed a kind of extra-textual symbolic identity, used to articulate political fears, frequently of a proletarian uprising (1987).[10]

The phrase 'my hideous progeny' suggests a monstrous birth, and as Ellen Moers and others have shown, *Frankenstein* is rich in its accounts of anxieties surrounding childbirth, gender and sexuality and also in its account of neglectful parenthood.[11] The novel genders scientific research as masculine, in a sexually invasive relationship with 'feminine' nature: scientists, Professor Waldman suggests, 'have indeed performed miracles. They penetrate into the recesses of nature and show how she works in her hiding places' (Shelley 1996: 28). Statistically, childbirth was by far the biggest killer of the eighteenth and nineteenth centuries, ten times deadlier than the next most virulent cause of death (syphilis), and of course affecting only one half of the population. Shelley's own mother, Mary Wollstonecraft, died of puerperal fever days after giving birth to her. By the publication of *Frankenstein* in 1818, Shelley herself had already lost one child. Wollstonecraft's last novel, *The Wrongs of Woman*, left unfinished at her death in 1797, is the story of Maria, incarcerated in a madhouse by her sadistic husband, whose baby, 'only four months old, had been torn from

her, even while she was discharging the tenderest maternal office'
(Wollstonecraft 1976: 80) (that is, breastfeeding), and who subsequently
writes the child a long letter, which comprises most of the action of the
novel, detailing her life, only to discover near the end that the child is dead.
That is to say, Wollstonecraft's novel, left unfinished because of her own
death in childbirth itself takes the form of a letter to a dead baby.
Furthermore, in her 'Author's Preface', Wollstonecraft writes of her fear
that the novel will simply be taken as 'the abortion of a distempered fancy'
(ibid.: 73). Like childbirth, in *Frankenstein* the Monster, or more properly
the novel itself, kills women – Frankenstein's mother and aunt, his wife
Elizabeth, the servant-girl Justine Moritz and her mother, Madame Moritz,
the female monster, whom Victor tears limb from limb – and it kills children
– little William Frankenstein. Of all subsequent versions of the novel, it is
Mary Shelley's Frankenstein, no doubt because it was produced with an
awareness of feminist interpretations of the novel, which most graphically
develops this theme. Victor (Kenneth Branagh) resolves to do away with
childbirth after witnessing the death of his own mother (Cherie Lunghi)
giving birth to his younger brother, and consequently goes around collecting
amniotic fluid in a bucket from women in childbirth: the Monster (Robert
de Niro) is 'gestated' in a vat of this fluid.

Immediately after creating the Monster, Victor collapses onto his bed
and has a wildly incestuous, necrophiliac dream in which his wife, his
mother, and the Monster are united:

> I thought I saw Elizabeth, in the bloom of health, walking in
> the streets of Ingolstadt. Delighted and surprised, I embraced
> her; but as I imprinted the first kiss on her lips, they became
> livid with the hue of death; her features appeared to change,
> and I thought that I held the corpse of my dead mother in my
> arms; a shroud enveloped her form, and I saw the grave-worms
> crawling in the fold of the flannel. I started from my sleep with
> horror; a cold dew covered my forehead, my teeth chattered,
> and every limb became convulsed; when, by the dim and
> yellow light of the moon, as it forced its way through the
> window-shutters, I beheld the wretch – the miserable monster
> whom I had created.
>
> (Shelley 1996: 34–5)

On top of its anxieties surrounding childbirth, the novel is shot through
with specifically male sexual anxieties. When Frankenstein resolves to create
a 'being of gigantic stature ... eight feet in height and proportionably large',
he means to endow the Monster with an enormous penis, perhaps as a
means of compensation for his own lack. In what may be the novel's single
most overdetermined moment, the Monster famously tells Victor that 'I
shall be with you on your wedding-night': unquestionably, this is an

invitation to read the Monster as Victor's alter-ego or *Döppelganger*, who performs the function of a murderous id, or a rampaging phallus (Shelley 1996: 32, 116). John Sutherland has suggested, ingeniously, that Victor's description of the process of creation as 'the work of my hands' implies that he creates life initially through masturbating, presumably into some kind of Petri dish, which is fertilized *in vitro*: 'Victor Frankenstein . . . is less the mad scientist than the reluctant parent, or semen donor' (Sutherland 2000: 33). I think certainly one can say that the Monster's creation is masturbatory in the sense of its being narcissistic: Victor creates life out of nothing, or creates himself. 'Such a man,' Walton says of Victor, 'has a double existence' (Shelley 1996: 16).

'I shall be with you on your wedding-night' also introduces a theme which, while certainly present in Shelley's novel (as a consequence of its narcissism), has really been developed by a number of film adaptations. This is the suggestion of a gay relationship between Frankenstein and his monster: that Frankenstein either creates for himself a lover, or that his creature's 'monstrosity' is a projection of his own guilt or self-loathing because of his 'deviant' sexuality. Male friendship seems to be the animating relationship behind Shelley's novel, between Walton and Victor – 'You may deem me romantic, my dear sister, but I bitterly feel the want of a friend,' Walton writes – between Victor and Henry Clerval, and between Victor and the Monster. Indeed, after creating the Monster, Victor says, 'I dreaded to behold this monster; but I feared still more that Henry should see him', which is strongly suggestive of Victor's repressed erotic desire for Clerval: he is afraid to let him see his 'monster' (Shelley 1996: 10, 37).

However, as I suggested, it is in the cinema that this theme has really been developed. We looked at the complex sexual relations between James Whale, his collaborators, and his work in the last chapter, but here I really want to note again the scene in *The Bride of Frankenstein* where Dr Pretorius (Ernest Thesiger), whom the maid describes as 'a very queer-looking old gentleman', dismisses Elizabeth from Frankenstein's bedroom so that the two men can get down to the business of creating life. *Gods and Monsters* has Ernest Thesiger saying to Colin Clive on the set of *The Bride*, 'What a couple of queens we are, Colin!' Whale (Ian McKellen) replies, 'Yes, that's right – a couple of flaming queens. Pretorius is a little bit in love with Dr Frankenstein, you know.' In *Frankenstein: The True Story*, Victor (Leonard Whiting) creates his monster (Michael Sarrazin), swathed in bandages (like Elsa Lanchester's Bride), which Victor removes, leaving only what looks like a giant white nappy. Victor embraces the Monster and exclaims, 'You're beautiful!' – which indeed he is, at first, before he begins to decompose. 'Beautiful' remains one of the Monster's few words throughout the film, which ends with Victor and the Monster embracing once again in the polar wastes before being crushed by a falling glacier. Probably the most explicit gay *Frankenstein* of all is Jim Sharman's *The Rocky Horror Picture Show* (1977), where the transsexual Dr Frank-N-

Furter (Tim Curry) creates his blonde, bronzed monster Rocky (Peter Hinwood) quite explicitly as a sex-toy. *Mary Shelley's Frankenstein* has Victor (Branagh), stripped to the waist, creating Robert de Niro's Monster with the aid of a gigantic set of bellows, which looks for all the world like a huge scrotum, and which expels (ejaculates) electric eels (spermatozoa) into the vat of amniotic fluid where the Monster lies, giving him life. The Monster then spills out of the vat of fluid, which is actually more like baby oil, and wrestles naked with Victor.[12]

'It's alive!'

Together, Whale's two *Frankenstein*-movies (and, to a much lesser extent, *Son of Frankenstein*) form the definitive interpretation of Shelley's novel, simplifying and in most ways improving upon Shelley's original. Shelley's Monster is required to shoulder too much significance, from the kinds of scientific, political and sexual meanings discussed earlier to Enlightenment debates on upbringing, education and language-acquisition, and to articulate much of this significance in some astoundingly portentous dialogue. While this has immeasurably enriched the novel's cultural afterlife, as argued above, it actually makes the novel itself somewhat preposterous. Whale's films seek to solidify the Monster's protean, shifting symbolic identity, and to a remarkable extent they succeed, largely because of Jack Pierce's iconic Modernist make-up and Boris Karloff's unforgettable central performance as the largely inarticulate Monster (Karloff thought he should be *completely* wordless, disapproving even of the few words the Monster speaks in *The Bride*) – and because of what has become the classic mad-science laboratory apparatus, designed by Kenneth Strickfaden as a combination of Tesla coils, Van Der Graaf generators, and a number of unique items which Strickfaden called a 'bariton generator', a 'nucleus analyser', and a 'vacuum electrolyser'![13]

Whale's *Frankenstein* pares away the novel's many other themes to become almost entirely a film about scientific ethics – the relationship between knowledge and 'madness'. Henry Frankenstein wishes to harness 'all the electrical secrets of heaven', and discovers 'the great ray which first brought life to the world': 'Crazy, am I?' he says, 'We'll see whether I'm crazy or not!' Establishing what was to become a requirement for mad science movies, the novel contains a conservative fellow-scientist (here, Dr Waldman, played by Edward Van Sloan) whose function is to embody or present an ethical counter-argument: 'Herr Frankenstein is greatly changed ... [by] his insane ambition to create life. ... Herr Frankenstein was only interested in human life – first to destroy it and then recreate it. There you have his mad dream.'

As is again compulsory, Frankenstein explains his motivation in Faustian terms, arguing that no limits should be set on human knowledge, and that scientific ethics and accusations of insanity are the weapons of a fundamentally conservative order afraid of progress or of radical individualism. When Waldman warns that the Monster 'will prove dangerous', Frankenstein replies: 'Dangerous? Poor old Waldman! Have you never wanted to do anything that was dangerous? Where should we be if nobody tried to find out what lies beyond? ... But if you talk like that, people call you crazy.'

To emphasize that this is truly *mad* science, the film incorporates a startling innovation, credited to the co-writer of the screenplay, Francis Edwards Faragoh – the 'abnormal brain', which the Monster gets following a mix-up by Fritz (Dwight Frye). The abnormal (or 'criminal') brain dooms the Monster to criminality from the outset, providing a eugenic subtext which was to be properly exploited later in the century by the Hammer *Frankenstein*-cycle, and theoretically diminishing the problem of social responsibility. Shelley's Monster argues that he has become monstrous because he has been rejected by a humanity, from Victor to the de Laceys, unable to see beneath his ugly exterior; the criminality or abnormality of the Monster's brain suggests, rather, that the whole enterprise, and the Monster which results, are inherently evil. This theory is problematized, however, by Karloff's profoundly sympathetic performance, and even more so in *The Bride* by Whale's habitual use of Christ-imagery to accompany the Monster: captured by the mob, the Monster is bound to a stake as if crucified; as the blind man (O.P. Heggie) plays the violin, tears roll down the Monster's cheek, and an icon of the crucifixion lights up, Vegas-style, to the accompaniment of cheesy organ-music; the Monster stumbles from the old man's cottage and into a roadside shrine, and from there into a graveyard, where he takes refuge in an open vault under a gravestone which again depicts the crucifixion.

Though they are, as I noted, pared down, Whale's *Frankenstein* does revisit some of the novel's sexual and familial themes, which it connects strongly with Henry's scientific endeavours. Waldman's remark in the novel about scientists who 'penetrate into the recesses of nature and show how she works in her hiding places' is echoed here by the Burgomeister's exhortation that the mob 'Search every ravine, every crevice.' Elizabeth tells Victor Moritz that 'The very day we announced our engagement he told me of his experiments. He said he was on the verge of a discovery so terrific that he doubted his own sanity.' The film actualizes the Monster's threat to 'be with you on your wedding-night' by having him interrupt Henry and Elizabeth's wedding-day, attacking Elizabeth in her bedchamber: 'There can be no wedding while this creation of mine is still alive,' Henry says. 'I made him with these hands, and with these hands I will destroy him.' Most notoriously, in a scene cut from the 1931 prints and not restored for many years, the film's monster is also a child-killer, albeit an inadvertent one: the Monster comes across a child throwing flowers into water, and thinking that she too is a flower, he throws *her* in too, and she drowns.

On its release in 1956, *The Curse of Frankenstein*, the first of Hammer Studios' numerous adaptations and free interpretations of Shelley's theme, was considered so visceral and repellent that the *Observer* newspaper's film-critic C.A. Lejeune, for one, thought it seemly to apologize to American audiences on Britain's behalf for what was 'Amongst the half-dozen most repulsive films I have encountered in the course of some 10,000 miles of film reviewing'! (Walker 2000: 189). Though it *is* unquestionably an extreme film, *The Curse of Frankenstein* nevertheless inaugurated one of the major contributions to 'Frankensteinism', and in Peter Cushing's several portrayals of Baron Frankenstein we have a powerful if not definitive instance of the mad scientist driven beyond ethical limits in the search for knowledge. Once again, the Hammer films are truly documents of *mad* science.

The films vary in tone and ethical position, from the Baron's dehumanizing slide charted in *Curse* to his straightforward evil in *Frankenstein Must Be Destroyed*, though he is also given honourable motives and a sympathetic performance in *Frankenstein Created Woman*. Interpretations of the Monster also vary, from the pity and tragedy of the readings of Michael Gwynn in *The Revenge of Frankenstein* or Freddie Jones in *Frankenstein Must Be Destroyed* to the brutishness of Christopher Lee in *Curse* or Dave Prowse in *Frankenstein and the Monster From Hell*. There are also differences in the *kinds* of mad science which Frankenstein practises. The stripped-down nastiness of *Frankenstein Must Be Destroyed* – a nastiness which Rigby suggests was Terence Fisher's response to the artistic if not commercial triumph of Michael Reeves's extraordinarily cynical *Witchfinder General* (Rigby 2000: 155) – leaves no place for elaborate laboratory apparatus, relying instead on unostentatious surgical brain-transplantation to create the Monster. Conversely, its predecessor, *Frankenstein Created Woman*, had shown Frankenstein at his most alchemical, with its theme of the transmutation of souls and its constant accusations of and allusions to sorcery, black magic, and devil-worship: 'Everything we don't understand is magic – until we understand it,' the Baron says, and later he tells a courtroom that 'To the best of my knowledge, doctorates are not awarded for witchcraft – but in the event that they are, no doubt I shall qualify for one.'

Nevertheless, I think one should view these films as a *cycle*, frequently (though not always) developing from and commenting on each other, and united by a single director, Terence Fisher, and most importantly by the recurring presence of Cushing himself in the lead role.[14] Given this consistency of vision and purpose, it is important to note here that the Hammer-cycle both begins (with *Curse*) and ends (*Monster From Hell*) in a lunatic asylum. Symbolically, it never leaves there.

By *Frankenstein and the Monster from Hell*, Cushing's Baron is irredeemably evil, a Mengele-style vivisectionist conducting dreadful experiments with the inmates of the lunatic asylum he runs. The opening scene of *Frankenstein Must Be Destroyed* has the Baron, wearing a mask that makes him look like a burns victim, beheading Dr Otto Heidecke with a gigantic sickle, to experiment with his brain. It is the Baron here, obviously, and not his Monster, who 'must be destroyed': indeed, Freddie Jones's wholly sympathetic performance as the Monster, an articulate, suffering combination of Doctors Richter and Brandt, two leading brain-doctors (Brandt's brain in Richter's body), leaves viewers in no doubt as to who the 'real' monster is. *The Curse of Frankenstein* shows the first development of this monstrosity in the Baron's obsessive commitment to scientific research at the expense of humane values. His colleague and former tutor, Paul Krempe (Robert Urquhart, in the role of warning scientist – M. Krempe was the name of one of Victor's tutors in Shelley's original) maintains that Victor is 'neither wicked nor insane – he's just so dedicated to his work that he can't see the terrible consequences that could result'. Victor's progressive corruption is indicated through an accumulation of telling details: he does not hesitate to cut the head off a corpse when its eyes have been eaten away by birds, and dissolve it in acid, while Paul is horrified (later in the cycle, as we have seen, he will be lopping the heads off *live* subjects); unthinkingly, he wipes his hand on his smart jacket, leaving a bloodstain. Paul argues that Victor is violating morality by mutilating corpses: 'Mutilating?' Victor replies, 'I've removed his brain. Mutilating has nothing to do with it.' Victor argues that transgression in the name of science is not only permissible but vital: 'I'm harming nobody. Just robbing a few graves – and what doctor or scientist doesn't? How else are we to learn the complexities of the human animal?'

Developing the eugenic subtext established by the 'abnormal brain' of Whale's films, *Curse* presents Victor as a full-blown adherent of nineteenth-century theories of criminal 'types' – Cesare Lombroso's theories of an inherently criminal physiognomy, and Paul Broca's ideas about the brains of criminals: 'One's facial character is built up of what lies behind it, in the brain – a benevolent mind, and the face assumes the patterns of benevolence; an evil mind, then an evil face.' In keeping with this, Lee's Monster is immediately violent and murderous, 'a criminal lunatic'. This contrasts strongly with Karloff's far more nuanced portrayal – Lee is far more brutish, as the film itself is far more brutal. The Monster's confrontation with the blind man here has none of the sympathy and humanity afforded Karloff and Heggie in *The Bride of Frankenstein* – here, it is simply another episode of terror and murder.

This terror and brutality extend to the sexual relations within the film. Victor has contracted an arranged marriage with Elizabeth, but is having a passionate affair with Justine the maid, whom he later gives to the Monster, who acts out Victor's violent sexual impulses by murdering her. Paul is clearly in love with Elizabeth. At one point, Victor sizes Elizabeth up for his experiments – when she says that she wants to help him with his work, he appears to examine her head, and says, 'Who knows, my dear, perhaps you will – some day.' In the film's equivalent of the Monster's threat to 'be with you on your wedding-night', Victor threatens to 'introduce Elizabeth to the world of science, and see how she likes it' – the implications here are twofold: that Victor will let the Monster loose on Elizabeth, and that she herself will be his next experimental subject. Victor's laboratory, with its permanently locked door, is the place where Justine meets her terrible fate, and the place which Elizabeth is forbidden from entering. Here, the mad science laboratory is a kind of Bluebeard's chamber, the secret room which it is death for women to enter.

Victor goes beyond the pale of obsessive scientific research 'for its own sake' and into genuine 'evil' with the murder of Professor Bernstein. Bernstein is apparently the finest scientific mind in Europe, and also a kindly Einstein-type figure, whose brain Victor wants to pilfer for the Monster (the brain is later damaged by shards of glass as Victor fights with Paul). It is Bernstein who proffers the film's classic note of warning:

> Is the world ready for the revelations scientists make? There's a great difference between knowing that a thing is so and knowing how to use that knowledge for the good of mankind. The trouble with us scientists is we quickly tire of our discoveries. We hand them over to people who are not ready for them, while we go off again into the darkness of ignorance, searching for other discoveries which will be mishandled in just the same way when the time comes.

As students of mad science, though, we know that Bernstein's wise words of caution are no match for the fiery Romanticism of Frankenstein's Promethean rhetoric. This is what we really want to hear:

> We hold in the palms of our hands such secrets that have never been dreamed of. Where nature puts up her own barriers to confine the scope of man, we've broken *through* those barriers. Nothing can stop us now!

Notes

1. Bobby 'Boris' Picket and the Crypt-Kickers, 'The Monster Mash', London HL 10320 (1973, recorded 1962).
2. Gould notes with approval that in Michael Crichton's original novel, 'Malcolm urges ... a single, devastating critique based on his knowledge of chaos and fractals: the park's safety system must collapse because it is too precariously complex in coordinating so many, and such intricate, fail-safe devices' (1997a: 228). Gould regrets what he sees as the infantilizing of this issue in Spielberg's hands, though from my own perspective Goldblum—Malcolm's 'evolutionary' critique is effective precisely because it taps into a tradition of cinematic warnings about the dangers of unchecked mad science.

3. See, for example, Paul Davies, *The Mind of God: Science and the Search for Ultimate Meaning* (1993); or the comments made by George Smoot in 1992 in the light of his discovery of cosmic 'ripples': 'like seeing the face of God'.
4. Peter Lorre was the undisputed king of hand-movies, having also starred in *The Beast with Five Fingers*, about a murderous amputated hand.
5. Freud (1990); Prawer (1980: 75); Skal (1998: 107).
6. For this, and a general discussion of Faust and modern mad science, see Skal (1998: 47–50).
7. Anon. (1824). The story was published anonymously, but is frequently taken to be by Shelley, although it is not collected in the definitive *Collected Tales and Stories* (Shelley 1976).
8. For Konrad Dippel, see Florescu (1996: 76–92).
9. See Florescu (1996: 225–6) for Frankenau.
10. As Baldick points out, by the time Shelley writes her novel, 'monster' already has an understood political context and significance, largely through the writings of Edmund Burke: 'the monster' was Burke's habitual metaphor for the French Revolution.
11. For the classic account of *Frankenstein* as a 'birth myth', see Ellen Moers, 'Female Gothic', in Moers (1978: 90–112).
12. De Niro here wears an absurdly bulked-up monster suit. However, a brief shot shows that, though hugely muscled, the Monster has a normal-sized penis, which in consequence looks rather small. To rectify this, Victor goes off to an antechamber and returns with a giant axe, or chopper!
13. Curtis (1998: 142). For an account of the electrical engineer Nicola Tesla and his influence on cinematic mad science, see Skal (1998: 88–91). Tesla is given a kind of immortality in *Return of the Vampire*, where Bela Lugosi plays Armand Tesla, described as 'the depraved Romanian scientist who died in 1744, shortly after publishing his work on vampirism. Tesla's morbid thirst for knowledge turned upon him, and after his death he himself became a vampire.' Who could ask for anything more?
14. This is not strictly true. The two weakest entries in the cycle, *The Evil of Frankenstein* and *The Horror of Frankenstein*, are not directed by Fisher but by Freddie Francis and Jimmy Sangster respectively; *Horror* does not star Cushing as Frankenstein, but Ralph Bates.

|3|

Vampires

Children of the night[1]

> 'Well, I don't know – I guess we are all solid here,' this
> gentleman replied, looking round him with a slow, deliberate
> smile, which made his mouth enormous, developed two
> wrinkles, as long as the wings of a bat, on either side of it, and
> showed a set of long, even, carnivorous teeth.
>
> (James 1966: 41)

The image is a familiar one. In this quotation, from Henry James's 1886
novel *The Bostonians*, 'this gentleman', Selah Tarrant, 'the mesmerist' (James
1966: 39), is clearly being likened to a vampire. Tarrant is metaphorically
part-vampire and literally all showman, part of 'a company of mountebanks
... he looked around at the company with all his teeth' (ibid.: 39, 49). Tarrant
performs a quasi-incestuous hypnotizing double-act with his mediumistic
daughter Verena: 'He threw up his arms at moments, to rid himself of the
wings of his long waterproof, which fell forward over his hands.... Tarrant's
grotesque manipulations ... seemed a dishonour to the passive maiden'
(ibid.: 51, 52). Tarrant's daughter Verena is also his victim: 'she was anaemic
... she was certainly very pale, white as women who have that shade of red
hair; they look as if their blood had gone into it' (ibid.: 51). Verena has herself
a vampiric, mesmerizing effect on her audience: 'At the end of ten minutes
Ransom became aware that the whole audience ... were under her charm. I
speak of ten minutes, but to tell the truth the young man lost all sense of
time' (ibid.: 53). Verena's performance leaves Basil Ransom with 'a vulgar
consciousness of being very thirsty' (ibid.: 51).

It is not, surely, Henry James's intention that we read Tarrant literally as
a vampire – that is to say, he does not in all probability sleep during the
daytime in a coffin laden with his native soil; nor, teeth notwithstanding, is
Verena's anaemia really caused by her father biting her neck and sucking her
blood; neither Ransom nor any of the other characters see the necessity of
dispatching him with a stake through the heart. Rather, vampirism is being

invoked here as a metaphor, a metaphor for an exploitative familial and commercial relationship: Tarrant is vampire-*like*. James was, though, interested in the supernatural in his writing – particularly in the ghost-story, of which he wrote a number (most notably his novella *The Turn of the Screw*, though also such stories as 'The Aspern Papers' and 'The Real Thing') – and at least one of his novels, *The Sacred Fount*, has been read in some detail (albeit rather implausibly) as a vampire novel by James B. Twitchell in his study of nineteenth-century vampire literature, *The Living Dead* (1981: 178–89). Twitchell's book offers a series of interesting and sometimes ingenious readings of vampirism in (mostly canonical) nineteenth-century writing (there is, for instance, a wonderful, *almost* convincing reading of 'The Rime of the Ancient Mariner' as an orthodox vampire tale),[2] though the book's very ingenuity is also its greatest weakness: Twitchell understands as vampiric any text in which there is 'the interchange of energy' (1981: 190).[3] That is, he literalizes the frequent metaphoric use of vampirism, thus tending to see vampires where I see only figures of speech.

This is not to say, of course, that vampires haven't been put to heavy metaphoric or symbolic use. On the contrary, part of the very appeal of the vampire is its symbolic flexibility and applicability: vampires have been made to mean many things. Thus we have, for example, the vampire as a symbol for pestilence, disease, or invasion; in an often related way we have the vampire as symbol for colonialism or nationalism (vampires and nationalists share the same language, the rhetoric of 'blood and soil'); we have vampirism as a metaphor for gender-relations or sexuality, for sexual repression, perversion, or dissidence – hence the frequent Freudian readings of vampirism (most famously those of Ernest Jones and of Maurice Richardson),[4] and we have the vampire as a symbol of class-relations, as the embodiment of aristocracy, or as a metaphor for the 'bloodsucking' process of capitalism (that is to say, a broadly Marxist reading of vampirism – indeed, a reading that was offered by Karl Marx himself) – and more generally, as above, for any exploitative human relationship.

A good deal of the power of James's depiction of Tarrant as a vampire lies in the very familiarity of the imagery – fangs and bat-wings, or the cloak (here, a 'waterproof') – an imagery as readily available to us now as it would have been to James's readership. This may be somewhat surprising, as these are images which are most strongly associated with Count Dracula, and Bram Stoker's *Dracula* was not published until 1897, that is, eleven years *after* James published *The Bostonians*. But the vampire metaphor recurs throughout the nineteenth century (and earlier), drawing upon a burgeoning library of vampire fiction and lore. Marx and Engels's *Communist Manifesto* (1848) famously opens with the image, 'A spectre is haunting Europe ...', while *Das Kapital* is suffused with vampiric images of labour-relations: 'Capital is dead labour which, vampire-like, lives only by sucking living labour, and lives the more, the more it sucks'; 'the prolongation of the working day ... only slightly quenches the vampire thirst for the living blood of labour' (Marx 1983: 203; Marx 1976: 242, 367).[5] As an embodiment of exploitative class relations, Marx refers readers to the example of the 'Wallachian Boyar' (Marx 1976: 344) – that is, Vlad the Impaler. As early as 1732, a correspondent in the *Gentleman's Magazine*, commenting on the current vampire epidemics in Eastern Europe, understood them quite clearly as articulating a political allegory (the article had first appeared that year in *The Craftsman*):

> This account of *Vampyres*, you'll observe, comes from the Eastern Part of the World, always remarkable for its *Allegorical Style*. The States of *Hungary* are in subjection to the *Turks* and *Germans*, and govern'd by a pretty hard Hand; which obliges them to couch all their Complaints under *Figures*. This Relation seems to be of the same kind.
>
> These *Vampyres* are said to torment and kill the *Living* by *sucking out all their Blood*; and a *ravenous Minister*, in this part of the World is compared to a *Leech* or *Bloodsucker*, and carries his Oppressions beyond the Grave, by anticipating the *publick Revenues*, and entailing a Perpetuity of *Taxes*, which must gradually drain the Body Politick of its Blood and Spirits. In like manner, Persons who groan under the Burthens of such a *Minister*, by selling or mortgaging their estates, torment their *unhappy Posterity*, and become *Vampyres* when dead.
>
> (Frayling 1992: 27)

Given this heavy metaphorical use to which vampirism has always been put, it is difficult to offer a coherent history of the subject – vampires are too varied, too disparate. As Nina Auerbach notes, 'Vampires, like other minorities, may look alike to outsiders, but the differences among them are more telling than the surface similarities' (1995: 194, n3). And vampires are so prodigiously, promiscuously different that for the purposes of this chapter, I shall be operating a door policy, looking mostly at 'real' rather than figurative vampires: that is to say, while I will be only too happy to tease out the vampires' metaphorical meanings, I shall only do so *after* they have shown me their fangs.

Corpses and Grand Tourists: Enlightenment and Romantic vampires

What I want to do now is to trace the path of vampires throughout the eighteenth and nineteenth centuries, to follow them, as it were, through their literary representations. Though vampires themselves are governed by a restricting series of rituals and structures, often regarding freedom of movement – they cannot cross running water, for example; you need to invite them across your threshold; they need to carry with them quantities of their native soil when travelling abroad – they nevertheless, for all this, get about a bit. Following them necessitates, like the vampire hunters at the end of *Dracula*, a somewhat breathless spatial and cultural tour.

The most important thing to say about the development of vampirology across these centuries was that there was a profound shift in forms of representation between the Enlightenment and the publication of *Dracula* in 1897, a shift which, broadly speaking, saw the vampire move from a creature of folklore to one of literature. In doing so, it also partook of a considerable upward social mobility, from peasant to aristocrat (there's also a concomitant geographical mobility – literary vampires have a fondness for the Grand Tour: class and mobility become important when the vampire is deployed metaphorically in narratives of invasion – peasants are simply not mobile enough to represent such fears), and importantly in doing so, became sexualized. We might want to see Romanticism as the Rubicon or threshold of this change, for Romantic writers (and, for that matter, painters) characteristically conflated two previously distinct supernatural entities – the revenant, or corpse returned from the grave, usually in search of blood (the 'traditional' vampire of folklore), and the demon lover, the incubus or succubus, the nightly visitant in the form of nightmares who simultaneously removed both their victims' semen or chastity (depends on gender) and their souls. With this shift there also came, as we have already seen, a greater awareness of the metaphorical possibilities of the vampire.

Though we do have examples of vampire folklore from classical and near- and far-eastern antiquity,[6] there are relatively few pre-Enlightenment vampires as we would recognize them today in English literature, though there are plenty of incubi and, importantly here, returned corpses or revenants. The great vampirologist Montague Summers suggests that, 'Although there is some evidence that the Vampire was by no means unknown in England during Anglo-Saxon times, the allusions are accidental and occasional, rather than detailed and direct' (1980: 78). For medieval British revenants, Summers directs our attention to William of Newburgh's *Historia Anglicana* (1196), which records three attested cases of vampirism, in Buckinghamshire, Melrose and Berwick (in each case, the vampire was a recently buried corpse returned to torment his community), and to Walter Map's eleventh-century *De Nugis Curialum* ('Of Courtiers' Trifles'), which has an anecdote about a female vampire who cut children's throats in the guise of a virtuous matron:

> this evil messenger ... this loathsome instrument of ... wrath
> has been fashioned as far as possible in the likeness of this noble
> lady, that this demon may cause this noble soul to be accused
> of the guilt of her heinous deeds.... Then the creature flew away
> through the window howling aloud and screeching terribly.
> (Summers 1980: 91)

This is another, literary, one, from the medieval romance *The Awntyrs of Arthur*:

> Bare was the body and blakke to the bone
> Al biclagged in clay uncomly cladde. . . .
> Hit waried, hit waymented, as a woman,
> But neither on hide ne on huwe no heling it hadde.
> Hit stemered, hit stonayed, hit stode as a stone;
> Hit marred, hit memered, hit mused for madde. . . .
> Serkeled with serpentes that sat to the sides –
> To tell the todes thereon my tonge wer ful tere.
> (Hanna 1974: ll. 105–21)[7]

Here, a corpse has disinterred itself, moving and moaning, from a marshy tarn, black and grimy and riddled with worms and toads. Corpses *do* moan and move, owing to a natural build-up and emission of gases, and *do* have a habit of disinterring themselves, especially if, as here, they've been placed in bodies of standing water. Decomposing bodies are astonishingly buoyant – there are records of murder victims floating to the surface even though they've been weighed down with a cast-iron electricity generator casing, or wholly sealed in a lead pipe (a note to murderers: you need to disembowel your victim first to prevent this) (Barber 1988: 142–3). Occasionally, if heavy rain causes the water-table to rise, corpses or coffins can disinter themselves from the ground, as in this Los Angeles coroner's report on the aftermath of Hurricane Jim in 1985:

> Down toward the city streets slid rotting caskets containing more than a hundred bodies borne on the lip of the mudslide. Within minutes, caskets and corpses engulfed the area, plunging through windows and into the living rooms of houses, into stores, and lodging against walls. One body ended up in the doorway of a supermarket. I drove with my staff to Verdugo Hills. And what I saw there was a scene I'll never forget. Mud had swept the corpses everywhere, some of them now standing grotesquely upright. . . . Most of them, even some buried for decades, were not skeletons, as most people would expect. The skin was gone, but not the muscle and the tissue . . . the fat on the corpses had changed to a soaplike texture when the bodies picked up sodium and moisture underground, and their color had become a grayish-white.
> (ibid.: 154)

Paul Barber, in his book *Vampires, Burial and Death* (1988), has suggested that *all* the practices, rituals and forms of behaviour associated with vampirism have their origins either in the natural decomposition processes, the way in which bodies normally behave, or else in traditional burial practices (ibid.: 102–77). Europe's periodic vampire crazes have all taken place during times of plague, when, accompanying hysteria and neuroses notwithstanding, the sheer volume of dead bodies made it difficult for proper burials to take place. Under these conditions, the bodies have a greater propensity to return, and, importantly, their return is likely to be interpreted supernaturally, as embodiments of pestilence, returning from the grave to bring death to the community. What tends to happen, then, with the vampire of folklore, is that supernatural explanations are offered for natural processes. And this is precisely what the anonymous author of *The Awntyrs of Arthur* does: the corpse is explained as a site of meaning, its significance imbued here with apocalyptic or prophetic overtones. The corpse is Guinevere's mother; her appearance is accompanied by an unnatural darkness at noon; she has returned to speak the future, to tell Arthur's court to mend its ways (Robson 2000).

The last great European vampire craze, and for my purposes the most important, took place in the first decades of the eighteenth century. The year 1727 saw the celebrated case of the Serbian vampire Arnod Paole, a soldier who returned from Turkey, died and rose from the grave to terrorize his village, being blamed for the death and subsequent return as vampires of thirteen villagers. An official investigation, by a team of doctors, jurists and high-ranking military officers, concluded that Paole's vampirism was indeed to blame, and ordered that the vampires be disinterred, beheaded and burnt, and their ashes scattered in the river.[8] (The first recorded English usage of the word 'vampire', incidentally, is in 1732, in a translation of this report from the German.)

This event, the most celebrated of several, was later to exercise several prominent Enlightenment thinkers, notably Diderot, Voltaire and Rousseau, not least because it enshrined the existence of vampires as a fact in law. It also exercised the Catholic Church. In 1746, Augustin Calmet, a Benedictine scholar celebrated for his work of biblical exegesis, published his treatise on vampires, later translated into English as *The Phantom World*, his attempt to formulate a coherent theological response to the vampire outbreaks:

> In this age, a new scene presents itself to our eyes, and has done for about sixty years in Hungary, Moravia, Silesia, and Poland; men, it is said, who have been dead for several months, come back to earth, talk, walk, infest villages, ill use both men and beasts, suck the blood of their near relations, destroy their health, and finally cause their death; so that people can only save themselves from their dangerous visits and hauntings by exhuming them, impaling them, cutting off their heads, tearing out their hearts, or burning them. These are called by the names of oupires or vampires, that is to say, leeches; and such

particulars are related of them, so singular, so detailed, and
attended by such probable circumstance, and such judicial
information, that one can hardly refuse to credit the belief
which is held in these countries, that they come out of their
tombs, and produce those effects which are claimed of them.

(Calmet 1850: 2: 2)

As Calmet noted, the existence of vampires as a fact provable in law had
potentially serious ramifications for the church: 'I lay it down as an undoubted
principle, that the resurrection of persons really dead is effected by the power
of God alone' (ibid.: 2: 7). Given that vampires were prowling Eastern Europe
in considerable numbers, and given that only God could cause the true
symptoms of vampirism (the resurrection of the body), then He had some
explaining to do. Calmet outlined what he saw as the three possible causes
of vampirism: (1) that vampires are not really dead, but have been buried
alive; (2) that they are caused by God; and (3) that they are caused by 'a
demon' (ibid.: 2: 6). Of these options, Calmet clearly favoured the first, not
only as the most plausible to a rational mind (the law of Occam's Razor
dictates that, given this choice, one should choose the first option as the
simplest – the one which does not require the multiplication of causes: human
error rather than divine intervention), and as the one which most readily lets
God off the hook. Nevertheless, he recognizes that there are problems here:
'But how can they come out of their graves without opening the earth, and
how re-enter them again with out its appearing ... neither revelation nor
reason throws any certain light on the subject' (ibid.: 2: 10–11). As the above
list of ways to dispose of vampires – exhumation, burning, beheading,
impaling, tearing out the heart – shows, and as numerous further instances
in his book demonstrate, Calmet was aware of the potentially widespread
violation of corpses (or, worse, the murder of living people who had already
been buried alive!), and the treatise ends inconclusively:

> The stories told of these apparitions, and all the distress caused
> by these supposed vampires, are totally without solid proof. I
> am not surprised that the Sorbonne has condemned the bloody
> and violent retribution wrought on these corpses; but it is
> astonishing that the magistrates and secular bodies have not
> employed their authority and legal force to put an end to it.
> This is a mysterious and difficult matter, and I leave bolder
> and more proficient minds to resolve it.

(ibid.: 2: 205)

If the succeeding generation of French Enlightenment thinkers came to
judge Calmet harshly, as, in Christopher Frayling's words, 'a plodding,
credulous and over-literal crank' (1992: 28), this may be because of his
sedulous refusal to commit himself to an opinion on the veracity of the very

subject he discusses at such length: either vampires exist or they do not, but after several hundred exhaustive pages the reader is none the wiser as to what Calmet himself thinks – which amounts to having it both ways. After reading Calmet, Pope Benedict XIV summed up the problem of vampires for the church in modernity:

> Whether the discussion is about corpses found in a state of incorruption, or about the blood which flows from them or about the growth of hair and nails after death, or about the decapitation of vampires or the cremation of their bodies, with the scattering of their ashes in water, *everything* seems to depend on how much faith, or trust, we have in those who witnessed the events.
>
> (Frayling 1992: 26)

Writing elsewhere, though, Benedict was more direct, blaming 'those priests who give credit to such stories, in order to encourage simple folk to pay them for exorcisms and masses' (ibid.).

While Voltaire and the other *philosophes* dismissed the phenomenon as just another example of credulity, Rousseau tended to view vampires almost as a test case for the Enlightenment project, and kept an open mind, concluding that no rational explanation (and thus ultimately no credibility) could be provided for a phenomenon for which there was nevertheless considerable testimony: 'No evidence is lacking – depositions, certificates of notables, surgeons, priests and magistrates. The proof *in law* is utterly complete. ... Yet with all this, who actually *believes* in vampires?' (Frayling 1992: 31).

It was with Romanticism, however, that the *literary* vampire really got going. The reasons for this are complex, but for now it's enough to say that, as Chapter 1 suggested, the Enlightenment had always had a kind of underside, or as it's sometimes characterized, an unconscious – in this sense, the Gothic novel is itself a product (or a by-product) of Enlightenment. It's no accident that the second half of the eighteenth century witnessed the rise in popularity of graveyard poetry, of the cult and fiction of sensibility, of the profoundly anti-rationalist theories of the sublime, and most importantly here of the Gothic novel. Where Enlightenment valued reason, order, modernity, the Gothic acted as a negative image, imaging forth the irrational, chaos, the past (see Chapter 1). It was the very popularity of this kind of Romantic Gothic which led Wordsworth, in his *Preface to the Lyrical Ballads*, famously to deplore the 'gross and violent stimulants' occasioned by 'frantic novels, sickly and stupid German Tragedies, and deluges of idle and extravagant stories in verse' (Wordsworth and Coleridge 1991: 248, 249).

Coleridge, Southey and Byron all wrote vampiric poetry, as did Goethe. There was also a fine tradition of Eastern European vampire literature throughout the nineteenth century, by writers such as Gogol and Alexis

Tolstoy, though as Frayling points out, these tend to be in the old folkloric mode – perhaps because their authors themselves come from vampire country (1992: 64). It's also worth pondering whether Wordsworth's 'Leech-Gatherer' constitutes his own contribution to the vampire genre: 'Such seemed this man, not all alive nor dead, / Nor all asleep' (Wordsworth 1977: 1: 533).[9]

But the image of the vampire in literature – the decadent, sexualized aristocrat – was really established in the popular imagination with the publication of Dr John Polidori's *The Vampyre* in the *New Monthly Magazine*, April 1819. This novella was a product of the celebrated ghost-story evening with Byron, Shelley and Mary Shelley at the Villa Diodati on the shores of Lake Geneva in 1816, which famously also produced *Frankenstein* (though the true circumstances of this event are a bit cloudy – certainly Mary Shelley's famous version of events, published some years later in the Preface to the 1831 edition of *Frankenstein*, doesn't always tally with the account offered in Polidori's journal, and omits the presence of a fifth member of the party, Claire Clairmont). The novella features Lord Ruthven, a charismatic aristocrat who goes on a Grand Tour of Europe – taking with him a young man named Aubrey – where he proceeds to seduce and corrupt the virtuous and aid the wicked. Mortally wounded in Greece, Ruthven makes Aubrey swear a solemn oath never to reveal his death. The action shifts to fashionable London: Ruthven returns, seduces and marries Aubrey's sister; because of the solemnity of the oath, Aubrey is powerless to intercede until on his own death-bed. The novella closes with this deathless paragraph: 'The guardians hastened to protect Miss Aubrey; but when they arrived, it was too late. Lord Ruthven had disappeared, and Aubrey's sister had glutted the thirst of a VAMPYRE!' (Ryan 1991: 24).

Initially, *The Vampyre* was assumed to be by Byron himself – indeed, Goethe (bizarrely) thought it was Byron's finest work, and it was collected with Byron's poetry well into the nineteenth century. This is unsurprising, as Byron certainly *did* have an interest in vampires (an interest he shared, though, with any number of Romantic writers). His 'Fragment of a Turkish Tale' entitled 'The Giaour' contains this famous curse:

> But first, on earth as Vampire sent,
> Thy corse shall from its tomb be rent;
> Then ghastly haunt thy native place,
> And suck the blood of all thy race,
> There from thy daughter, sister, wife,
> At midnight drain the stream of life;
> Yet loathe the banquet which perforce
> Must feed thy livid living corse; ...
> Wet with thine own best blood shall drip,
> Thy gnashing tooth and haggard lip.
>
> (Byron 1997: 28–9)

As his notes to the poem demonstrate, Byron had done some homework on the subject of vampires:

> The Vampire superstition is still general in the Levant. Honest Tournefort tells a long story, which Mr Southey, in the notes on Thalaba, quotes about these 'Vroucolochas', as he calls them. The Romaic term is 'Vardoloucha'. I recollect a whole family being terrified by the scream of a child, which they imagined must proceed from such a visitation. The Greeks never mention the word without horror. ... The freshness of the face, and the wetness of the lip with blood, are the never-failing signs of a Vampire. The stories told in Hungary and Greece of these foul feeders are singular, and some of them most *incredibly* attested.
>
> (Byron 1997: 46–7)

'Vroucolochas', or 'vrykolakas', and its analogue, 'vardoloucha', surface today only in anthologized vampire stories from the nineteenth century, in Alexis Tolstoy's 'The Family of the Vourdalek', and Count Eric Stenbock's 'A True Story of a Vampire' with its Hungarian protagonist, Count Vardalek.

In 1717 the French botanist M. Pitton de Tournefort published the first volume of his *Relation d'un voyage du Levant*, which contained an account of a 'vrykolakas', or vampire, whose dissection the author had witnessed on the Greek island of Mykonos:

> The body was disinterred after the mass, and they set about the task of tearing out its heart. The butcher of the town, quite old and very maladroit, began by opening the belly rather than the chest. He rummaged about for a long time in the entrails, without finding what he sought, and finally someone informed him that it was necessary to cut into the diaphragm. The heart was torn out to the admiration of all the bystanders. But the body stank so terribly that incense had to be burned, but the smoke, mixed with the exhalations of this carrion, did nothing but increase the stench, and it began to inflame the minds of those poor people. Their imagination, struck by the spectacle, filled with visions.
>
> (Barber 1988: 22)

The 'vrykolakas' was in life a 'sullen and quarrelsome man', and a murder victim; in death he does not return to drink the blood of his victims nor otherwise to prey upon them, but 'he had been seen walking during the night, taking long strides; ... he came into houses and turned over furniture, extinguished lamps, embraced people from behind, and played a thousand little roguish tricks' (ibid.: 21).

Byron, though he obviously knew of Tournefort's account, had read it most selectively, leaving out Tournefort's central contention that what he had witnessed was not the destruction of a revenant but the violation of a corpse: 'When they asked us what we thought of the deceased, we answered that we thought him quite adequately dead'; the stench, so bad that Tournefort, standing nearby, 'almost perished' from it, and the warmth which the butcher claims to feel inside the body, are (correctly) adduced to be part of the natural decomposition process, not signs of supernatural activity, 'and as for the pretended red blood, it was still evident on the hands of the butcher that this was nothing but a stinking mess' (Barber 1988: 22).

However, such sceptical Enlightenment scientism, although remarkably gory, does not make for a bloodcurdling Romantic tale of terror. As Byron himself notes, his own researches come via Robert Southey's account of Tournefort in his notes to his massive 'Thalaba the Destroyer', which contains, amongst much else, a vampire whose existence Southey felt needed to be justified at great length:

> It was She ...
> Her very lineaments ... and such as death
> Had changed them, livid cheeks, and lips of blue;
> But in her eyes there dwelt
> Brightness more terrible
> Than all the loathsomeness of death.
> 'Still art thou living, wretch?'
> In hollow tones she cried to Thalaba;
> And I must nightly leave my grave
> To tell thee, still in vain,
> God hath abandoned thee?'
>
> (Southey 1838: 4: 280)

Southey accompanied this passage with an eight-page explanatory gloss, excerpting five eighteenth-century accounts of vampirism, including the Arnod Paole case and, by far the longest, Tournefort's 'vrykolakas', given in its entirety (1838: 4: 297–305). What's most striking, I think, about Southey's vampire is how *un*-Byronic it is, how unseductive (radically so compared to the many Romantic lamias – female vampires, succubi – in, for example, the poetry of Coleridge or Keats): Tournefort's 'vrykolakas' was, the botanist was convinced, no more than a corpse, and very dead indeed; Southey's 'vampire corpse', clearly modelled on Tournefort's account, and on the account of Arnod Paole, is very much a creature of the eighteenth-century vampire epidemics, and thus emphatically a revenant, a 'vrykolakas' of folklore rather than a vampire of literature. Where Southey's vampire looks back on, and comments upon, an older tradition, Byron's looks forward to, and inaugurates, a new one.

Even after Dr Polidori was generally accepted as the author of *The Vampyre*, he was frequently accused of simply plagiarizing Byron. Certainly, there are similarities between *The Vampyre* and a prose fragment Byron composed in 1816 – the Grand Tour, the solemn oath: though in Byron the vampire (if he is one) is called Darvell. What's incontrovertible is that Polidori based the figure of Ruthven on Lord Byron, even down to the name: Ruthven is the family name of the protagonist of Lady Caroline Lamb's scandalous 1816 *roman-à-clef, Glenarvon*, a thinly fictionalized account of her celebrated affair with Byron. (Grey de Ruthvyn, the actual, historical Lord Ruthven, incidentally, was once Byron's tenant at Newstead Abbey; Byron's mother fell in love with Ruthvyn, causing animosity between the two men.) Glenarvon's ancestor, John de Ruthven, 'drank hot blood from the skull of his enemy and died' (Byron *did* use a human skull as a wine-goblet at Newstead Abbey, and in Thomas Love Peacock's comic-satiric *roman-à-clef, Nightmare Abbey*, Scythrop Glowry, based on Percy Shelley, drinks Madeira from a human skull in his lonely tower); on first meeting Glenarvon, the narrative records Calantha's (ie, Lady Caroline Lamb's) response: 'The day, the hour, the very moment of time was marked and destined. It was Glenarvon – it was that spirit of evil whom she beheld; and her soul trembled within her, and felt its danger'; Glenarvon tells Calantha, 'Unblessed myself, I can but give misery to all who approach me. All that follow after me come to this pass; for my love is death' (Lamb 1995: 123, 148, 229). Though the novel is, notwithstanding its Gothic trappings, its references to superstition and ghostly hauntings, fundamentally a secular one, nevertheless its closure *does* finally admit the existence of the supernatural, and allow for the possibility that Glenarvon is an actual, and not just a metaphorical vampire. He meets his end by drowning, fleeing from a ghost-ship crewed by his victims.

Penny dreadfuls and melodramas: the Victorian vampire

The classic nineteenth-century vampire text is of course Stoker's *Dracula*, but between *The Vampyre* in 1819 and *Dracula* in 1897, vampires stalked the nineteenth century in prose fiction, and also upon the stage. While Bram Stoker's sources for *Dracula* have been extensively studied, including his modelling of the Count's physical appearance on Henry Irving, the great Victorian actor-manager (Stoker was for years his secretary, personal assistant and business manager), relatively little attention has been drawn to the fact that Stoker, professionally engaged in the theatre, had very nearly a century of stage vampires to draw on for inspiration. He even oversaw one theatrical production (actually a staged reading) of his novel, *Dracula or The Un-dead, in a prologue and five acts*, in order to secure copyright, in May 1897. Eric Bentley, musing on the popularity of vampires in the theatre, writes:

> In the theatre, phenomena like ... *Dracula* are not
> eccentricities but prototypes ... There is no comparison ...
> between the potency of the novel and the acted play. Physical
> presence on the stage makes an essential difference here. It is
> not in the quiet of libraries, bedrooms or kitchens that
> devotees of bloodsucking swoon. It is in the theatre.
>
> (Stuart 1992: 223)

Theatrical versions of Polidori came almost immediately. Charles Nodier's hugely successful *Le Vampire* (co-written with Achille Jouffrey and Pierre Carmouche – the three also collaborated on a stage version of *Frankenstein* in 1826) was first performed in Paris in June 1820, occasioning a craze for vampire plays in the city: a contemporary critic remarked, 'There is not a theatre in Paris without its Vampire! At the Porte-Saint-Martin we have *Le Vampire*; at the Vaudeville *Le Vampire* again; at the Varieties, *Les Trois Vampires ou le clair de la lune*' (Skal 1990: 14). The critic underestimated: there were at least three more vampire productions in 1820, including operas. (This phenomenon, incidentally, provides the source for Anne Rice's Paris theatre of vampires, a theatre which is actually populated by vampires.)

Nodier was immediately adapted into English: James Robinson Planché's *The Vampire, or, The Bride of the Isles* was performed in London's Lyceum in August 1820, incorporating a sensational new stage device, a trapdoor in the stage which allowed the vampire seemingly to disappear in an accompanying puff of smoke (in theatrical parlance, this trapdoor is still known as a 'vampire'). In both Nodier and Planché, Ruthven was played by the same actor, the Englishman T.P. Cooke.[10] Planché's melodrama revisits and freely adapts the Byron–Polidori original, opening with an 'Introductory Vision' which takes place in 'the Basaltic Caverns of Staffa', where the sleeping form of Lady Margaret lies, while Unda ('The Spirit of the Flood') helpfully explicates:

> Beneath this stone the relics lie
> Of Cromal, called the Bloody. Staffa still
> His reign of fear remembers. For his crimes
> His spirit roams, a vampire, in the form
> Of Marsden's Earl; to count his victims o'er,
> Would be an endless task – suffice to say,
> His race of terror will to-morrow end,
> Unless he wins some virgin for his prey,
> Ere sets the full-orb'd moon.
>
> (Planché 1820: 14–15)

The 'full-orb'd moon' is important here – as Auerbach has noted, the reviving power of the moon is the defining characteristic of vampire narratives in the first half of the nineteenth century, and 'the presiding moon is Planché's most important addition to the vampire legend' (Auerbach 1995: 24). (*Varney the Vampyre*, for example, undergoes any number of narrative contortions in order to effect its protagonist's revival by moonbeams – though so dementedly incoherent is that novel that this seems hardly to matter.) Planché also introduces in this play the trope of the vampire's sense of remorse or even disgust at his own lot:

> Demon as I am, that walk the earth to slaughter and devour!
> The little bit that remains of heart within this wizard frame,
> sustained alone by human blood, shrinks from the appalling
> act of planting misery in the bosom of this veteran chieftain.
>
> (1820: 26–7)

It is this weary disgust which finally does for Sir Francis Varney at the end of 900 double-columned pages of *Varney the Vampyre*, and which, though absent from *Dracula* itself, is certainly present in Lugosi's 1931 portrayal – 'To die, to be really dead, that must be glorious' – and which recurs most strongly in one strain of modern vampire narrative of the Romantic-psychological variety, as exemplified by Anne Rice's *Interview with the Vampire* (1976). There, the vampire-narrator, Louis, is motivated almost entirely by self-loathing – such, indeed, is the disgust he initially feels at his predatory condition that he is unable to feed on humans, choosing instead to drink the blood of animals.

In 1852 the Dublin dramatist Dion Boucicault wrote and starred in another adaptation, again called *The Vampire* (abridged from three to two acts for its 1856 New York production, and renamed *The Phantom*; while *The Phantom* was playing at Wallace's Theatre, another version of the story, *Ruthven*, by A. Harris, was also in New York, playing at the Grecian). Boucicault shifts the action from Scotland to Wales (and Planché's 'original' had only been given a Scottish setting because the Lyceum Theatre had a ready supply of kilts!), and divides the action (and, in *The Phantom*, the acts) between the time of Charles II and the mid-Victorian present. Once again, the vampire, here called Alan Raby, attempts to inveigle his way into a marriage, here with the beauteous Ada, whom Raby has miraculously brought back from the dead. Ada has died of a 'brain fever', that favourite but mysterious nineteenth-century malady, occasioned by hearing the report of the death in battle of her beloved Captain Edgar Peveryl – though this report is premature as Edgar has himself been 'snatched from the grave' by 'the wondrous skill of a strange physician' (presumably Raby again). As ever on the nineteenth-century stage, Raby can be revived by the rays of the moon: he is finally destroyed by being cast into a chasm 'where the light of heaven never visited' (Boucicault 1856: 9, 14).

In 1845, Edward Lloyd, printer, of Fleet Street, London, published the first of what was to be 109 weekly episodes of a 'penny dreadful' romance, *Varney the Vampyre; or, The Feast of Blood. A Romance of Exciting Interest*. The publisher, Lloyd, specialized in serialized penny-dreadfuls, usually of the Gothic or supernatural variety. It was a success, so much so that in September 1847, immediately after the final instalment was published, Lloyd reprinted the whole novel as a full-blown triple-decker, winding its way, as noted, through nearly 900 double-columned pages.

The authorship of *Varney* is a thorny and confused issue. It was published anonymously, and where the title page of the 1847 complete novel gives no indication of authorship at all, the title-page of the first serialized edition in 1845, in which for 1d a reader got not only part 1, but 'Nos. 2, 3 and 4 are Presented, Gratis, with this No.', has *Varney* as being 'by the author of 'Grace Rivers; or, The Merchant's Daughter'. However, following the work of Louis James on his papers, most scholars now attribute *Varney* to James Malcolm Rymer, a trained civil engineer and mechanical draughtsman from the Scottish highlands, and a prolific author of serial fiction for Lloyd, who wrote under at least five different names (James 1963: 37–8).

Given its huge length, the simple fact of reading *Varney the Vampyre* is itself a minor sort of a triumph. Rymer was paid per line of typeface – little wonder, then, that the novel is so long, for in it Rymer hit upon the perfect model for an endless plot: like the vampire himself, the novel is potentially everlasting. What's perhaps best known about the novel is that, at its close, Varney, sickened by his eternal existence and bloodlust, flings himself into Mount Vesuvius, thus putting an end both to himself and his narrative. What's less well known is that Varney was killed off at the insistence of the publisher, Lloyd, who didn't want to continue financing a novel which potentially spun itself out to the cracks of doom.[11] This is an extreme example of the marketplace controlling the content of fiction in the nineteenth century – as John Sutherland notes in his study *Victorian Novelists and Publishers* (1976), the role of the publisher in shaping the content of Victorian fiction is considerable. Varney, of all the vampires that I have ever come across in film, literature or folklore, is easily the most difficult to kill: he is variously stabbed, staked, shot (many times), hanged, burned, and drowned, but never dies for in true Victorian fashion he too can be restored to full health by the rays of the full moon (which somehow always manage to alight on him). As we have seen, Karl Marx habitually noted that capital is itself vampiric:

> Capital posits the permanence of value ... by incarnating itself in fleeting commodities and taking on their form, but at the same time changing them just as constantly. ... But capital obtains this ability only by constantly sucking in living labour as its soul, vampire-like.
>
> (Marx 1973: 646)

Varney, indestructible by physically coercive human agency, is a product or embodiment of capitalism, and it is only capitalism that can destroy him.

It is virtually impossible to give a coherent synopsis of the plot of *Varney*, which duplicates, further redoubles and contradicts itself many times. The novel does not, in fact, have a 'plot' at all in the normal sense of the word.[12] I think what's important to remember here is that Rymer was, in the deepest sense, a professional author, paid, as I noted, by the line, and that at the time Varney was being serialized in weekly instalments, he was also working on at least three more serials for Lloyd, and perhaps others as well. The novel's contradictions, lacunae and many digressions (the narrative constantly interrupts itself with irrelevant tales within the tale, usually of a supernatural kind) are to a large extent a consequence of this. Indeed, one wonders whether it is not in fact the product of *more than one* writer – if so, they do not seem to have communicated much.

'Dracula should only go for women and not men!' (Skal 1994: 126). This is what the producer Carl Laemmle Jr. wrote in the margin of his copy of the final draft of the screenplay for Tod Browning's *Dracula* (1931). But from its very beginnings as a literary trope, vampirism has always been used as a vehicle for more-or-less encoded articulations of sexuality and desire (as a way of writing about sex without writing about sex), and importantly (though not exclusively) of articulating *homosexual* desire, thus operating on a dialectic of vampirism as dissident or deviant and thus forbidden and silenced (hence the need for metaphor, for a form made of encoded meanings, a kind of secret language, a supernatural polari), but also as desirable, wished-for: a version of the standard Gothic dialectic of desire and repulsion, extant at least since the novels of Ann Radcliffe, displacing or projecting outwards the repressed desires of its readership.

The ability of the vampire to signify deviant or polymorphous sexuality is symbolically in-built, already embodied by the image of the fanged, penetrating mouth which metonymically represents vampirism. In his frequently cited essay, '"Kiss Me With Those Red Lips": Gender and Inversion in Bram Stoker's *Dracula*', Christopher Craft writes:

> As the primary site of erotic experience in *Dracula*, the mouth equivocates, giving the lie to the easy separation of the masculine and the feminine. ... Are we male or are we female? Do we have penetrators or orifices? And if both, what does that mean?
>
> (1997: 445–6)

We shall discuss the encoded sexuality of *Dracula* later, but for now I want to note that the image discussed here in all its complexity, the penetrating mouth, is a displaced version of the familiar phobic image of the *vagina dentata*, the vagina with teeth, simultaneously enveloping and castrating (see Chapter 4 for more on this). This fear of the emasculating power of an uncontrolled female sexuality is one aspect – there are others – of the fears embodied in the figure of the lesbian vampire.

J. Sheridan Le Fanu's 'Carmilla', published in 1872 as the last of the interlinked stories in the collection *In a Glass Darkly*, is by far the most celebrated of all lesbian vampire narratives, and as such completes our picture of pre-*Dracula* nineteenth-century vampires, as what we have seen thus far in this chapter is a powerful reminder both of the pervasiveness of the vampire throughout that century (a pervasiveness which Bram Stoker's magisterial novel, coming at the very end of its century, tends to obscure) and of the fact that *Dracula* itself constitutes not so much the beginning of a tradition as the end of one, the culmination of over a century of vampiric representation.

Both texts present vampirism in terms of the dream. This is from *Carmilla*:

> I can't have been more than six years old when one night I awoke, and looking around the room from my bed, failed to see the nursery-maid. ... [T]o my surprise, I saw a solemn, but very pretty face looking at me from the side of the bed. It was that of a young lady who was kneeling, with her hands under the coverlet. I looked at her with a kind of pleased wonder, and ceased whimpering. She caressed me with her hands, and lay down beside me on the bed, and drew me towards her, smiling; I felt immediately delightfully soothed, and fell asleep again. I was wakened by a sensation as if two needles ran into my breast very deep at the same moment, and I cried loudly.
>
> (Le Fanu 1993: 246)

In *Dracula*, the narrative of the Count's first preying on Lucy Westenra, in Whitby, is offered as a phallic nightmare:

> I have a vague memory of something long and dark with red eyes ... and something very sweet and bitter all around me at once. Then I seemed sinking into deep green water, and there was a singing in my ears, as I have heard there is to drowning men; and then everything seemed passing away from me; my soul seemed to go out of my body and float about the air. I seemed to remember that once the West Lighthouse was right under me, and there was a sort of agonising feeling, as if I were in an earthquake.
>
> (Stoker 1997: 94)

(It's worth noting that here Stoker takes his one liberty with the otherwise map-like accuracy with which he depicts the town of Whitby: Lucy is up in the graveyard by the Abbey on the East Cliff; it should therefore be the *East* Lighthouse that's under her. The problem here is that the East Lighthouse is rather smaller than the West Lighthouse, and you can't have the Count with a small lighthouse.) At the same time as Stoker was researching into mesmerism, sleepwalking and dreams for *Dracula*, Sigmund Freud was beginning to publish the accounts of his own researches into the meaning of dreams. It's no accident, I think, that so much critical work on Gothic literature has been from a psychoanalytic perspective. Indeed, Freud's disciple Ernest Jones wrote a whole monograph on nightmares, containing considerable research into vampires and incubi, which concludes quite straightforwardly that nightmares spring from sexual repression (though one has to note the questionable assumptions which underlie some of his premises, such as that those most prone to nightmares are virgins, widows and nuns – this particular neurosis, then, is easily remedied by the love of a good, or bad, man). Jones does, I think, make one especially germane observation, on the etymology of the name Lilith, which means in Hebrew 'lasciviousness' (Jones 1949: 125). Lilith was originally the Babylonian Queen of the Vampires; though she comes down to us today in Judaic folklore, as Adam's first wife, dismissed from the job for lustfulness and a desire for power: she wanted to have sex on top. This is of course what happens to female vampires, they become pure lasciviousness, caring about neither age nor gender. This happens to Carmilla, who is for Le Fanu an embodiment, simultaneously enticing and terrifying, of dangerous ideas about sex and power. It also happens to *Dracula*'s Lucy Westenra, who is in a sense punished for her initial free thinking about sexual propriety – 'Why can't they let a girl marry three men, or as many as want her?' she asks (Stoker 1997: 60) – by being held down by her one-time suitors Seward and Morris, as well as Professor Van Helsing (who's already commented that, in giving Lucy his blood in transfusion, he's symbolically become a bigamist), while her fiancée Holmwood penetrates her with a stake.

So dangerous is the novel's conception of female sexuality, or even of independent womanhood, that Lucy, after her death, becomes not merely the demonic embodiment of undiscriminating lasciviousness, but a paedophile, the 'Bloofer Lady', abducting children on Hampstead Heath:

> She seemed like a nightmare of Lucy as she lay there; the pointed teeth, the bloodstained, voluptuous mouth – which it made one shudder to see, the whole carnal and unspiritual appearance, seeming like a devilish mockery of Lucy's sweet purity.
>
> (Stoker 1997: 190)

This is why female sexuality needs to be controlled so tightly, for unchecked it runs riot. The killing of Lucy is, in fact, the novel's great set-piece, complete with dripping wax candles: a violent reinstatement of male sexual dominance. The preliminary visit to Lucy's tomb sets up the scene as a sexual violation:

Van Helsing went about his work systematically. Holding his candle so that he could read the coffin plates, and so holding it that the sperm dropped in white patches which congealed as they touched the metal, he made assurance of Lucy's coffin. Another search in his bag, and he took out a turnscrew. ... Straightway he began taking out the screws, and finally lifted off the lid, showing the casing of lead beneath. The sight was almost too much for me. It seemed to be as much of an affront to the dead as it would have been to have stripped off her clothing in her sleep whilst living; I actually took hold of his hand to stop him.

(ibid.: 175–6)

The phallic imagery here – candles, sperm (that is, candlegrease), screws – is repeated and intensified as Holmwood kills Lucy, aided and surrounded by her former suitors and protectors, who will him on. The image here is a powerful one of traditional masculinity, the god Thor with his mighty hammer, and the tableau is that of a violent gang-rape:

Then he struck with all his might.
    The Thing in the coffin writhed; and a hideous blood-curdling screech came from the opened red lips. The body shook and quivered and twisted in wild contortions; the sharp white teeth champed together till the lips were cut, and the mouth was smeared with a crimson foam. But Arthur never faltered. ... He looked like a figure of Thor as his untrembling arm rose and fell, driving deeper and deeper the mercy-bearing stake, whilst the blood from the pierced heart welled and spurted up around it.

(ibid.: 192)

By contrast, the killing of Dracula himself is given far less attention, though it's worth remembering that Quincey Morris, who actually does the deed, is the only one of the vampire hunters to die – men can't penetrate men, and live.

Dracula stands poised, quite self-consciously, on the cusp of modernity. Technological advancements – blood transfusions, stenographs, train timetables, typewriters, Kodak cameras – all have their place in killing the vampire, though recourse is also needed to the old ways: the host, the cross, the stake. Professor Van Helsing straddles these worlds. Francis Ford Coppola's *Bram Stoker's Dracula* also introduces us to that other *fin-de-siècle* invention, the cinematograph (Gary Oldman's Count goes to see one in London). Importantly, this alludes to the future of *Dracula* in 1897, on the big screen: what we now know about *Dracula*, we know from the movies. With this in mind, I'd like to close this section with a quote from

Maxim Gorky, who went to see the Lumière Cinematograph in Moscow in 1896, and was horrified by what he saw. What he saw was a procession of the Undead:

> Your nerves are strained, imagination carries you to some unnaturally monotonous life, a life without colour and without sound, but full of movement, the life of ghosts, or of people, *damned* to the damnation of eternal silence, people who have been deprived of all the colours of life.
>
> (Skal 1990: 4)

We are Dracula: Lugosi, Lee, and the classic cinema vampire

Vampires found their true home in the cinema, but the twentieth-century history of vampire movies almost did not happen at all – or anyway, it almost happened in a rather different way. Florence Stoker, Bram's widow, clung tenaciously to the rights for adaptations of *Dracula* as a source of income in her last years – rights which, you'll remember, Stoker himself had secured with a dramatized reading in 1897. Thus, when in 1922 F.W. Murnau directed *Nosferatu: Ein Symphonie des Grauens* (*Nosferatu: A Symphony of Horror*) – an unauthorized adaptation (by Henrik Galeen) of *Dracula* which changed the title, changed the location from London to Bremen, and changed the characters' names, so that Count Dracula becomes Graf Orlock and Harker becomes Hutter – Florence Stoker sued, demanding that all extant prints be destroyed.[13] Which they were – almost. One print remained undiscovered, and thus the film survives, a source of endless fascination to students of the genre, despite being dismissed by André Gide as 'heavy-handed, absurd and unimaginative', and by the great historian of the horror film Carlos Clarens as 'crude, unsubtle and illogical' (1997: 21).

What's most indelible about *Nosferatu* is the embodiment of the vampire himself, by Max Schreck after the astounding production designs of the artist and occultist Albin Grau, as a disturbing combination of a rat and a penis. Laurence A. Rickels suggests that the film's very title gives it a sexual specificity: 'in Romanian *nosferatu* is the name of a type of vampire specialising in making husbands impotent' (Rickels 1999: 95). (Although, in *Shadow of the Vampire*, Willem Dafoe's vampiric Max Schreck claims *himself* to be impotent – too old for that sort of thing, and dried up.) Thus, when Orlock springs up from his coffin, stiff-jointed and erect, his symbolic potency is obvious, and favourably contrasted to the flabby (flaccid?) Hutter, whose wife Ellen entices the nosferatu to her bed and keeps him there *all night*, until the cock crows. (QED, if you ask me.)

This nosferatu, or feral vampire, more animalistic by far than the Count, is a recurring minor theme and image in twentieth-century vampire representation, all derived from Schreck and Grau. Other than Schreck himself, the notable screen nosferatus (or is it nosferati?) have been Klaus Kinski in Werner Herzog's remake of Murnau, and Reggie Nalder's truly horrid, blue-faced Mr Barlow in the TV movie of Stephen King's *'Salem's Lot*. Graf Orlock, the nosferatu, also makes a memorable appearance in Kim Newman's brilliant *Anno Dracula* (1992), a revisionist vampire novel which amounts to a compendium of vampirism:

> At the end of the corridor, framed by an arch, stood a tall, hunched *nosferatu* in a long, shabby frock coat. His head was swollen and rodent-like with huge pointed ears and prominent front fangs. His eyes, set in black caverns that obscured his cheeks, were constantly liquid, darting here and there. Even his fellow elders found Graf Orlok [sic] . . . a disquieting presence. He was a crawling reminder of how remote they all were from the warm [i.e., the living].
>
> (Newman 1992: 341)

At the same time as Graf Orlock was retreating from humanity in Germany, John L. Balderston and Hamilton Deane were preparing their authorized stage version of *Dracula*, showcasing an altogether more socialized vampire. The play was previewed in the Grand Theatre, Derby, in August 1924, with Edmund Blake as the Count, moving on to performances in Wimbledon the next Spring. The play's West End debut came in February 1927, when the 22-year-old Raymond Huntley donned an opera cloak over his own evening suit to play the Count at the Little Theatre. In the same year, the play opened in New York, with the lead taken by a little-known Hungarian actor called Bela Lugosi (Skal 1990: 65–91).

When Universal Studios bought the screen rights to the Balderston–Deane *Dracula* in 1929, they did not have Bela Lugosi, who barely spoke English and memorized his lines phonetically, in mind for the lead: Conrad Veidt was originally mooted for the part. While Veidt, with his background in German expressionist horror, would have been a fine choice, twentieth-century popular culture might have been rather different had Tod Browning's *Dracula not* starred Bela Lugosi. As Clarens writes:

> If *Dracula*, the film, has retained any power to impress after . . . years of repeated showings, it is due in the main to Lugosi himself. It is useless to debate whether he was a good actor or not; Lugosi *was* Dracula: the actor's identification with the part is complete.
>
> (1997: 62)

As indeed it was, despite being the only time Lugosi was to play Dracula on screen, unless one counts the ignominious *Abbot and Costello meet*

Frankenstein – though he did play the vampires Count Mora (in an incestuous relationship with his daughter Luna) in Browning's *Mark of the Vampire*, and Armand Tesla in *Return of the Vampire*. On his death in 1956, age 72, Lugosi was buried in full Dracula regalia.

Browning's *Dracula* has often been criticized for its staginess and lack of action, especially at the end, where the Count is dispatched offscreen, to the accompaniment of a rather pathetic moan (thus betraying its stage origins – in the original 1924 production, the censor, in the only cut he made to the play, insisted that the Count's death not be shown explicitly) (Skal 1990: 70). Nevertheless, much about the film remains fascinating – it has what is still the best-ever Castle Dracula, with cobwebs, a monumental staircase out of a Borgesian nightmare, and the famous armadillo (what *is* it doing there?). There is also an outrageous, scenery-chewing performance from Dwight Frye as the fly-eating Renfield, who here takes Harker's part as the first visitor to Castle Dracula. It is also Renfield who plays a major part in the film's fascinating take on the sexual politics of Stoker's original novel. In the novel, the Count furiously interrupts Harker's willing seduction by the three female vampires: 'But the Count! Never did I imagine such wrath and fury, even to the demons of the pit. His eyes were positively blazing. ... "How dare you touch him, any of you? ... This man belongs to me!"' (Stoker 1997: 43). As Frayling has shown in his study of Stoker's working-notes for *Dracula*, the phrase 'This man belongs to me!' is more-or-less the only consistent feature amongst Stoker's many textual revisions: it is there from the very start, obviously central to Stoker's conception of his novel (1992: 303–16). Frye's Renfield is a high-camp Englishman abroad, complete with spats and homburg; the kind that seems to believe that talking more loudly in English will get you understood in Transylvania (and it does!). This gay dandy is a ready victim of the Count's seduction. More troublesome is Dr Van Helsing. Edward Van Sloan's performance as Van Helsing (he is another survivor from the 1927 Broadway production) is usually dismissed as wooden, which it is, but this only serves to heighten the contrast between the stolid, puritanical, Protestant Van Helsing on the one side, and the colourful, Catholic, dissident Count and his bug-eating toyboy Renfield, a pair of flaming queens to match Henry Frankenstein and Dr Pretorius, on the other. The pivotal moment in the film comes with Dracula's attempted seduction of Van Helsing: the pair lock eyes for an eternity, and it takes all of Van Helsing's resolve not to succumb. As classic Hollywood cinema invariably found ways of circumventing the censorious Hays Code, so too does the practice of Browning's film belie Laemmle's injunction that 'Dracula should only go for women and not men!'

Released the year after *Dracula*, but of considerably greater cinematic merit, Carl Dreyer's icy, dreamlike *Vampyr* took as its source not Stoker but Le Fanu, as an extremely circuitous adaptation of 'Carmilla', with touches of *In a Glass Darkly*'s longest tale, 'The Room at the Dragon Volant'.[14] A young man, David Gray (called Allan Gray in the opening credits and the film's subtitle, 'The Dream of Allan Gray'), arrives at a mysterious inn on a riverbank, his arrival cross-cut with shots of a (grim?) reaper ringing for the ferry. The opening scene establishes an atmosphere of uncanniness which the film maintains with remarkable consistency throughout (in part because the whole thing was shot through a filter of white gauze, giving it a vague, washed-out air): the inn is full of deformed men and of shadows acting independently of those who cast them; there is a gravedigger whose earth seems to be flying *from* the ground *to* the spade, and a sinister doctor from whose rooms seem to come the cries of children and the barking of dogs. Clearly visible in the doctor's rooms are bottles of poison and a closet full of children's shoes. Gray receives a parcel containing a treatise on vampirism and a note, 'You can help free us from our affliction.' The afflicted one is Léone, a young woman under the care of her sister Gisèle, and apparently undergoing a gradual transformation into vampirism: in one memorable close-up, Léone looks at her sister, her expression changing from sweetness to a very disquieting combination of fury and lust, and then back again. Gray donates blood to aid Léone, and the film's most celebrated passage has him out in the antechamber after the transfusion, saying weakly to the doctor, 'I've lost my blood', before splitting himself in two, his ghostly double bearing witness to his own funeral where, in yet another memorable shot (the film is full of them), events are viewed from the point of view of Gray inside his own coffin, through a glass panel in the top. The vampire herself is an aged crone, Marguerite Chopin, who died in mortal sin, unrepentant; she is aided by the sinister doctor, who meets his own end in a flour-mill, a blizzard of white filling the already whited screen.

On its release in 1956 *Curse of Frankenstein* proved to be a great success for Hammer studios, which was understandably keen to follow it up with an adaptation of another great canonical work of nineteenth-century horror. Thus, the following year, Hammer gave the world *Dracula*, again directed by Terence Fisher, and with Christopher Lee as the Count. While he may not have had Schreck's uncanny otherness or Lugosi's exotic suavity, Lee brought to the role an unmatched sense of magnetic power – by comparison, most subsequent vampires are minnows, or children. Very effectively, the film dispenses with much of the accepted supernatural paraphernalia of vampirism, notably the bat-transformation, presenting the Count at his most aristocratic, as pure, commanding ego. Thus, when, dressed all in black, the Count greets Jonathan Harker (John Van Eyssen) – 'Mr Harker, I'm glad that you arrived safely. I am Dracula and I welcome you to my house' – his vampirism almost seems beside the point. Lee also brings to the Count a greater sense of Stoker's 'wrath and fury' than any of his predecessors, as the red-eyed vampire roars and snarls at his harem as they attempt to seduce Harker: Lee's Dracula does not *need* to transform into a beast, as he carries that transformation within himself at all times.

Hammer's take on sexual politics was often troubling, if only because it so closely resembled Stoker's own. This is perhaps most notoriously exemplified in their next film in the cycle, *Dracula – Prince of Darkness*. Here, Lee's Count is given no dialogue at all, having instead a purely iconic role: thus, much of the focus of the film shifts to his first vampirized victim, Helen – a very fine performance from Barbara Shelley, resurrected (or more properly liberated) from a prim and rather sour Victorian matron to a lascivious vamp with flowing hair and diaphanous nightgown, and much the better for it: 'You don't need Charles!' she says to her sister-in-law Diana, in what is simultaneously a statement of desire and of liberation. It can't last, of course, and in what is the film's most notorious scene (so notorious, in fact that one critic, S.S. Prawer, has devoted a whole chapter to its study) (1980: 240–69), Helen is held down on a table, writhing and screaming, by a group of monks, while the imperious, rifle-wielding Father Sandor (Andrew Keir) drives a stake through her heart and her brother-in-law Charles looks on, horrified and excited by what he sees. It is, of course, a gang-rape, and a very brutal one, drawing directly on the death of Lucy in Stoker's original, though this time given full ecclesiastical sanction. Indeed, although he earlier dismisses a village priest who is about to violate the corpse of a dead (as opposed to undead) girl with a stake through the heart as 'a superstitious, frightened idiot', Father Sandor's activities here do not greatly differ from those of the puritanical witch-hunter Gustav Weil (Peter Cushing) in *Twins of Evil*, far more terrifying than the vampires he hunts.[15]

Hammer studios, and Terence Fisher in particular, have long divided critical opinion. While Robin Wood considers Fisher's films to be the work of a moral simpleton, the equally influential David Pirie has taken very seriously the dualistic view of good and evil which he sees in his work – though Fisher himself resisted such auteurist approaches to his work, preferring instead to see himself as a skilled craftsman-for-hire.[16] Certainly there is a kind of conservative Puritanism visible in Fisher's work, as there is throughout the Hammer *œuvre* generally. In part, this is because of the studio's continuing commitment to traditional Gothicism, its habitual reliance on accepted templates for horror (perhaps best exemplified by its many versions of the *Dracula* and *Frankenstein* stories), and consequently its reluctance, in narrative and metaphorical terms, to leave the nineteenth century. Thus, in 1968, when George A. Romero was changing the face of horror with *Night of the Living Dead*, Hammer's best effort was probably *Dracula Has Risen From the Grave* – a fine film, but hardly revolutionary, as its title implies only too clearly.

None of which is to argue that Hammer's films are without merit – far from it – merely that they occupy the conservative pole of modern horror. Certainly, Hammer could, at times, be perverse. The highly Freudian *Brides of Dracula* is a vampiric rewriting of Tennessee Williams's *Suddenly Last Summer*, with David Peel's very gay Baron Meinster, a peroxide Dorian Gray, vampirizing both his own mother (Martita Hunt) and Dr Van Helsing (Peter Cushing) – who recovers by cauterizing his own wound with a red-hot poker (!). Also Freudian is *Taste the Blood of Dracula*, a study of

Victorian sexual hypocrisy in which a trio of tyrannical Victorian patriarchs are killed by their own children: Hargood (Geoffrey Keen) lusts drunkenly after his daughter Alice (Linda Hayden), whom he wants to beat with a riding crop, until she dispatches him with a shovel; the vampirized Lucy (Isla Blair) grins deliciously as she drives a stake through her father's (Peter Sallis) heart. Such delights notwithstanding, by the 1970s Romero and a new generation of film-makers were making Hammer's output increasingly anachronistic. The studio's last film, *To the Devil a Daughter*, was released in 1975.

1975 and after: vampire circus

That same year, 1975, was to prove singularly important for vampires, the beginning of a new era for the Children of the Night. The late 1970s in general saw a number of highly influential books and films which together succeeded in reinventing the vampire for modernity: Stephen King's *'Salem's Lot* (1975); Fred Saberhagen's *The Dracula Tape* (1975); Anne Rice's *Interview with the Vampire* (1976); George A. Romero's characteristically distinctive take on the vampire legend, *Martin* (1976); Chelsea Quinn Yarbro's *Hotel Transylvania* (1978), the first in her 'Saint-Germain' series; Suzy McKee Charnas's *The Vampire Tapestry* (1980). All of these texts can, singularly and taken as a body, justifiably be described as revisionist, and led the way to a proliferation of vampires so great that I can do little more here than glance at some of them (to do them justice would require a whole book, not one section of one chapter). While there certainly *were* some more traditional conceptions of the vampire produced during this period, the most distinctive of them tend either to be self-consciously old-fashioned, like Frank Langella's Byronic Count in *Dracula* (1979), a filmed version of the successful Broadway revival of the Balderston–Deane play, or Werner Herzog's stylish *Nosferatu: Phantom Der Nacht* (1979), a remake of Murnau; or else knowing and parodic, like George Hamilton's genuinely brilliant take on Lugosi in *Love at First Bite* (1979). All three of these films are characterized by a wistful, backward-looking romanticism, coming at the end of a decade in which things had changed dramatically in the world of vampires.

'When I conceived of the vampire novel which became *'Salem's Lot*,' King has written, 'I decided I wanted to try to use the book partially as a form of literary homage ... So my novel bears an intentional similarity to Bram Stoker's *Dracula*' (King 1982: 40). Combined with this attempt at a revision of the traditional vampire canon was a distrust of traditional structures of power and authority. The book was written, says King, in the shadow of the Watergate affair:

> In my novel *'Salem's Lot*, the thing that really scared me was not vampires, but the town in the daytime, the town that was empty, knowing that there were things in closets, that there

> were people tucked under beds, under the concrete pilings of
> all those trailers. And all the time I was writing that, the
> Watergate hearings were pouring out of the TV ... During that
> time I was thinking about secrets, things that have been hidden
> and were being dragged out into the light.
>
> (Underwood and Miller 1988: 5)

As Nina Auerbach, who also makes use of this passage, notes, it is surely no
accident that at the very same time that tapes incriminating Richard Nixon
were being played on American television, at least two vampire novels were
themselves to take the form of taped confessions: Saberhagen's *The Dracula
Tape*, a radical retelling of Stoker from the Count's point of view, and Rice's
Interview (Auerbach 1995: 152).

Unquestionably, the citizens of 'Salem's Lot are, on the whole, as vile a
bunch as you'd care to meet, a motley collection of wife-beaters, sadists,
racists, paedophiles, homophobes and other 'preeverts' (King 1976: 84).
Their priest, Father Callahan, muses on contemporary America's 'banality
of evil': 'he was being forced into the conclusion that there was no EVIL in
the world at all but only evil – or perhaps (evil)' (ibid.: 164). Into this climate
of small-town American (evil) comes an invader, the embodiment of old-
school European EVIL, the vampire Mr Barlow, an illegal immigrant in a
box that has 'No customs stamp ... a hell of a funny thing' (ibid.: 98).
Barlow and his associate Mr Straker have come to this small American town
from the Old World, posing as antiques dealers selling 'old things, fine
things', and probably, in the view of the authorities, 'queer for each other':
certainly, Mr Barlow has an 'almost effeminate face' (ibid.: 112, 156, 363).
Though Barlow affects to scorn American life, he is drawn and fascinated by
it – and eventually destroyed by it, unable to cope with American modernity:

> I am from many lands, but to me this country ... this town ...
> seems full of foreigners ... but beautiful, enticing foreigners,
> bursting with vitality, full-blooded and full of life. Do you
> know how beautiful the people of your country and your town
> are, Mr. Bryant? ... How should a poor rustic like myself deal
> with the hollow sophistication of a great city ... even an
> American city? No! And no and no! I *spit* on your cities!
>
> (ibid.: 245–6)

But it is to the cities that the vampire was destined to go, and *Martin*
opens with John Amplas's quasi-vampire arriving in a working-class
neighbourhood in Pittsburgh, come to stay with his elderly cousin Cudo
(Lincoln Maazel). Martin sedates his female victims, rapes them and opens
their veins with a straight razor to drink their blood, and the prosaic reality
of 1970s' Pittsburgh is intercut with monochrome visions of Martin, in frilly
vampire garb, pursued by angry villagers. Are these memories or fantasies?

The film maintains its ambivalence as to Martin's status throughout: Cudo is convinced that Martin is an 84-year-old nosferatu, and festoons their home with crucifixes and garlic, to which Martin is immune; the reality may be more straightforwardly secular, that he is a delusional sex-killer. As ever, I think both interpretations are simultaneously valid, and the film closes with Cudo killing his young (or ancient) cousin in the traditional way, with a stake through the heart.

Count Dracula makes a dramatic entrance in Jonathan Harker's journal at the beginning of Stoker's novel, but notably barely appears after that – the novel's focus shifts to his victims and hunters. His *presence* is felt throughout, however, as threatening otherness, in inverse proportion to the frequency of his appearances. For some, exploring this otherness has proven irresistible, and thus from the mid-1970s we have been given a series of accounts which have effectively attempted to psychologize the vampire, with a life, a history, a 'personality', as best exemplified, perhaps, in Charnas's excellent *Vampire Tapestry*, whose vampire, Weyland, is at one point put on the couch (and seduced) by a psychoanalyst, Floria.

The problem with most other attempts to psychologize the vampire is their fundamental shallowness or even banality. When the Count delivers the long speech to Jonathan which begins, 'We Szekelys have a right to be proud, for in our veins flows the blood of many brave races who fought as the lion fights, for lordship' (Stoker 1997: 33), it is to convey the fact that he, Dracula, *is* history – he contains within himself an aristocratic tradition of European history; he is both himself and his own bloodline, his ancestors, and, in true aristocratic fashion, blood is all to him. While Yarbro's novels display the 4,000-year-old Saint-Germain as an active and benign agent across the span of human history, the vampires of Anne Rice's *Interview* and the rest of her numerous 'Vampire Chronicles' seem barely engaged at all in human affairs, which impinge on them only as a vision of changing fashions and interior design, and increased opportunities for consumerism. Rice may have been the first vampire-writer deliberately to make a play for cult status, to present vampirism as a desirable lifestyle choice, an idea continued in the 1980s with the vapid *The Hunger*, and in 1990s with the Goth radical chic of *Lost Souls* (1992) and the other vampire novels of Poppy Z. Brite.[17] At the beginning of *The Vampire Lestat* (1985), Rice's eponymous vampire awakens in New Orleans:

> People were adventurous and erotic again in the way they'd been in the old days, before the middle-class revolutions of the late 1700s. They even *looked* the way they had in those times. ... And these were just the common people of America. Not just the rich who've always achieved a certain androgyny, a certain joie de vivre that the middle-class revolutionaries called decadence in the past.

> The old aristocratic sensuality now belonged to everybody.
> It was wed to the promises of middle-class revolution, and all
> the people had the right to love and to luxury and to graceful
> things.
>   Department stores had become places of near Oriental
> loveliness – merchandise displayed amid soft tinted carpeting,
> eerie music, amber light. In the all-night drugstores, bottles of
> violet and green shampoos gleamed like gems on the sparkling
> glass shelves.
>
> (Rice 1994: 14)

Well, it *was* the 1980s! More disturbing, though, is the sense that it is
somehow entirely proper that Rice's vampires treat the rest of us as cattle,
simply because they are beautiful and we are not. It is tempting to view
Rice's novels as the work of a Marxist satirist – tempting but, alas,
wrong.

As Chapter 5 will argue, Stephen King's commitment to pre-adulthood
was to shape the face of horror in the 1980s, influencing a series of
vampire movies for and about adolescents: the stonking *Fright Night*,
Vamp, *The Lost Boys*, the lauded *Near Dark* – a series of films which
leads logically to the teenie-babe shenanigans of *Buffy the Vampire Slayer*.
While *Vamp* is mainly for fans of Grace Jones in her underwear, the
others do deal, with varying success, with issues of familial anxiety and
breakdown: both *Fright Night* and *The Lost Boys* are concerned with
single parenthood and its effects on teenage children, and both feature
identical scenes where separated mothers inadvertently invite into their
homes vampires posing as suitors, replacement fathers for mixed-up teens.
Likewise, *Near Dark* posits a family of vampires (led by Lance Henriksen)
as a competing (and compelling) alternative to the traditional American
nuclear family.

No account of the modern vampire movie would be complete without
a discussion, however brief, of Coppola's horror for the carriage-trade,
Bram Stoker's Dracula. Though undeniably overwrought and almost
sabotaged by some completely useless acting (notably from Keanu Reeves
as the screen's worst-ever Jonathan Harker), the film belongs alongside
Murnau's and Browning's in an honourable tradition of fascinatingly
flawed versions of Stoker. Anthony Hopkins's unhinged performance as
Van Helsing raises the possibility – a possibility that Stoker also entertains
– that the doctor may in fact be a deranged maniac, and thus the vampire
hunters are far more dangerous than the vampire himself. Also of note is
the fact that Gary Oldman's Count Dracula is a changeling. Here, it is a
question of the nature or source of the gaze, for Oldman's Dracula looks
different depending on who does the looking. To Jonathan Harker, he is,
like his performer, an Old Man – more precisely, with his ridiculous
pompadour hairstyle, candelabrum, robe, and general air of high camp,

he is Liberace, and thus entirely in keeping with the homoerotic subtext of this section of both the novel and the film, and with the film's connection of vampirism and AIDS (Liberace was one of a number of high-profile victims of the disease). To the film's highly sexualized Lucy, he is the wolf, or more specifically the wolf-man, lusty, animalistic, even priapic – in one notable scene he has sex with Lucy on a grave. To Mina, he is the handsome young man, a delicate aesthete, in keeping with Winona Ryder's performance of propriety.

Vampires showed no signs of expiring with the millennium. The 1990s, indeed, saw a number of highly inventive takes on the old stories. Newman's *Anno Dracula* rewrites the end of Stoker's novel to have the Count achieve his aim of conquering England, allowing Newman to indulge in an encyclopaedic orgy of late-Victorian popular culture – and to produce in the process what may be the finest vampire novel since 1897. Tom Holland's *The Vampyre: The Secret History of Lord Byron* (1995) goes back even further, with the appealing hypothesis that Byron may really all along have been what Lady Caroline Lamb said he was, a vampire. Like Van Helsing, the psychotic sex-killer of Roderick Anscombe's *The Secret Life of Laszlo, Count Dracula* (1994) is a disciple of the Victorian hypnotist, mind doctor, and quack, Charcot. Dan Simmons's *Carrion Comfort* (1989) has a global conspiracy theory of 'mind vampires', the Island Club, malevolently intervening in human history (they are behind, for example, the assassination of John Lennon), while his *Children of the Night* (1992) has Count Dracula as naturalized American industrialist Vernor Deacon Trent, returning to the post-Ceauşescu Romania of orphanages and AIDS, going home to die.

On film, vampires had a less successful decade. *Blade* is an uneasy combination of the vampire and action movies, though it is far preferable to John Carpenter's viciously homophobic *Vampires*. Like *Near Dark*, *Vampires* is a strange hybrid, a Tex-Mex vampire road movie. Astonishingly enough, this has proven quite a lively sub-genre: much more fun than any recent vampire movie is Robert Rodriguez's similarly hybrid *From Dusk Till Dawn*. *From Dusk Till Dawn*, indeed, went even further, combining the Tex-Mex vampire road movie with the splatter movie to often hilarious effect, with a notable cameo from Tom Savini as 'Sex Machine', a biker with a machine-gun in his codpiece. Best of all, though, was *From Dusk Till Dawn*'s tag-line: 'No interviews. Just vampires.' Thank goodness for that.

Notes

1. 'Listen to them – the children of the night. What music they make!' (Stoker 1997: 24). I am aware, *pace* Nina Auerbach's rather tart remark that the 'children of the night' to whom the count refers here are wolves, not vampires (Auerbach 1995: 211n38). Nevertheless, as *Dracula* itself makes clear (and 'Dracula's Guest' even more so), wolves and vampires are at the very least metonymically linked, the one a symbol for the other, if not literally interchangeable: Dracula himself, at least, is capable of transforming into a wolf, though not all vampires are.

2. Twitchell (1981: 145–60). Samuel Taylor Coleridge did of course write one unproblematic vampire-poem, 'Christabel', which Twitchell duly, and splendidly, discusses on pp. 40–8.
3. On the same page, Twitchell offers a schematic account of vampirism in his texts, complete with '+ ENERGY GAINER' AND '– ENERGY LOSER' for the 'vampire' and its victim.
4. See Jones (1949); Maurice Richardson, 'The Psychoanalysis of Count Dracula', in Frayling (1992: 418–22). It was Richardson who famously wrote of *Dracula* that 'From a Freudian standpoint – and from no other does the story really make any sense – it is seen as a kind of incestuous, necrophilious, oral-anal-sadistic all-in wrestling match' (Frayling 1992: 418–19).
5. For the best analysis of Marx's vampire-imagery, see the chapter 'Karl Marx's Vampires and Grave-diggers', in Baldick (1987: 121–40); see also Frayling (1992: 83–4), who notes that 'Karl Marx enjoyed reading the horror tales of Hoffmann and Dumas père for relaxation at bedtime.'
6. For a discussion of these figures and legends, usually taking the form of gods of death and blood rites, see Devendra P. Varma, 'The Vampire in Legend, Lore and Literature', in Prest (1998: 1: xiii–xxx).
7. A loose translation into modern English:
   All bare was the body and black to the bone
   All bogged down with clay, horribly covered
   It wailed and lamented like a woman
   But neither on the body nor the face was there a covering
   It shook. It was bewildered, it stood like a stone
   It moaned, it murmured, it muttered like a lunatic
   Circled with serpents that clung to its sides
   To count the toads on it is too difficult for my tongue.
8. The case of Arnod Paole (or Arnold Paul) is discussed by a number of modern commentators: see, for example, Barber (1988: 15–20) (who reproduces the original report, *Visum et Repertum* – 'Seen and Destroyed' – in its entirety); Frayling (1992: 21–3).
9. Characteristically, Twitchell has attempted a reading of the entire poem in vampiric terms (1981: 160–6).
10. See Stuart (1992: 226). Stuart also notes that in 1823, the Royal Court Theatre staged a version of Southey's *Thalaba the Destroyer*, which played in a double-bill with *Frankenstein; or, The Demon of Switzerland* (ibid.: 231). Cooke was most famous for his performance as Frankenstein's Monster, a performance which Mary Shelley saw and admired.
11. Bunson (1993: 271). As Auerbach notes, Bunson is not always reliable (Auerbach 1995: 206, n1), but this account certainly tallies with what we know about the practices of Victorian serial-fiction publishing, as well as having a certain symbolic appropriateness.
12. Readers who are curious but lack stamina should note that Twitchell (1981: 207–14) gives a detailed plot-synopsis of *Varney*.
13. For the definitive account of this case, see Skal (1990: 43–63).
14. *Vampyr* is usually dated 1932, though Skal claims to have found an illustrated review in a Portuguese film magazine dated January 1931 (Skal 1996: 206).
15. *Twins of Evil*, starring *Playboy* centrefolds Mary and Madeleine Collinson, was the final leg of Hammer's enjoyably sordid 'Karnstein Trilogy' all based, more or less, on *Carmilla*. The others were *The Vampire Lovers*, which stuck very closely to its source and starred the great Ingrid Pitt as Carmilla Karnstein, and *Lust for a Vampire*.
16. In 1973, Wood wrote, 'Fisher is certainly consistent – the consistency being mainly a matter of unremitting crudeness of sensibility. The most striking thing about the world he creates is its moral squalor. His characters have no aliveness, no complexity' (Prawer 1980: 268). For David Pirie on Fisher, see Pirie (1973: 51–2).
17. Ken Gelder, in his analysis of Rice's relationship with her audience, cites a question put to her by an interviewer: 'You now have a rather large cult of fans – people obsessed with your work. Does that excite you?' (1994: 114).

|4|

Monsters from the id

Horror, madness and the mind

Interviewed about his performance as the psychopathic psychiatrist Dr Hannibal Lecter in *Manhunter*, and on Anthony Hopkins's Oscar-winning performance in the same role in *The Silence of the Lambs*, Brian Cox suggested that 'the difference between Anthony Hopkins's performance and my performance is that Tony Hopkins is mad and I am insane!' (O'Brien 2001: 115).[1] Cox's distinction here is not quite as fanciful as it appears, and indeed it reflects two very different attitudes to madness and its portrayal within the horror genre. The first, that which Cox calls 'madness', is florid and melodramatic, typified by grandiose gestures and aims, and reflects that conception of madness (and monstrosity, which shares an etymology with 'demonstrate' – display) as *performative* or spectacular (that is, constituting a spectacle to be witnessed) which Michel Foucault examines in *Madness and Civilization*:

> [madness] is judged only by its acts ... Madness no longer exists except as *seen*. The proximity instituted by the asylum ... does not allow reciprocity: only the nearness of observation that watches, that spies, that comes closer in order to see better, but moves ever farther away, since it accepts and acknowledges only the values of the Stranger.
>
> (Foucault 1967: 250)

In the eighteenth century, for example, visits to bedlams – madhouses – to view the inmates were considered as entertainments, akin to viewing theatrical performances. If this 'madness' might be considered the result of having 'too much' personality, then 'insanity', conversely, signifies an absence of personality, usually manifested as unindividuated, unmotivated destructiveness.[2]

The former strain has a rich history in horror, and in cinema stretches back at least as far as *The Cabinet of Dr Caligari*. *Caligari*'s dreamlike

narrative logic and imagery unfurls some way beyond sanity, seemingly a
tale told by the inmate of a lunatic asylum. Caligari himself (Werner Krauss)
is simultaneously a seedy sideshow huckster at whose behest the clairvoyant
somnambulist, Cesare (Conrad Veidt), strangles his victims, and also the
director of the lunatic asylum, a mad doctor out to prove that minds can be
controlled to commit murder (little wonder, perhaps, that the film has been
read as a prefiguring allegory of Hitler's Germany).[3] While the cinematic
dominance of this kind of 'madness' has been challenged in recent years by
the largely characterless killers of the slasher movie (the exception here,
Freddy Krueger, is something of a problem case, as we shall see: his
wisecracking murderous trickster persona developed with the *Nightmare on
Elm Street* series; his supernaturalism makes him a problematic slasher,
though ultimately a slasher nevertheless), traditional madmen still
occasionally rear their ugly heads, as with Jack Nicholson's outrageously
unrestrained performance as the axe-wielding Jack Torrance in *The Shining*
(a film with innumerable redoubling emblems of the twisted state of Jack's
mind – the Overlook Hotel's maze from which he, finally, cannot escape,
the model of the maze in the lobby, the labyrinthine corridors of the hotel
itself, the mazelike patterns on the carpets), John Lithgow's barking turn as
Carter Nix in *Raising Cain* (see below for more on this), and, of course,
Anthony Hopkins's three outings as Hannibal Lecter, the maddest of mad
doctors.

The writer whose work best exemplifies this tradition of 'madness' is
Edgar Allan Poe: 'And much of Madness and more of Sin / And Horror the
soul of the plot', as the verses from 'Ligeia' famously have it (Poe 1977b:
161). Poe's stories tend to be unsettlingly monologic, with no external
referent, and thus dependent on the veracity of narrators who are frequently
highly unreliable, not least because they are frequently highly mad. This
unreliability threatens totally to destabilize the already unstable world of
'The Fall of the House of Usher', where Roderick Usher, in an incestuous
relationship with his sister and suffering, as do many of Poe's protagonists,
from an acute heightening of the senses, hears the catatonic Madeline rise
from her tomb, and exclaims to his friend the narrator: 'MADMAN! ...
MADMAN! I TELL YOU THAT SHE NOW STANDS WITHOUT THE
DOOR!' (ibid.: 144) Who is the 'madman' here? Is it Usher himself, or is it
the narrator? If the narrator, then what effect might this knowledge have on
our reading of the story? Less ambiguously, 'The Tell-Tale Heart' is told
solely from the perspective of its deranged protagonist, attempting to justify
to the police who visit him, to the reader who hears his confession, and to
himself, the rationale behind his killing and dismembering a blind old man:

> TRUE! – nervous – very, very dreadfully nervous I had been
> and am; but why *will* you say that I am mad? The disease had
> sharpened my senses – not destroyed – not dulled them. Above
> all was the sense of hearing acute. I heard all things in the

> heaven and in the earth. I heard many things in hell. How,
> then, am I mad? Hearken! and observe how healthily – how
> calmly I can tell you the whole story.
>
> (ibid.: 289)

Unsurprisingly, Poe has provided rich material for film-makers interested in
madness, most notably in the impressive series of loose adaptations made by
Roger Corman for AIP in the early 1960s, distinguished by the lurid
camerawork of Floyd Crosby (and later of Nicholas Roeg), and, of course,
the extraordinary presence of Vincent Price: *The Fall of the House of Usher*,
The Pit and the Pendulum, *Tales of Terror*, *The Raven*, *The Haunted
Palace*, *The Tomb of Ligeia*, and *The Masque of the Red Death*. But the
shift in the representation of horror madness is perhaps best exemplified by
a comparison of two films, one based (very loosely indeed) on Poe and both
starring one of the screen's greatest madmen, Boris Karloff: *The Black Cat*
(1934) and *Targets* (1968).

The Black Cat posits a sense of warped, heightened reality as the norm
for continental Europe in the inter-war years, and for a sense of quite how
demented this film is, it is really necessary only to recount the plot – surely
the greatest plot in cinema (if not world) history. Dr Vitus Werdegast (Bela
Lugosi), 'one of Hungary's greatest psychiatrists', travels across central
Europe by train 'to visit an old friend', Hjalmar Poelzig (Karloff), 'one of
Austria's greatest architects'. During World War I, Poelzig betrayed his
country to the Russians – an action which led directly to the death of
Werdegast's wife and to Werdegast's own imprisonment for fifteen years –
and has subsequently built himself a beautiful Art Deco palace literally on
top of a battlefield graveyard: 'The masterpiece of construction built upon
the ruins of the masterpiece of destruction, the masterpiece of murder. The
murderer of ten thousand men returns to the place of his crime.' As well as
being a murderous traitor (and a chess-master with a passion for playing
Bach's 'Toccata and Fugue', that classic madman's favourite, on a huge
pipe-organ), Poelzig is also (of course!) a Satanist, who conducts a black
mass in 'Latin', and a kind of mad scientist who keeps a series of women in
suspended animation in his basement – including Werdegast's late wife,
who did not die in World War I, but instead lived on to marry Poelzig
himself. After her death, Poelzig married Karen, Werdegast's daughter.
Poelzig murders Karen sooner than have her rescued by her father, but is
then himself captured by Werdegast, who skins him alive before blowing up
the house, killing them both.

Targets stars an elderly Karloff as elderly horror-star Byron Orlok, who
has come to believe that 'My kind of horror isn't horror any more. ... No
one's afraid of a painted monster', and so announces his retirement: 'I'm an
antique, out of date. ... I'm an anachronism. ... The world belongs to the
young. Make way for them, let them have it.' This speech is immediately
followed by a shot of Orlok's head framed in the telescopic sights of Bobby

(Tim O'Kelly), a gun-maniac who lives with his wife and parents (including a domineering father, whom he contemplates murdering) in a freaky pastel blue and lilac house (very different from the bright reds and greens of the Corman Poes), the TV permanently on. One day, and for no explained reason, Bobby simply flips, killing his wife, his mother, and a delivery-man, before gunning down passing motorists from the top of an industrial plant. It is all random, undiscriminating, pointlessly unmotivated. At the close of the film, Bobby heads to the drive-in cinema which is premiering Orlok's latest film, *The Terror*, and sits behind the screen, the barrel of his gun pointing through a small hole, out at the audience. Orlok, doubled as his screen character, Baron von Leppe, advances on Bobby, overpowering him. Looking down at the cowering Bobby – bland, characterless, the polar opposite of the polymathically dotty Hjalmar Poelzig – Orlok asks, 'Is *this* what I was afraid of?'

When did *you* get out?': doubles, split personalities, and evil twins

The image of the double – the *Döppelganger* or second self, the mirror image, the Other who is also Oneself – tracks, haunts, or shadows cultural production in the nineteenth century, and on into the twentieth. Proverbially, an encounter with the double portends the death of the self. In his important study of the theme and idea of the double, the psychoanalyst Otto Rank suggests that the fear of the double has at least some of its origins in beliefs surrounding the human shadow – and superstitions remain about the misfortune which results from stepping on shadows, or casting shadows in inappropriate places or at unpropitious times. The shadow thus symbolizes, or exists in, another world parallel with our own, a non-material or spirit world. To cross over into that world is to die. Rank notes: 'From this shadow-superstition, some scholars believe, developed the belief in a guardian spirit, which in its turn is closely related to the double-motif' (1979: 50).

Closely allied to this are fears of the portrait, or of the mirror, as displaying a corrupt or evil image of the self. Puritan iconoclasts destroyed such images and mirrors, believing them to be a debased form of a creation which was God's alone. Jorge Luis Borges's classic, playful examination of idealism and reality, 'Tlön, Uqbar, Orbis Tertius', posits the shadow-world of Tlön, 'the work of a secret society of astronomers, biologists, engineers, metaphysicians, poets, chemists, algebraists, moralists, painters, geometers', existing alongside of, gradually contaminating, and eventually consuming our own reality. The existence of such a world is announced by means of a mirror: 'one of the heresiarchs of Uqbar had declared that mirrors and copulation are abominable, because they increase the number of men' (Borges 1970: 32, 27). To go through the looking glass is to enter a new world, a world of danger, of inversion, of the upsetting of norms and conventions. It is also, as the theorist Rosemary Jackson has suggested, specifically to enter the world of fantasy, the world of the *paraxis*:

> The term paraxis is … a technical one employed in optics. A paraxial region is an area in which light rays *seem* to unite at a point after refraction. In this area, object and image seem to collide, but in fact neither object nor reconstituted image reside there: nothing does. … This paraxial area could be taken to represent the spectral region of the fantastic, whose imaginary world is neither entirely 'real' (object), nor entirely 'unreal' (image), but is located somewhere between the two.
>
> (1988: 19)

As Rank further notes, the double/mirror motif is importantly also connected to ideas of *narcissism*, ideas which will be important for our discussion here (1979: 69–86). Narcissus, on seeing his reflection in a pool, was so entranced by its beauty that he was unable to remove his gaze, and thus withered away and died. From a psychoanalytic perspective, this myth is significant first of all as it emblematizes the splitting or doubling of the self into subject and object and, second, as Rank reminds us, the Narcissus legend associates the sight of the double not only with self-love but with death. From this follows what appears from a socially licensed, 'heteronormative' position to be the *morbid* pattern of narcissism – egotism, self-love, 'abnormal' sexual relations, and homoeroticism – which characterizes so many narratives of the double, from *Jekyll and Hyde* and *Dorian Gray* to *Fight Club*.

In Chapter 1 we discussed the doubled narrative of James Hogg's *Private Memoirs and Confessions of a Justified Sinner*, looking particularly at the relationship between doubleness and complex national identities and affiliations in this and other texts. *Justified Sinner* is indeed a promiscuously doubled text – not only Robert/Gil-Martin, but also, as noted earlier, the two narratives and their authors (Robert and the Editor), and the competing versions of national identity they embody – as well as the split national identity embodied by the Editor and 'James Hogg'. But Robert and Gil-Martin themselves also double, or shadow, Robert's (half-)brother George: 'But the next day, and every succeeding one, the same devilish-looking youth attended him as constantly as his shadow; … the sight of this moody and hellish-looking student affected him in no very pleasant manner'; 'The attendance of that brother,' George feels, 'was now become like the attendance of a demon on some devoted being that had sold himself to destruction; his approaches as undiscerned, and his looks as fraught with hideous malignity' (Hogg 1981: 21–2, 37–8). In his twice-told tale, Hogg *twice* uses the same metaphor, the cast shadow, to describe Robert and George:

there was the self-same being, always in the same position with regard to himself, as regularly as the shadow is cast from the substance ... George then perceived that it was his brother; and, being confounded between the shadow and the substance, he knew not what he was doing or what he had done.

(ibid.: 36, 42)

In like manner, Gil-Martin also doubles *George* – who in his own turn is described by Robert as 'a limb of Satan' – and is himself doubled by M'Gill, Robert's hated school rival (Gil-Martin at first introduces himself to Robert only as 'Gil') (ibid.: 45, 129).

Gil-Martin's name derives from Scottish folklore, as 'Gil-Moules', a Scottish Border name for the devil (Gifford 1976: 165). He has no intrinsic, authentic form within the text – only appearing in the guise of others, he is pure doubleness (as Satan, pure duplicity). Gil-Martin explains these chameleon-like tendencies to Robert, suggesting that he is, in effect, a universal double: 'by looking at a person attentively, I by degrees assume his likeness, and by assuming his likeness I attain to the possession of his most secret thoughts' (Hogg 1981: 124–5). Crucially, Robert first encounters Gil-Martin immediately after his (step-)father, the Rev. Wringhim, has announced that Robert is indeed, after all, one of the elect, one of *'the just made perfect* ... my name written into the Lamb's book of life, and that no bypast transgression, nor any future act of my own, or of other men, could be instrumental in altering the decree'. The Rev. Wringhim says to Robert, 'Set your face against sin, and sinful men, and resist even to blood, as many of the faithful of this land have done, *and your reward shall be double*' (ibid.: 115, my emphasis). Certainly, his immediate reward is *a* double: 'What was my astonishment on perceiving that he was the same being as myself! ... I conceived at first, that I saw a vision, and that my guardian angel had appeared to me at this important era of my life'; 'You think I am your brother,' Gil-Martin says to him, 'or that I am your second self' (ibid.: 116–17). This section of the novel, rich as it is in its implications, even contains suggestions that it is not Gil-Martin who is the double here, but Robert himself. Returning from his meeting with Gil-Martin, Robert's parents barely recognize him: 'you are quite changed; your very voice and manner are changed ... translated ... transformed, since this morning, that I could not have known you for the same person' (ibid.: 120). Be this as it may, it is certain that Gil-Martin tempts Robert largely through appealing to his narcissism, telling him what he wants to hear, that as one of the elect, there is literally nothing he can do to damn himself: 'There was something so flattering in all this, that I could not resist it' (ibid.: 127).

It is necessary here to reiterate a point made in Chapter 1: *Justified Sinner* is an *interpretively* doubled text. That is to say, it is a novel whose dynamic is motivated by the play of two competing interpretations: that the novel is fundamentally supernatural, and therefore that Gil-Martin is the devil; or, that the novel is secular, and that Gil-Martin is a psychological projection, Robert's 'second self', split from his ego as a psychological defence mechanism, to protect Robert from the unacceptable implications of his own psychosis (this, as we shall see later in the chapter, is a classic form of horror 'madness'). Robert suffers from blackouts, and when he comes to, sometimes months later, his life is littered with inexplicable disappearances and corpses: the devil made him do it, he says, or the devil did it himself; he is innocent, and being framed. What's important to remember here, though, is that *both* of these interpretations are simultaneously correct. In a manner analogous to Henry James's *The Turn of the Screw*, this is a text which derives its power from its ambiguity, and it is this which motivates interpretation. While, as readers, we are certainly free to 'choose' or 'prefer' one interpretation over the other (that Robert suffers from paranoid schizophrenia; that the James's 'ghosts' have indeed come over from the other side, a supernatural spirit-world), nevertheless these novels' strictly Freudian *uncanniness* derives precisely from the very plausibility of both interpretations. Thus, and significantly, Gil-Martin is *both* Satan and the second-self embodiment of Robert's madness. (*Pace* all of this, it may be pointed out that there are independent witnesses in the novel, Mrs Logan and Mrs Calvert, who give ample testimony to having seen Gil-Martin with Robert, thus suggesting that Gil-Martin is indeed an autonomous agent – Satan, rather than a figment of Robert's twisted mind. However, it should be noted that this testimony forms a part of the 'Editor's Narrative' within the novel, and that as I argued earlier, the Editor is hardly an impartial reporter, but instead predisposed to interpret pre-Enlightenment Scotland as backward, tradition-haunted. The Editor, in other words, specifically comes to these events in search of superstition and belief in the supernatural, and that, unsurprisingly, is what he finds.)

Karl Miller in his influential study *Doubles* suggests that Hogg's interest in the subject of diabolic temptation may have been prompted by the republishing of *The Confession of Nichol Muschett of Boghall* in 1818. 'Muschett', Miller writes, 'was executed for murdering his wife in 1721. The crime was committed in the valley below the hill of Arthur's Seat in Edinburgh, on the summit of which is located a crucial violence in Hogg's novel'. Muschett claims in his *Confession* to have been persuaded to murder by a Satanic figure, James Campbell of Burnbank, who

> was the only viceregent of the devil to prompt me to be guilty
> of the following wickedness; which I greedily went on in, being
> so far inebriate with these wicked principles, which by degrees
> (after he understood how my natural temper was to be
> prevailed upon) he instilled into me.
>
> (Miller 1985: 3)

Even more significant for Hogg, it has been suggested, was the publication in 1824 of an abridged, anonymous translation of E.T.A. Hoffmann's 'The

Devil's Elixir' in *Blackwood's Edinburgh Magazine*. The translation was actually by R.P. Gillies, a literary acquaintance of Hogg's in Edinburgh between 1813 and 1827 (Hogg 1981: xxi—xxii). Hoffmann's tale of demonic doubling and antinomian dogma does indeed resemble Hogg's novel in many of its details: it is the tale of one of the elect, Medardus, haunted by a sinister figure whom he believes to be the Devil, who commits a number of crimes, including murder, for which Medardus is blamed.[4]

No discussion of the double in horror would be complete without an account of 'William Wilson'. Poe's tale of a man haunted from schoolboy to *roué* by his double, namesake, and conscience might serve as a distillation of the recurring themes and concerns of *Döppelganger* narratives. The narrator's very name, William Wilson, is a double, although we are told – in a manner typical of Poe's narrators, who tend to be slippery, unreliable, or barking mad – that 'William Wilson' is an alias, 'a fictitious title not very dissimilar to the real', and signifying only, then, itself, the name of a mirror, or double:

> when, upon the day of my arrival, a second William Wilson came also into the academy, I felt angry with him for bearing the name, and *doubly disgusted* with the name because a stranger bore it, *who would be the cause of its twofold repetition*
>
> (Poe 1977b: 7, 9, my emphasis)

Both Wilsons are 'singularly alike' – doubles who are single, who together make one person, the same person (this word 'singular' recurs throughout the story) – and their relationship is articulated using the classic images of our subject: 'if we *had* been brothers we must have been twins'; 'an imitation of myself ... it was identical; *and his singular whisper, it grew the very echo of my own*'; 'this most exquisite portraiture'; 'my arch-enemy and evil genius' (ibid.: 8, 9, 10, 19). Like Gil-Martin, Wilson the double may have no intrinsic form. Gazing at his sleeping enemy, Wilson the narrator sees only pure terror or monstrosity, the face, perhaps, of his own moral degeneration, which the second half of the story charts:

> Were these – *these* the lineaments of William Wilson? I saw, indeed, that they were his, but I shook as if with a fit of ague in fancying they were not. What *was* there about them to confound me in this manner? I gazed, – while my brain reeled with a multitude of incoherent thoughts. Not thus he appeared – assuredly not *thus* – in the vivacity of his waking hours. The same name! the same contour of person! the same day of arrival in the academy! And then his dogged and meaningless imitation of my gait, my voice, my habits, and my manner! Was it, in truth, within the bounds of human possibility, that

what I now saw was the result, merely, of the habitual practice
of this sarcastic imitation? Awestricken, and with a creeping
shudder, I extinguished the lamp, passed silently from the
chamber, and left, at once, the halls of that old academy, never
to enter them again.

(ibid.: 12)

It is worth dwelling on the implications of this passage. What is going on
here? Is Wilson gazing in horror at his own image, seeing for the first time
the horrifying reality of his own Self? ('Were these – *these* – the lineaments
of William Wilson?') In which case, 'William Wilson' is an 'orthodox'
psychological fable of the split self. Can it be that the face upon which
Wilson gazes here is not really his double at all? ('Was it, in truth, within the
bounds of human possibility, that *what I now saw* was the result, merely, of
the habitual practice of this sarcastic imitation?') In which case, the narrator
is straightforwardly paranoid, delusional, and psychotic. Or can it be that
the face upon which Wilson gazes has no features at all, or indefinable,
unstable features? In which case, the locus of this story might well be
supernatural. Typically, the answer, it seems to me, is all of these things
(and perhaps more) simultaneously. The story thus ends in ambiguity, with
Wilson murdering what appears to be his mirror-image, but is seemingly
rather his conscience or soul.

There is further, it is strongly implied, a sexual relationship between the
two Wilsons: 'To the moralist it will be unnecessary to say, in addition, that
Wilson and I were the most inseparable of companions. . . . I was galled, too,
by the rumour touching a relationship, which had grown current in the
upper forms' (ibid.: 8–9). This narcissistic or masturbatory sexuality
develops, while the narrator is at Eton, into his membership of a decadent,
gay fraternity:

I invited a small party of the most dissolute students to a secret
carousal in my chambers. We met at a late hour of the night;
for our debaucheries were to be faithfully protracted until
morning. The wine flowed freely, and we were not wanting
other and perhaps more dangerous seductions.

(This passage, of course, taps into a long history of fact and rumour about
same-sex relationships in England's public schools.) The double interrupts
this night of 'more than wonted profanity', and whispers the name 'William
Wilson!' in the narrator's ear: 'I grew perfectly sober in an instant'
(ibid.: 13).

It is this theme of the double intruding himself into an enclosed all-male
order which animates Stevenson's *Dr Jekyll and Mr Hyde*. The novella's
entire action takes place within a community of single, middle-aged, largely

professional men: Jekyll himself, his former colleague Dr Lanyon, the lawyer Utterson, and his friend Enfield, 'the well-known man about town' (Stevenson 1994: 10). It is a community characterized by repression: Utterson 'was austere with himself; drank gin when he was alone, to mortify a taste for vintages; and though he enjoyed the theatre, had not crossed the door of one for twenty years'. Enfield and Utterson are given to taking long walks together through seedy parts of town: 'the two men put the greatest store by these excursions, counted them the chief jewel of each week, and not only set aside occasions of pleasure, but even resisted the calls of business, that they might enjoy them uninterrupted' (ibid.: 9, 10). Sir Danvers Carew, the 'aged and beautiful gentleman' murdered by Hyde, is himself given to solitary walks late at night through sleazy neighbourhoods: he is beaten to death in a 'dismal quarter of Soho', which 'with its muddy ways and slatternly passages ... seemed, in the lawyer's eyes, like a district of some city in a nightmare' (ibid.: 31–2).

'When they had come within speech ... the older man bowed and accosted the other with a very pretty manner of politeness' (Stevenson 1994: 29): the insinuation here, that Sir Danvers is beaten to death by Hyde after soliciting him for sex, is borne out by the other men's suspicions about *Jekyll's* relationship with Hyde. Utterson, a professional keeper of other men's secrets, 'the last reputable acquaintance, and the last good influence in the lives of down-going men' (that is, men who go down on each other?), immediately assumes that the relationship between Jekyll and Hyde, a financial relationship with Hyde drawing cheques on Jekyll's bank account, is based on blackmail: 'Blackmail, I suppose; an honest man paying through the nose for some of the capers of his youth. Blackmail House is what I call the place with the door, in consequence' (I shall examine the symbolic significance of this door shortly):

> 'Poor Harry Jekyll,' he thought, 'my mind misgives me he is in deep waters! He was wild when he was young; a long while ago, to be sure; but in the law of God there is no statute of limitations. Ah, it must be that; the ghost of some old sin, the cancer of some concealed disgrace; punishment coming, *pede claudo*, years after memory has forgotten and self-love condoned the fault.'
>
> (ibid.: 9, 13)

For Enfield, this is a familiar story, indicative of secret lives and double standards: 'I make it a rule of mine: the more it looks like Queer Street, the less I ask' (ibid.: 14). Hyde's very name, of course, suggests that Jekyll has something to hide, or that he is what Jekyll denies, keeps repressed – a suggestion confirmed within the text by Utterson's remark that 'If he be Mr Hyde, ... I shall be Mr Seek' (ibid.: 21).[5]

The fact that, for Enfield, the site of Hyde's discovery 'looks like Queer

Street' – that is, a site simultaneously of uncanniness and of homosexuality
– is one of a number of cues within the text that are indicative of the way
that its community of bachelors perceives Jekyll and Hyde's relationship.
That is, they take Hyde for 'rough trade' from the East End, a Rent Boy
whom Jekyll keeps financially. Jekyll's powerfully symbolic house has two
entrances: the front door, which Jekyll uses, opens out onto a respectable
West End square, while somehow the back door, which is Hyde's, leads to
a seedy East End street. The fact of Hyde's entry into Jekyll's property
through the back door is reiterated several times throughout the text, as a
clear euphemism for buggery, culminating in the less ambiguous 'through
the back passage' (ibid.: 77). Certainly, Hyde is a much younger man than
Jekyll, and, as James B. Twitchell suggests, Hyde therefore represents
Jekyll's wayward youth, that which he has long repressed, and which he
now has the means to recapture (Twitchell 1985). In his youth, Jekyll
writes, 'my pleasures were (to say the least) undignified'; he now feels that
'To cast my lot in with Jekyll was to die to those appetites which I had long
secretly indulged and had of late begun to pamper' (Stevenson 1994: 74,
79). Symbolically, Hyde is also, however, the *product* of Jekyll's wayward
youth – that is to say, his illegitimate son. Hyde is made Jekyll's major
beneficiary, due to inherit his considerable fortune of a quarter of a million
pounds (a vast sum in the 1880s).

What *Jekyll and Hyde* does, of course, is to provide both an examination
of and an indelible metaphor for the notorious Victorian double standard,
respectability and hypocrisy, and for the repression that this entails: Jekyll
'stood already committed to a profound duplicity of life'; he writes of his
desire to contain his transformations into Hyde, which become
progressively more involuntary, that 'My devil had been long caged, he
came out roaring' (ibid.: 69, 80). This develops into full-blown Freudianism
in many of the film versions of Stevenson's text, and is in turn coupled with
a habitual conflation of *Jekyll and Hyde* with the Jack the Ripper murders
of 1888, in which five women were brutally murdered and disembowelled
in the East End of London. At the same time, in the West End, the actor
Richard Mansfield was starring in a celebrated stage adaptation of *Jekyll
and Hyde*, which showcased startling transformation scenes courtesy of
photo-sensitive make-up. In yet another precursor of the 'video nasty'
debates, the Ripper murders were blamed in some quarters on the Mansfield
production, and the actor found himself, briefly, the prime suspect in the
case (Frayling 1996: 153–60). What this identification with the Ripper did
was to make Hyde in the public imagination what he emphatically was not
in Stevenson's original – a heterosexual sex-killer. In Rouben Mamoulian's
great film version, Jekyll's (Fredric March) motivation seems purely borne
of sexual frustration, partly because of the domineering presence of his
fiancée's father, Sir Danvers Carew, thus providing a heterosexual rationale
for his murder by Hyde. March's apelike Hyde is pure id, and it's great to
be him, as he has a fantastic time, all the time – 'Free at last!' he exclaims,

with genuine glee, before heading off for the nearest prostitute. The Ripper is an explicit part of Hammer's gloriously perverse (but thematically quite faithful) *Dr Jekyll and Sister Hyde* – he *is*, in fact, Dr Jekyll himself (Ralph Bates), who happens upon the elixir of life in a hormone found only in a woman's pancreas (hence the need for disembowelment). The obvious side-effect here is that Jekyll transforms into *Mrs* Hyde (Martine Beswick), giving the film ample opportunity to explore a number of issues present in Stevenson's original, as Mrs Hyde allows the effete Jekyll to realize his desire for men, while she herself leers desiringly at Jekyll's young female neighbour. As Jekyll's mentor Professor Robertson (Gerald Sim) proclaims, 'It's a very queer business, Sergeant. Very queer.'

Closely allied to the double is the twin. It is believed that as many as 25 per cent of pregnancies begin with twins. In the majority of cases, the weaker twin is absorbed into the stronger: '71 per cent of twin gestations diagnosed before ten weeks were singletons when delivered', according to one medical report (Schwartz 1996: 20). That is to say, many of us begin life by *eating our own twin!* Ideas such as this have obviously proven very fruitful in the horror genre, where evil or murderous twins have found their true home. The acclaimed *Sisters* has Margot Kidder as murder-suspect Danielle Breton and her evil identical twin, Dominique Blanchion – conjoined twins separated at birth, as are the Bradley brothers, Duane and Belial, in the wonderfully grotty *Basket Case*. The titular basket is where Duane keeps Belial, little more than a deformed growth removed from his side, who occasionally escapes to wreak mayhem and murder. In Stephen King's *The Dark Half* (1989), young Thad Beaumont suffers from crippling migraines, diagnosed as the product of a brain tumour. Thad undergoes brain-surgery, and the doctors remove from his brain not a tumour, but the living remains of his absorbed twin: 'a single blind and malformed human eye ... part of a nostril, three fingernails, and two teeth' (King 1989: 9). Thad's twin later rises from the grave as 'George Stark', his pseudonymous alter-ego.

Considerably more sophisticated than *Basket Case*, though commensurately less fun, is David Cronenberg's tale of indistinguishable twin gynaecologists Elliot and Beverly Mantle (both played by Jeremy Irons), *Dead Ringers*: 'The truth is,' says Elliot, 'nobody can tell us apart. We are perceived as one person.' At the beginning of the film, Elliot, the dominant, 'evil' twin, returns from a prizegiving, saying to his brother, 'Bev, you should have been there.' 'I was,' Beverly answers. Tension develops between the brothers when Beverly begins a relationship with Claire Niveau (Genevieve Bujold), but refuses to tell Elliot about it. 'I want to keep it – for myself': 'Listen,' Elliot tells him, 'you haven't had any experience until I've had it too. You haven't fucked Claire Niveau until you tell *me* about it.' (Later, Elliot has sex with twin prostitutes, Mimsy and Coral, and asks one to call him 'Elly' and the other 'Bev'.) Beverly becomes addicted to prescription drugs, as in turn does Elliot: 'Whatever is in his bloodstream goes directly into mine.' Beverly has a nightmare in which he and Elliot *are* conjoined twins, physically joined by connective tissue, which Claire (bloodily) bites in half: coming to believe that they actually are in need of separation, Beverly operates on Elliot with the sadomasochistic gynaecological instruments he has designed, and kills him.

As noted at the beginning of this chapter, the hilarious *Raising Cain* features an outrageously flamboyant, Jacobean performance from John Lithgow (one of the few modern actors genuinely unafraid of ridiculousness), alternately gurning, sneering, and cackling as Carter Nix, an eminent child-psychologist, and his evil (and imaginary) twin, Cain: 'When did *you* get out?' are Carter's first words to his brother. (It's worth dwelling on the significance of the name Carter Nix here for a moment: first, it is self-negating, with 'nix' meaning 'nothing' – this man of many selves is thus nobody; but also, and interestingly, this demented schizo is named at least in part after two recent American presidents!) Carter/Cain was traumatized in childhood because of experiments performed on him by his father, a deranged Norwegian child-psychologist (Lithgow again!) who deliberately split his son's personalities and wrote up his research in a pioneering book, also called *Raising Cain*. Amongst Carter's multiple personalities is 'Margo', a sinisterly protective mother-figure, and the film has one undeniably great moment where, in this female persona, mincing and preening, Nix headbutts his father's collaborator Dr Waldheim unconscious, and then steals her wig (she's undergoing chemotherapy) and makes good his/her escape from the police station, off to kill Dr Nix Senior with a scalpel. The film's closing shot is of Nix as Margo, still wearing Dr Waldheim's wig, appearing behind Jenny (Nix's wife) with an evil smile on her face.

Cain/Margo, like *Dr Jekyll and Sister Hyde*, returns us to the anxieties of masculinity and sexuality explored in Stevenson and Wilde. Our true contemporary *Jekyll and Hyde*, *Fight Club* revisits, a century on, Stevenson's theme of alienated metropolitan masculinity. Specifically, this is a masculinity alienated by modern consumer capitalism, and the film counterpoints the colourless sterility of corporate identity (the grey business suit) with the vigorous, violent, colourful display of male bodies in the Fight Club, which itself develops into an underground anarchist organization attempting to dismantle modern capitalism. The narrator (Edward Norton), a corporate drone who fetishistically collects Ikea home furnishings, finds himself on a business-trip seated next to Tyler Durden (Brad Pitt), who manufactures and sells soap made from human fat, the discarded by-product of liposuction operations, and itself a powerful encapsulating symbol of contemporary luxury, waste, and decadence. The outrageously charismatic, and even (for this is a millennial text) messianic Tyler/Pitt is, of course, a projection of Tyler/Norton's repressions, the embodied discontents of this civilized modern man, his id. As Tyler/Pitt explains, he looks and dresses as Tyler/Norton would like to, acts as he wishes he could, and is, we are told, a 'spectacular' sexual athlete: more succinctly, Marla (Helena Bonham Carter) refers to the Tylers as 'Dr Jekyll and Mr Jackass'.

The relationship between the Tylers is powerfully homoerotic – that is to say, masturbatory, self-desiring – and Pitt, with his absurd glistening torso, makes a glorious Narcissus. This sexual organization places *Fight Club* in that tradition of classic American fiction famously identified by Leslie Fiedler, narratives which posit a 'flight from womanhood', an escape into all-boy fantasies and networks (Huck and Jim adrift on their raft in *Huckleberry Finn*; the all-male crew of the Pequod in *Moby Dick*) (Fiedler 1952). The economy of the Fight Club itself is, to use Eve Kosofsky Sedgwick's term, rigorously *homosocial*, comprised of relations of eroticism and power between men, which exclude women even (and especially) while asserting an aggressive heterosexuality (Sedgwick 1985). The film is thus full of images and episodes symbolic of sexual anxiety and gender ambiguity. Tyler/Norton takes to haunting recovery programmes and twelve-step groups, and in one such programme, a testicular-cancer support group, he meets (and is continually, crushingly embraced by) Bob (Meat Loaf), a former champion bodybuilder who has grown 'bitch tits' because of oestrogen levels in his body and who, like the rest of the men in the group (including, symbolically, Tyler/Norton), has no balls. The film visits and revisits images of castration and its threat: in the men's toilets, Tyler/Pitt attacks the police chief and threatens to cut off his testicles with a knife, a scene which is doubled and reversed when the cop Fight-Clubbers try to do the same thing to Tyler/Norton. Both Tylers have vagina-shaped acid-burns on their hands, scars which are subsequently displayed by other Fight-Clubbers, an emblem of their newly empowered masculinity, devious and ambiguous.

'He knows you're alone': psychos and slashers

In the 1985 film *Fright Night*, young Charley Brewster (William Ragsdale), who has a vampire for a next-door neighbour, asks the television vampire-hunter Peter Vincent (Roddy McDowell) – the faded 1980s' equivalent of such horror icons as Vampira or Zacherley – whether he is 'serious' about his belief in vampires. 'Oh, absolutely,' Vincent replies:

> Unfortunately none of *your* generation seems to be. ... *I* have just been fired because nobody wants to see vampire killers any more, or vampires either. Apparently all *they* want are demented madmen running around in ski masks hacking up young virgins.

This is of course an accurate account of the dominant mode of the horror movie in the early and mid-1980s, the slasher-movie, flourishing from approximately 1978–84, and then again, to a much lesser extent, and partly as nostalgia, in the late 1990s (as the teenage consumers of the first wave of slashers became themselves cultural producers, bent on revisiting, as it were, their own adolescence). Though the genre has clear antecedents – in Alfred Hitchcock's *Psycho* and *Frenzy*, for example, and in *Peeping Tom*, *Black Christmas*, *The Texas Chain Saw Massacre*, and the Italian Grand Guignol *giallo* thrillers of Mario Bava and Dario Argento – the history of the modern slasher really dates from the release of John Carpenter's *Halloween* in late 1978.

Made for a reported $320,000 and grossing over $75,000,000 worldwide at the box-office, *Halloween* was at the time the most successful independent movie ever made, and had its success redoubled in the then-new medium of home video (the slasher and the video arrived together – it is tempting, and not altogether untrue, to say that the success of each was dependent upon the other).[6] In its wake followed the similarly successful *Friday the 13th*, and from there innumerable others, frequently deploying calendrical or celebratory motifs in their titles.

Bound up with their cheapness (young, inexperienced actors; very few requirements by way of locations, or even necessarily effects – *Halloween* itself, for example, has *no gore at all!*) and amenability to video, the success of the slashers also lay in their very formulaic nature. In essence, all slashers utilize the same, simple narrative paradigms:

1. A past misdeed creates a psychopathic killer.
2. In the present, on a specific date, the killer returns to the site of the misdeed.
3. He stalks and kills with a knife (or some kind of blade) a group of teenagers of both sexes.
4. One girl survives to thwart the killer, at least temporarily.[7]

This, precisely, is the narrative grammar of *Halloween*, and it is a narrative revisited, usually with great fidelity, by most slashers. What this means in practice is that these movies presuppose a high degree of genre-competence in their audiences, and therefore that audiences for these movies *already* know *exactly* what to expect (it is this sense of genre-awareness which drives Wes Craven's *Scream*-cycle, whose success lies largely in recognition, in articulating for its audience things it already knew), thus offering a participatory, ritualistic, or even sacramental experience. Consequently, the slasher genre is characterized by a deliberate lack of originality and a high degree of repetition, with only slight deviations within a rigid formal template. What this means, as Twitchell has noted, is that the dominant auteur-theory of film criticism, positing the director as creative centre, is quite beside the point in accounting for the slasher genre (Twitchell 1985: 84).[8] This also accounts for the genre's high degree of self-referentiality, not only in the *Screams* but from the very beginning. *Halloween* famously stars

Jamie Lee Curtis, daughter of Janet Leigh, who played Marion Crane in *Psycho* – Curtis went on to become the most celebrated of all 1980s' 'scream queens', starring in *The Fog, Prom Night, Terror Train*, and *Halloween II* (all 1980–1). *Halloween H20* (1997) reintroduces Curtis as Laurie Strode, now dependent on prescription drugs and alcohol to control her nightmares and psychological problems, formerly married to 'an abusive chain-smoking methodone addict', calling herself Keri Tate, and working as the principal of an exclusive private school; her Personal Assistant, Norma Crane, is played by Janet Leigh (the two had also starred together in Carpenter's *The Fog*). In *Halloween*, Donald Pleasance played the haunted psychiatrist Dr Sam Loomis – Sam Loomis was the name of Marion Crane's boyfriend in *Psycho* (the Loomises, in fact, are a venerable slasher dynasty, now in their third generation with *Scream*'s Billy Loomis; furthermore, *Halloween*'s Annie, Michael's first victim on returning to Haddonfield, is played by Nancy Loomis!)

In his comment about 'demented madmen running around in ski-masks', Peter Vincent is no doubt alluding to Jason Voorhees, resident slasher of the *Friday the 13th* series, who wears an ice-hockey mask rather than a ski mask – though *Halloween*'s Michael Myers is also masked, as is *The Texas Chain Saw Massacre*'s Leatherface – slashers love their masks. In the 1990s, the *Scream*-cycle revisited the trope by having its killer(s) don a mask based on Edvard Munch's *The Scream*, while Mary Harron's *American Psycho*, based on Bret Easton Ellis's notorious satire of 1980s' consumerist mores, has Patrick Bateman (Christian Bale), obsessed with surfaces, with his own aesthetic appearance, removing a clear, gelatinous skin-cleansing mask from his face while discussing his non-existence: 'I'm simply not there.' This is the mask which resembles, but is not, the killer's own face, like Leatherface's mask of human skin, or Michael Myers's mask of a white, featureless human face; Hannibal Lecter, too, escapes from custody in *The Silence of the Lambs* by disguising himself as one of his captors, and literally wearing his face – and by the sequel, *Hannibal*, Lecter's metonymic muzzle-mask has become a prized item in its own right, sold to his nemesis Mason Verger as both fetish and icon. Under the slasher's mask there may be no face at all, for the killer may have no identity other than as an embodiment of unmotivated destructiveness. This is certainly the premise behind Ellis's *American Psycho*, where Bateman is perpetually being mistaken for any number of his Wall Street colleagues, all of whom are indistinguishable from each other – the same horn-rimmed Oliver Peoples glasses, the same slicked-back hair.

Linked to these issues and problems of identity are problems of *identification*, problems which have been discussed by a number of commentators, most notably Carol J. Clover in her *Men, Women and Chain Saws* (Clover 1992; see also Creed 1993; Dika 1987). Following the work of Laura Mulvey on the gendered (male) cinematic gaze (Mulvey 1975), Clover and others have commented on, for example, the slashers' heavy use of subjective camerawork, which theoretically at least invites viewer-identification with the killer himself. This is quite startlingly exemplified in the opening scene of *Halloween*, a celebrated tracking-shot from the perspective of young Michael Myers, who takes a carving-knife from the kitchen and climbs the stairs to his sister's bedroom, pausing to pick up and put on a clown's mask. From this moment until the end of the shot, screen-space is reduced to two eye-shapes (representing the mask's eyeholes), suggesting that we are quite literally viewing events – the murder of his naked sister, who has just had sex with her boyfriend – through Michael's own eyes. 'Horror,' Clover suggests, 'privileges eyes because, more crucially than any other kind of cinema, it is about eyes. More particularly, it is about eyes watching horror' (1992: 167). This kind of identificatory voyeurism, it is often noted, has generic sources in *Psycho*, where Norman watches Marion showering through a hole in the wall immediately prior to killing her, and in *Peeping Tom*, where Mark (Karl Boehm) has a camera-tripod-spear on which he impales his victims while filming their deaths. Both of these, in turn, have a common source in Hitchcock's *Rear Window*, which plays out the connections between film-making, voyeurism and murder.

This straightforward identification of an implied audience, which is male, and which in turn is expected or encouraged to identify with the slasher, who is predominantly male and who predominantly kills women, has led to understandable accusations that the genre is inherently a misogynistic one, and as such a reactionary response to the feminist movement emergent in the 1960s and 1970s. Robin Wood, one of the most influential of all theorists of the horror movie, considers the slashers a 'sinister and disturbing' genre where 'the monster, while still "produced by" repression, has become essentially a superego figure, avenging itself on liberated female sexuality of the sexual freedom of the young' (Wood 1987: 80). Stephen King explicitly considers his own *Carrie* to be 'an uneasy masculine shrinking from a future of female equality', noting that 'writing the book in 1973 and only out of college three years, I was fully aware of what Women's Liberation meant for me and others of my sex' (King 1982: 198).

This misogyny is in turn exacerbated by an ostensible sexual morality frequently described as conventional, orthodox, or conservative, but which in fact gives convention, orthodoxy and even conservatism an unwarranted bad name: this is the celebrated association of sex with death, and most particularly the suspicion that the slasher himself metes out a bloody punishment for sexual transgression, pre-marital sex, or the loss of (female) virginity. Both *Candyman* and *I Know What You Did Last Summer* take as their impetus the celebrated urban legend of 'The Hook', in which a courting couple, hearing on the car-radio the story of an escaped lunatic with a hook for a hand, are spooked by noises outside, drive off, and on returning home discover a bloody hook hanging from the car door-handle – a tale which *I Know What You Did Last Summer*'s 'intellectual' heroine Julie (Jennifer Love Hewitt) understands as 'a fictional story created to warn young girls of the dangers of having sex'. Smarter and much more interesting is *Candyman*, a quasi-slasher about a ghostly black avenger in the Chicago housing projects (and thus one of the few slashers with genuine social concerns, or perhaps even radical political commitments), summoned through the mirror. Quite explicitly, the film deals not only with issues of black disenfranchisement but with fears of miscegenation (in turn confronting one of *Hollywood's* most powerfully residual taboos, the romantic attachment of black men and white women). The Candyman himself was a nineteenth-century portrait-painter, 'punished' for his affair with a white woman by having his hand cut off (once again, the hand is the organ of forbidden knowledge), getting smeared in honey and stung to death by bees. Returning from the grave, the Candyman sports a deadly hook in place of a hand, which itself stands as a displacement or metonym for the forbidden black penis.

It is also certainly the case that in *Halloween*, for example, Michael's victims are his sister, brushing her hair after sex with her boyfriend; Annie, dressed in her underwear and off to pick up her boyfriend Paul; and Lynda and Bob, who have also just had sex; while the presumably virginal Laurie, who cannot get a date, survives. In this, as in virtually all other aspects of the genre, *Halloween* provides a template for all subsequent examples (the far cruder *Friday the 13th*, for instance, is more overt and explicit still in its condemnation to butchery of sexually active teenagers). Interviewed on this subject, Carpenter himself was jokingly regretful: 'I didn't mean to put an end to the sexual revolution – and for that I deeply apologize!'[9]

However, and as ever, this straightforward association of the slasher-movie and misogyny turns out to be highly problematic, and that for a number of reasons. First, as Clover has suggested, it may be that the implied audience, although male, is encouraged by the genre to identify not with the slasher himself, but with the victim, or more precisely with the surviving 'Final Girl' – or, in a more complex fashion, that the process of identification is shifting and unstable, moving from killer to victim and often encompassing both. At any rate, this implies a willingness on the part of the 'male' audience to adopt a 'female' point of view: as a paradigm of this process, Clover opens her study by citing King's remark on the appeal of *Carrie*: 'Carrie's revenge is something that any student who has ever had his gym-shorts pulled down in Phys Ed or his glasses thumb-rubbed in study hall could approve of' (King 1982: 201). Clover comments on this:

> the 'any student' in question here looks a lot like an adolescent boy. Pulling gym-shorts down and thumb-rubbing glasses are things boys do to each other, not, by and large, things that girls do to each other or that boys do to girls. They are oblique sexual gestures, the one threatening sodomy or damage to the genitals or both, the other threatening damage to the eyes – a castration of sorts. ... The boy so threatened and humiliated,

King seems to be saying, is a boy who recognizes himself in a girl who finds herself bleeding from her crotch in the gym shower, pelted with tampons, and sloshed with pig's blood at the senior prom.

(1992: 4–5)

That is to say, the identification here involves a willing feminization, or even perhaps a willing castration of the male viewer. This process is further problematized since according to at least one source, Vera Dika, the *actual*, as opposed to implied, cinematic audiences for the slasher movie may be predominantly, though not overwhelmingly, female.[10]

The slashers themselves are often characterized by a good deal of gender-ambiguity or slipperiness. Though predominantly male, they are not exclusively so, and certainly not exclusively masculine. In *Psycho*, for example, Norman Bates murders while dressed as his mother, while *Dressed to Kill* has as its killer the transvestite psychiatrist Dr Elliott (played, would you believe, by Michael Caine in drag). *Chain Saw*'s Leatherface fusses around the family dinner-table wearing a curly woman's wig and a little apron, and with make-up on his mask – obviously, his role in this, cinema's most dysfunctional family, is as mother, and like *Psycho*, the family keeps its actual skeletal matriarch at home in a rocking-chair. Furthermore, the male authority-figures in that family are emasculated (partly for the economic reasons discussed in Chapter 1): the Grandfather is too weak to lift the hammer and kill Sally, while the Old Man is taunted by his son, Hitchhiker, with insinuations of impotence for his unwillingness to kill ('I don't take no pleasure in it,' he says). *Friday the 13th* reverses the pattern established in *Psycho* – the killer is assumed to be Jason Voorhees (who does, in fact, rise from the grave to kill again in all subsequent sequels) but is, in fact, his mother, Mrs Voorhees; similarly, *Scream 2*'s ultimate killer turns out to be Mrs Loomis, the vengeful mother of Billy, one of the first instalment's two slashers.

In turn, it is incorrect simply to assume that the slasher kills women. Slashers kill both sexes in more-or-less equal numbers, and the survivor, who thwarts the slasher, is almost invariably female. This 'Final Girl', as Clover has noted, is herself characterized by a sexual- or gender-ambiguity (Clover 1992: 35–41). She tends, first, to be virginal, like Laurie Strode, or at least not to have sex during the course of the film. Though terrified, she has sufficient physical resources repeatedly to beat off the slasher's attacks, if not actually to kill 'him'. This 'boyishness' which Clover identifies tends to be reflected in the 'Final Girl's' name, which is non-gender-specific: Stevie, Marti, Terry, Laurie, Stretch, Will, Joey, Max (Clover 1992: 40) – a tradition continued by *Scream*'s Sidney.

What is more, the very act of slashing itself may be feminizing. As Barbara Creed has suggested, it has at least some of its origins in (male) fears of castration – and specifically in fears of the castrating woman:

Male castration anxiety has given rise to two of the most powerful representations of the monstrous-feminine in the horror film: women as castrator and woman as castrated. Woman is represented as castrated either literally or symbolically. Her literal castration is represented in films in which she is usually a victim, such as the slasher film, where her body is repeatedly knifed until it becomes a bleeding wound. In other horror films woman is transformed into a psychotic monster because she has been symbolically castrated, that is, she feels she has been robbed unjustly of her rightful destiny. ... This version of the female psychopath represents a more conventional view of female monstrosity in that woman transforms into a monster when she is sexually and emotionally unfulfilled. She seeks revenge on society, particularly the heterosexual nuclear family, because of her lack, her symbolic castration.

(1993: 122)

Creed's interpretation here is a directly Freudian one, echoing Freud's own assertion that 'women are castrated, that instead of a male organ they have a wound which serves for sexual intercourse, and that castration is the necessary condition of femininity' (Freud 1979: 315). The implication of this reading, it seems to me, is that *both* the slasher and his victims are feminized here, the slasher by acting out the role of (female) castrator, the victim by the act of castration, by having his or her body reduced to a 'bleeding wound' – symbolically, by being given a vagina.

There are, of course, a small number of actual castrating female killers, though these tend to be confined to an even more disreputable sub-genre of the slasher, the rape-revenge movie. Thus, in Craven's *The Last House on the Left*, Mrs Collingwood avenges herself on Fred 'Weasel' Podowski – convicted child-molester and one of the gang of crazies responsible for the rape and murder of her daughter – by biting off his penis during fellatio. (Fred's gang is led by the psychopathic Krug Stillo: Fred the child-molester and Krug the psycho were later to be fused and raised from the dead in the person of Craven's ghostly psychopathic child-molester Fred Krueger.) Even more notorious, if that's possible, is *I Spit on Your Grave*, whose most frequently discussed scene has the brutally raped novelist Jennifer (Camille Keaton – Buster's grandniece) having her revenge on the leader of her attackers by cutting off his testicles in the bath.

Intimately linked to these castration anxieties are fears of the 'vagina dentata', the castrating vagina often symbolically represented as the bloody mouth full of deadly teeth. Perhaps the most striking of such images comes not in a slasher-movie (nor even, as might be expected, in the vampire-movie, though Amanda Bearse's terrifying female vampire in *Fright Night*, her mouth almost as large as her whole face, surely comes close),[11] but in Carpenter's astounding body-horror, *The Thing*, where at one point, a victim's whole torso opens up into a horrifying mouth/vagina, full of huge fangs, which then bites off the hands of the doctor who is trying to save him (which again returns us to the handless motif of mad science, which, as Chapter 2 noted, is itself a metonym for lack, or displaced castration). Within our specific genre, Francis Dolarhyde, the psychopathic 'Tooth Fairy' of Thomas Harris's *Red Dragon*, is traumatized by a childhood of abuse because of his deformed mouth. Born with a cleft palate, the orphaned Dolarhyde is tormented with the nickname 'Cunt Face', which he believes to be his real name (Harris 1991: 158). When the infant Dolarhyde, under the care of his grandmother, wets the bed because he is afraid of the dark, she puts his penis between the blades of a pair of scissors and threatens to castrate him; as an adult, he keeps his dead grandmother's false teeth, and has himself made a set of carnivorous dentures based on these, transforming his own mouth into a murderous, fanged vagina, and becoming in the process an embodiment of the gender-dislocation so typical of the slasher.

Wes Craven works from an intricate knowledge of his genre, as the *Scream* series was to demonstrate. *Scream 3* acknowledges, to no-one's surprise, that, for all his apparently secular origins in the crazed human psyche, the slasher was always, ever since *Halloween*, a fundamentally *supernatural* threat. First, he is essentially indestructible, able to shrug off massive amounts of damage – beatings, stabbings, shootings. Indeed, as the subsequent careers of both Michael Myers and Jason Voorhees were to prove, the slasher could be *absolutely* indestructible: rather in the manner of Sir Francis Varney, his survival was governed economically – depending on the success of the franchise, he could *always* be counted on to return. Second, and more profoundly, in his very use of cinematic space, the slasher habitually contravenes normal human conventions. He can appear from anywhere, out of the shadows, at any time, seemingly capable of becoming invisible and moving with absolute silence. Furthermore, any space *inhabited* by the slasher immediately contravenes the laws of physics, becomes a kind of haunted house. Thus, enclosed and relatively confined spaces such as the basements of suburban houses, become utterly impervious to sound: screams or cries for help are inaudible to the victim's friends, rarely more than 20 feet away; the houses themselves become seemingly endless labyrinths, full of darkened spaces out of which the slasher may, and will, strike. He is, in other words, and always was, what Laurie Strode and Dr Loomis acknowledge him to be in *Halloween*: the 'boogeyman', the unstoppable pursuer from all our nightmares.

Craven's most successful film of the 1980s thus offers the slasher as supernatural dream-demon in the unforgettable form of Freddy Krueger (or, more properly, Fred Krueger – it was only as the series progressed that the cuddly diminutive was habitually adopted, as Freddy, dripping mordant one-liners, became a bizarre anti-hero for the late 1980s: a horrid icon for a horrid time).[12] In spite of Fred Krueger's supernaturalism, *A Nightmare on Elm Street* follows the narrative pattern of the classic slasher-movie very closely, from the past misdeed (Krueger, a serial child-murderer who escapes justice on a technicality, is burned to death by an angry lynch-mob of Elm Street parents) to the rigorous sexual economy and use of sexual imagery. Tina (Amanda Wyss), the sexually active girl from a broken home, is Fred's first victim. When chaste final girl Nancy (Heather Langenkamp) falls asleep in the bath, Fred's taloned hand appears between her legs; later, Fred rises from under the bedsheets like a gigantic phallus, while her boyfriend Glen (a very juvenile Johnny Depp) is sucked into his own bed down a very vaginal hole, which then spews out an enormous geyser of blood.

A Nightmare on Elm Street is in fact one of a small series of films from its period to feature dream-demons, and to unfold with the narrative logic of a nightmare. In *Dreamscape*, Dennis Quaid plays a telepath able to enter and influence other people's dreams, who does battle with his evil counterpart, a CIA-trained telepathic hit-man (David Patrick Kelly): the film is based, as is *Nightmare*, on the old belief that, if you die in your dreams, you die in reality. Don Coscarelli's startlingly inventive *Phantasm* predates these, and it is worth dwelling for a moment on this remarkable, unclassifiable film, in which heroic, gun-totin' rock-n-roller Jody, his resourceful teenage brother Mike, and bald ice cream man Reggie battle against the Tall Man (Angus Scrimm), a demon undertaker with a spiked silver flying sphere, an army of hooded zombie dwarves, and a big fly. Much of the action takes place in a white-walled mausoleum which is both a Borgesian labyrinth and the portal to another world. The dwarves – reanimated dead from the graveyard – are used as slave-labour on an alien world (the zombies are compacted to dwarf-size to cope with the gravity on the alien planet), and their number includes Jody and Mike's parents. Mike, consequently, is terrified that Jody will abandon him, and follows him everywhere. This sense of familial anxiety is heightened at the end of the film, when it is revealed that Jody has died in a car accident the previous year, and that Mike, an orphan, lives as Reggie's ward, and suffers from chronic nightmares – of which *Phantasm* itself is one. The closing shot has the Tall Man, seemingly destroyed, reappearing, and a dwarf-hand dragging Mike through a window. This exact same closing shot was to feature in *A Nightmare on Elm Street*, where Fred's hand smashes through a glass pane in the door, dragging Nancy's mother through it. Fred had apparently been destroyed shortly before, when Nancy had simply turned her back on him, refusing to acknowledge his existence or his power, recognizing that the boogeyman is really, after all, only the visible sum of our fears. But then again, we all knew he'd be back ...

Notes

1. This is not the only difference: in *Manhunter*, the character's name is spelled 'Lecktor'. It's also worth noting here, as emblematic of the differences between the two Lecters, that Cox is never referred to as a cannibal – he is a dangerous, deadly psychopath, but not cannibalistic, and certainly not yet the quasi-Satan of *Hannibal*.
2. A similar distinction is offered by Tudor (1989: 185–210), though Tudor calls it 'madness' and 'psychosis'.
3. Kracauer (1947). For an opposing view, see Prawer (1980: 164–200).
4. For the connection between Hoffmann and Hogg here, see also, for example, Miller (1985: 2); Herdman (1991: 69).
5. Christopher Frayling further suggests that the original, but now discarded pronunciation of Jekyll as 'Jeekyll' means that the book's very title contains the pun which animates it: 'Hyde and Jekyll could rhyme with Hyde and Seek' (Frayling 1996: 122).
6. A large number of the 'video nasties' banned by the Video Recordings Act of 1984 were slashers, including such obvious *Halloween*-clones as *The Bogey Man*, as well as *The Burning*, closely modelled on *Friday the 13th*. For an account of the rise of both the video and the nasty, see Kerekes and Slater (2000).
7. For a slightly more complex narratology of the slasher, see Dika (1987: 93–4).
8. Twitchell's argument is made for horror *tout court*, and is thus highly debatable – though as a point specifically about the slasher movie, it is unarguable.
9. John Carpenter, interviewed in Adam Simon's *American Nightmare*.
10. Dika (1987: 87): 'these films of excessive violence against women found an audience that was 55 per cent female'. Nina Auerbach has also suggested that criticism of horror has been skewed by a too-ready association of the form with problems of masculinity and 'boy's game[s]' (1995: 3).
11. The *New York Post*'s review claimed that Bearse 'sports the champ vamp choppers of all time – stalactitic fangs gleaming from a crimson kisser that take up half her face' (Skal 1996: 106). One of my (female) students, on being shown a photograph of Bearse, exclaimed 'You could get two fists in there!'
12. In the original *Nightmare*, the nearest Fred comes to witticism is 'I'm gonna kill you *slow*!' In 1994, Craven returned to the franchise, recreating the original, nasty Fred in *Wes Craven's New Nightmare*. With series regulars Heather Langenkamp, John Saxon, and Robert Englund all playing themselves (as too does Wes Craven) haunted by the 'real' Fred Krueger, *New Nightmare* is a kind of trial-run for the metafictional horror Craven was to produce in the *Scream* series.

|5|

Forbidden knowledge

Textuality, metafiction and books

> Some books are dangerous, not to be opened with impunity.
>
> Victor Fargas[1]

In 1765, Thomas Lowndes of Fleet Street, London, published the first English translation of a tale found in an old Italian manuscript. The original Italian was penned by Onuphrio Muralto, and the translation into English was by William Marshall, Gent., who also provided an explanatory introduction:

> The following work was found in the library of an ancient catholic family in the north of England. It was printed at Naples, in the black letter, in the year 1529. How much sooner it was written does not appear. The principal incidents are such as were believed in the darkest ages of Christianity; but the language and content have nothing that savours of barbarism. The style is the purest Italian. If the story was written near the time when it is supposed to have happened, it must have been between 1095, the æra of the first crusade, and 1243, the date of the last, or not long afterwards.
>
> (Walpole 1968: 39)

The tale was entitled *The Castle of Otranto*, and was by neither Muralto nor Marshall, since neither of these people existed, but by the eccentric man of letters Horace Walpole, who came clean about his own authorship in the preface to the second edition.

Generally considered to be the first English Gothic novel, *The Castle of Otranto* is a hugely improbable tale (even by the loose standards of its genre) of usurpation, supernatural revenge and the workings of a malign providence set in medieval Italy, and historically important for its introduction into horror of two interconnected tropes, the Gothic castle and – what is most significant here – the found manuscript. Horror's metafictional tendencies, its structural use of mysterious manuscripts or books, and from there its more general reliance on the theme of the dangerous or forbidden knowledge to be found in these texts, has its roots here in *Otranto*, which is itself a rather wild product of eighteenth-century theories of fiction.

In his study *The Origins of the English Novel*, Michael McKeon (1988) examines the early history of the form in the seventeenth and eighteenth centuries, paying particular attention to the ways in which these early novels disguised their fictionality, presenting themselves as documentary works. The novel as we understand it was, in fact, a *product* or development of these kinds of documentary writings, McKeon suggests, growing particularly out of early Protestant 'spiritual autobiographies', first-hand accounts of the workings of God's grace upon the individual, which were then fictionalized and secularized while retaining the original overarching structure. Thus, for example, a number of Daniel Defoe's novels take the form of memoirs (*Robinson Crusoe, Moll Flanders, Roxana*) or journals (*Journal of the Plague Year*), while Samuel Richardson's epistolary novel *Pamela* grew out of a series of 'familiar letters' (specimen letters for literate, though formally uneducated, young women) upon which he was engaged: Richardson was most insistent on his own status as the *editor* rather than the author of *Pamela* – the collator of documents rather than the creator of fictions.

Following Ian Watt's monumental *The Rise of the Novel* (1957), it has become almost proverbial to theorize the novel as in its origins a fundamentally *Protestant* form, most particularly in its concentration on (some would say its creation of) the struggles of the individual character as a central fact of existence. McKeon goes further, suggesting that the secularization of the form, its shift from spiritual autobiography to individual history, was an inevitable consequence of Protestant scepticism towards traditional religious authority and its concentration instead on the unmediated individual interpretive act, and thus its focus on the text of the Bible: 'In England, if not in Roman Catholic Italy, the vulnerability of Scripture itself was paradoxically a clear consequence of Protestant and typographical bibliolatry' (McKeon 1988: 77). (That is, it created the conditions for individual interpretations of scriptural authority, thus, paradoxically – to use McKeon's word – creating an interpretive technique for the questioning of that authority.) McKeon's subordinate clause, 'if not in Roman Catholic Italy', is obviously an interesting one here, returning us to the subject-matter of Chapter 1, Protestant Britishness and anti-Catholicism. As I suggested in that chapter, the Gothic novel had a clear function in the late eighteenth and early nineteenth centuries, shoring up British identity by its creation of a barbarous, past-ridden, superstitious Catholic Europe. *Otranto* itself is an early example of just such a technique: the tale, with its dark doings and supernaturalism, is set in a medieval Italy silently counterpointed with modern, civilized Britain. More than this, however, the tale's fabricated provenance, its very documentary status, is highly revelatory: the original manuscript 'was found in the library of an ancient catholic family in the north of England'. This suggests a kind of domestic otherness at the heart of regional Gothic – not only are the manuscript's owners 'ancient' and 'catholic', but they are also from 'the north of England', far removed from metropolitan cultural centres.

While 'mainstream' realist fiction in the nineteenth century developed a flexible, powerful, even normative narrative technique – the third-person, 'omniscient' narrative perhaps best exemplified by the works of George Eliot – the Gothic novel continued, as horror generally continues, to deploy documentary narrative techniques and self-consciously to explore metafictional possibilities, the relationship between the texts it presents and the reality they represent. One of the most celebrated works of and about Romantic Gothic is the richly textual *Northanger Abbey*, a novel which not only offers an early sociological account of the audience for horror (predominantly young and female), but which, in its very concern with reading and readings, readers and the readership, exploits its own fictionality from its very opening sentence, 'No one who had ever seen Catherine Morland in her infancy, would have supposed her born to be an heroine' (Austen 1972: 37). The novel habitually blurs the boundaries between reality and (Gothic) fiction as Catherine continually interprets the events of her own life in the light of her reading of Ann Radcliffe. Furthermore, the novel implies, she is not entirely wrong to do so: General Tilney, for example, may not be a wife-murderer after all, but he *is* a mercenary and tyrannical father, quite capable of throwing the teenage Catherine out of his house when he discovers that she has no money. As suggested earlier, there is a strong sense in which the rhetoric and imagery of the Gothic (imprisonment, victimization, monstrous patriarchs) is the only language available to Catherine to describe her situation, and is certainly not inappropriate to the case.

As we saw in Chapter 1, Le Fanu's *In a Glass Darkly* and the posthumous *Purcell Papers* both contain framing narratives accounting for the provenance of the tales collected within, as the medical case-histories of Dr Hesselius or the antiquarian scholarship of Father Purcell. Furthermore, the three great canonical texts of nineteenth-century British-Irish Gothic, *Frankenstein*, *Dr Jekyll and Mr Hyde*, and *Dracula*, all deploy forms of documentary narrative techniques. Indeed, it seems that by the nineteenth century, with the realist novel and the industrial-capitalist utilitarian philosophy which underpins it both working at full power, there is considerable formal pressure to suggest or guarantee the veracity of one's subject matter, in direct proportion to the degree to which that subject was removed from a quotidian 'reality'. That is, the more implausible the subject, the greater the degree of evidence required, and thus the heavier the reliance on documentary techniques to provide (rather, to give the impression of providing) proof that what we are reading is not fiction but *truth*. Thus, *Frankenstein* is an epistolary novel, comprising the letters of

Robert Walton the polar explorer to his sister Margaret Savile – Walton's story provides the framing narrative to the novel's real interests. *Frankenstein*'s structure is analogous to a series of concentric circles, with each circle representing the narrative of a particular character – thus, the outer circle is that of Margaret Savile, presumably the collator of the novel's documents; this surrounds and contains the narrative of Walton himself, which in turn contains Victor Frankenstein's narrative; in the innermost circle, circumscribed by three mediating voices, the Monster speaks his own history. *Dr Jekyll and Mr Hyde* is presented as a legal as well as a medical case, *The Strange Case of Dr Jekyll and Mr Hyde*, a collection of documents held and presented by the lawyer Utterson, the nearest thing the novella has to a guiding central consciousness, in which each of the disparate narrators gives evidence, partial accounts of the same story from a number of different witnesses, culminating in 'Henry Jekyll's Full Statement of the Case'. (In this, Stevenson's Calvinist horror recalls the Protestant Gothics of the 1790s, the novels of Radcliffe and Lewis, typically climaxing in trial scenes, and in Radcliffe's case rejecting the supernatural evidence given in favour of a rational, sceptical, secular interpretation of events. A number of quasi-Gothic Jacobin novels from the same decade, such as William Godwin's *Caleb Williams*, also climax in court scenes, and indeed predicate their entire narratives on the potential iniquities of the English legal system.) *Dracula*, poised on the cusp on the twentieth century, presents a great number of documents and media – journals in long- and short-hand, newspapers, stenographs and phonographs, typewriters, Kodak cameras – to such effect that the technology of representation becomes a major factor (perhaps *the* major factor) in the defeat of the Count himself.

In the first half of the nineteenth century, *Blackwood's Edinburgh Magazine* was a major vehicle for the publication of the 'Tale of Terror', bloodcurdling short-stories which appeared alongside, were often informed by, and frequently took the guise of *Blackwood's* celebrated medical reports and histories. Edgar Allan Poe wrote a notable parody of this, 'How to Write a Blackwood Article', and indeed the horror story as a verifiable medical 'case' brings us back to Poe, and 'The Facts in the Case of M. Valdemar'. This extremely gruesome narrative of a New York intellectual dying of phthisis (wasting disease), hypnotized at the moment of death, opens with a characteristic assertion of the veracity of the account which follows, setting the record straight in the form of confronting the sceptical reader:

> Of course, I shall not pretend to consider it any matter for wonder, that the extraordinary case of M. Valdemar has excited discussion ... and very naturally ... a great deal of disbelief.
>
> It is now rendered necessary that I give the *facts* – as far as I comprehend them myself.
>
> (Poe 1977b: 280–1)

Poe's narrator, a radical clinician, puts M. Valdemar into a mesmeric trance at the moment of his death, where he remains able to respond to questioning: '*I have been* sleeping – and now – now – *I am dead*.' Released from his trance after an interval of several months, 'his whole frame at once, within a single minute, or even less, shrunk – crumbled – absolutely *rotted* away beneath my hands. Upon the bed, before that whole company, there lay a nearly liquid mass of loathsome – of detestable putridity' (ibid.: 287, 289). What's even more interesting is that the Valdemar case had already been written up by Poe, not as fiction, but as a factual essay, 'Mesmeric Revelation', whose narrator hypnotizes his terminally ill subject (again dying of phthisis), 'Mr. Vankirk', with whom he then has a metaphysical discourse on death and the immortality of the soul. 'Mesmeric Revelation' opens in familiar fashion: 'Whatever doubt may still envelop the *rationale* of mesmerism, its startling *facts* are now almost universally admitted' (Poe 1977a: 290).

It is difficult to over-estimate Poe's contribution to modern narrative fiction. He was, famously, a pioneer of the detective story, itself a model for the sceptical analytical process, with the detective as a kind of ideal reader able to interpret the often arcane or occult codes of the narrative. Thus his own master detective, Auguste Dupin, is also a master rationalist, forever seeking the material reality behind the mysterious and ostensibly supernatural events his stories witness. Poe himself was fascinated by secret codes and cryptograms – as a journalist and editor, he partly made a living devising codes and puzzles for his readers to crack – and the key to his story 'The Gold-Bug' is just such an apparently uncrackable cryptogram, while 'The Purloined Letter' concentrates on a missing document, whose possession signifies power, hidden in plain sight. His first published story, 'MS Found in a Bottle' – which in many ways operates as a sketch for his later novel, *Arthur Gordon Pym* – is, as its title suggests, an archetype of the found manuscript narrative, the message in a bottle. A shipwrecked sailor finds himself on a gigantic ghost ship sailing through Antarctic waters, and the tale closes with the ship's being sucked into a gigantic whirlpool, the moment of death, or possibly of discovery, when communication ceases. (The question of how the bottle survives the vortex where the ship does not is an interesting one, and not irrelevant.)

Libraries and labyrinths: Lovecraft, James, Borges

Operating at one perceived limit of popular culture, horror is often characterized as a debased if not unhealthy genre. Yet I would contend that it is a genre which takes knowledge and learning unusually seriously, recognizing that knowledge, invested as it is here with great power, can be both enlightening and deadly. While it is certainly the case that one kind of horror 'knowledge narrative' (the term in this context is Andrew Tudor's, 1989: 83–90), mad science, *is* animated by a conservative scepticism towards knowledge – while still recognizing its power – it remains true that no other genre elevates academics, librarians and other scholars to such central and indeed heroic status (my fictional colleagues are strangely absent from other genres, such as the western, war story, or romance), just as no other genre has with quite such frequency featured the library as its locus.

In the 1990s, for example, *Se7en* presented a Poe-like detective narrative in which a knowledge of intellectual arcana is required to catch Kevin Spacey's demonic everyman-killer (his name, John Doe, is anonymously generic; he has no fingerprints). In keeping with the film's apocalyptic vision of the modern city, it is Dante and Milton that are required reading to catch the killer: the film takes place in a nameless American city which is actually an amalgam of New York and Los Angeles (the character of urban life recalls New York, but the Mojave Desert is just down the road) but symbolically Hell, or more specifically *Paradise Lost*'s Pandemonium, the City of Many Demons. The sage Detective William Somerset (Morgan Freeman) is at home in the killer's high-cultural milieu, spending a good deal of his time cracking the case in the library, to the accompaniment of classical music (though he also orders an illegal surveillance of library withdrawals), while his partner, the more straightforward Mills (played by the more straightforward Brad Pitt), has to resort to Cole's Notes, at one point exclaiming in frustration, 'Fuck Dante!' (I know the feeling.)

Though he worked in isolation and relative obscurity in Rhode Island, not receiving any degree of widespread recognition until after his death in 1937, H.P. Lovecraft was a contemporary of European and American Modernist writers, and his work should properly, I think, be viewed in this context, as a bizarre but nevertheless significant contribution to High Modernism. Like Yeats, Lovecraft straddles the worlds of *fin-de-siècle* decadent occultism (Aleister Crowley and Arthur Machen are figures who link Yeats with Lovecraft here) and the literature of the 1920s and 1930s. Like any number of Modernists, Lovecraft's work exhibits a profound dislike of modernity, and ideologically he shares a typical interest in far-right politics, a contempt for 'the masses', and a dubious interest in eugenics and ideas of racial purity.[2] And Lovecraft's views on race were, to say the least, unambiguous: in New York in the 1920s, he wrote of the 'loathsome Asiatic hordes who drag their dirty carcasses over streets where white men once moved'! (Lovecraft 1992: Introduction, n.p.)

In the best of Lovecraft's work, these prejudices resulted in some powerful regional Gothic, and even a few forays into Celticism, of a kind which should be familiar. 'The Dunwich Horror' (1928), surely his finest story, opens with a remarkable descriptive passage, suggestive of a sense of uncanniness and spatial dislocation brought about by a distance from centres of culture: 'When a traveler in north central Massachusetts takes the wrong fork at the junction of the Aylesbury pike just beyond Dean's Corner he comes upon a lonely and curious country', peopled with 'figures [who] are so silent and furtive that one feels somehow confronted by forbidden things, with which it would be better to have nothing to do' (Lovecraft 1994b: 99–100). As with the Gothic locales of Wales, Scotland and Ireland from Chapter 1, once again here we are not on any map – 'all the signboards pointing towards [Dunwich] have been taken down' – and in a region where

> the natives are now repellently decadent, having gone far along the path of retrogression common in many New England backwaters. They have come to form a race by themselves, with the well-defined mental and physical stigmata of degeneracy and in-breeding. The average of their intelligence is woefully low, whilst their annals reek of overt viciousness and of half-hidden murders, incests, and deeds of almost unnameable violence and perversity.
>
> (ibid.: 101)

Given Lovecraft's industrial-strength eugenics, the human denizens of Dunwich seem hardly better than the monstrous, other-dimensional creatures – nine-foot-tall, twenty-penised Wilbur Whately, and his house-sized invisible twin brother – who live amongst them: indeed, for Lovecraft the Dunwichers seem to be of a comparable order of monstrosity, and it is their very incestuous degeneracy which produces the monstrous births. As the tag-line to the poster for Daniel Haller's film version succinctly puts it: 'A few years ago in Dunwich a half-witted girl bore illegitimate twins. One of them was almost human!'[3]

Virtually all of Lovecraft's work draws on his complex invented cosmology, later dubbed the 'Cthulhu Mythos', which postulates a universe governed by a monstrous race of 'elder gods' now banished to another dimension but forever threatening to return, bringing chaos with them, through ruptures in our own reality:

> These Great Old Ones ... were not composed altogether of flesh and blood. They had shape ... but that shape was not made of matter. When the stars were right, They could plunge from world to world through the sky; but when the stars were wrong, They could not live. But although They no longer lived, They would never really die. They all lay in stone houses in Their great city of R'lyeh, preserved by the spells of mighty Cthulhu for a glorious resurrection when the stars and the earth might once more be ready for Them. But at that time some force from outside must serve to liberate Their bodies. The spells that preserved Them intact likewise prevented Them from making the initial move, and They could only lie awake in the dark and think whilst uncounted millions of years rolled by.
>
> (ibid.: 80)

The Whately brothers are the product of a union between the half-witted albino Lavinia Whately and one such creature through the agency of Lavinia's father, Wizard Whately – thus the Whatelys' birth is doubly monstrous, both demonic and incestuous. In 'The Call of Cthulhu' (1926) such a rupture once again occurs, culminating in the appearance of the 'Great Cthulhu' himself (he is some kind of gigantic octopus-creature, or perhaps a terrifying vagina) on a fantastic multi-dimensional island in the South Seas. Cthulhu's arrival is anticipated in the dreams of artists and poets, in tune with the terrifying reality which lies behind our material world (an idea which Lovecraft seems to have lifted wholesale from Machen's *The Great God Pan*), and by heightened unrest amongst the 'degenerate races':

> Here was a nocturnal suicide in London, where a lone sleeper had leaped from a window after a shocking cry. Here likewise a rambling letter to the editor of a paper in South America, where a fanatic deduces a dire future from visions he has seen. A dispatch from California describes a theosophist colony as donning white robes en masse for some 'glorious fulfilment' which never arrives, whilst items from India speak guardedly of serious native unrest towards the end of March. Voodoo orgies multiply in Haiti, and African outposts report ominous mutterings. American officers in the Philippines find certain tribes bothersome about this time, and New York policemen are mobbed by hysterical Levantines on the night of 22–23 March. The west of Ireland, too, is full of wild rumour and legendry.
>
> (ibid.: 69–70)

The occult Celticism of this last sentence recurs far more powerfully in Lovecraft's 'The Rats in the Walls' (1923), where the heavy influence of Poe is covertly acknowledged in the narrator's surname, Delapore – originally de la Poer. (Jorge Luis Borges, of whom more later, was to describe Lovecraft as 'an unwitting parodist of Poe') (Borges 1998: 485). Stricken with grief after losing his son in the First World War, Delapore returns from America to his ancestral seat in Wales, Exham Priory, with its 'Gothic towers resting on a Saxon or Romanesque substructure, whose foundation in turn was of a still earlier blend of orders – Roman, and even Druidic or native Cymric, if legends speak truly' (Lovecraft 1994b: 19). In Exham, Delapore gradually succumbs to the ancestral curse of cannibalism, discovering a forbidden subterranean cavern beneath Exham, 'choked with the pithecanthropoid, Celtic, Roman, and English bones of countless unhallowed centuries' (ibid.: 41). The story closes with Delapore devouring his neighbour, the 'flabby' Captain Norrys, while undergoing a dramatic linguistic reverse-evolution, backwards from modernity to chaos, reverting (as Lovecraft understands it) from modern English, through Renaissance English, to Middle English, Latin, Irish, and finally gibberish:

> Who says I am a de la Poer. He lived, but my boy died! Shall a Norrys hold the land of a de la Poer? ... It's voodoo, I tell you ... that spotted snake ... Curse you, Thornton, I'll teach you to faint at what my family do! 'Sblood, thou stinkard, I'll learn ye how to gust ... wolde ye swynke me thilke wys? ... *Magna Mater! Magna Mater!* ... *Atys* ... *Dia ad aghaidh's ad aodaun* ... *agus bach dunach ort! Dhonas 's dholas ort, leat-sa!* ... *Ungl ... unl ... rrlh ... chchch* ...
>
> (ibid.: 42)

'The Call of Cthulhu', a tale of arcane forbidden knowledge, begins with a warning of the dubious benefits of intellectual investigation:

> The sciences, each straining in its own direction, have hitherto harmed us little; but some day the piecing together of dissociated knowledge will open up such terrifying vistas of reality, and of our frightful position therein, that we shall either go mad from the revelation or flee from the deadly light into the peace and safety of a new dark age.
>
> (ibid.: 61)

Like *Jekyll and Hyde* or *Dracula*, 'The Call of Cthulhu' takes the form of a tale collated from a number of manuscript sources and partial testimonies. The documents, concerning the barbaric 'Cthulhu Cult' and drawing heavily on *The Golden Bough*, are in part the research of the narrator's great uncle, George Gammell Angell, 'Professor of Semitic Languages at Brown University, Providence, Rhode Island', who dies mysteriously 'after having been jostled by a nautical-looking negro' (ibid.: 62). Underpinning all of the scholarship in Lovecraft's work is a forbidden 'book of books', 'the *Necronomicon* of the mad Arab Alhazred which the initiated might read as they chose' (ibid.: 81). Originally entitled the *Al Azif*, the *Necronomicon* gets its familiar name, meaning 'The Book of Dead Names', from the Latin translation of Olaus Wormius, 'as printed in Spain in the seventeenth century' (ibid.: 116). Abdul Alhazred, a visionary poet, first appears in Lovecraft's 'The Nameless City' (1921), as the author of the couplet 'That is not dead which can eternal lie / And with strange aeons even death may die' (Lovecraft 1994a: 129, 142), revisited in 'The Call of Cthulhu' where it is clearly understood as referring to the 'Great Old Ones' (Lovecraft 1994b: 81). It is to consult this Wormius edition, 'the dreaded volume kept under lock and key', that Wilbur travels to the library of Miskatonic (that is, Brown) University, to collate it with 'the priceless but imperfect copy of Dr [John] Dee's English version which his grandfather had bequeathed him ... with the aim of discovering a certain passage which would have come on the 751st page of his own defective volume', in order to find the incantation to give form to the 'Great Old Ones' (ibid.: 116, 117).

The *Necronomicon* is a fiction, a product of Lovecraft's imagination, though there seems to be a great desire that it should exist, and thus, in true *grimoire* (spell-book) fashion, it has taken on a life of its own beyond the boundaries of Lovecraft's work. Lovecraft has his imitators and disciples, who have effectively continued his work, perpetuating and developing the 'Cthulhu Mythos', and delving deeper into the mysteries of the *Necronomicon*. Borges, a grudging admirer (as are we all), inscribed his 'There Are More Things' 'To the memory of H.P. Lovecraft', noting that 'Fate, which is widely known to be inscrutable, would not leave me in peace until I had perpetrated a posthumous story by Lovecraft' (Borges 1998: 437, 484).[4] More directly, Lin Cooper's 'The Doom of Yakthoob' (1971), for example, takes the form of a passage from the text, and the book makes an appearance in numerous stories and films, including *The Haunted Palace*, based on a combination of Poe and of Lovecraft's *The Case of Charles Dexter Ward*, and *Necronomicon*, with Jeffrey Combs as Lovecraft.[5] Even more gloriously, an attempt has been made to reconstitute the 'original' *Necronomicon* itself, now readily available in a paperback edition presenting itself as an authentic occult document, complete with 'The Testimony of the Mad Arab', Abdul Alhazred himself! (Simon 1980).[6] The substance of the book itself, all symbols and incantations, is, as far as I can tell, incomprehensible. But I may be wrong ...

As variously Provost of King's College, Cambridge, Vice-Chancellor of Cambridge University and director of its Fitzwilliam Museum, and Headmaster of Eton, M.R. James knew more than most about the scholarly life. His celebrated ghost stories were created as scholarly diversions or amusements to be read aloud to students and colleagues in front of the fire in his study. His stories are reserved, ambiguous, highly formalized exercises in the creation of an unsettling mood, which sometimes infuriatingly refuse to commit themselves as to the status of the events they recount, and invariably take place within James's own cloistered world of ancient universities, old country houses and priories, and great libraries. Thus, 'Oh, Whistle, and I'll Come to You, My Lad' (the title is from Burns) opens with a High Table dispute between the rationalist Professor Parkins and his colleague, Mr Rogers, on the existence of ghosts: 'I hold,' says Parkins, 'that any semblance, any appearance of concession to the view that such things exist is equivalent to a renunciation of all that I hold most sacred.' This certainty is called into question by his encounter with the most stereotypical of ghosts, an animated sheet with 'a horrible, an intensely horrible, face *of crumpled linen*', following which 'the Professor's views on certain points are less clear-cut than they used to be' (James 1992: 67, 80, 81). (This is about as direct a statement as James's stories ever make.) The truly creepy 'Count

Magnus', a variant on the vampire story, has its academic traveller Mr Wraxall inadvertently reanimating the long-dead corpse of an evil Swedish nobleman, a Satanist who 'had been on the Black Pilgrimage, and had brought something or someone back with him' (ibid.: 57), which then pursues him back to his terrified death in England. (This 'Black Pilgrimage' is the 'Scholomance' to the city of Chorazin, birthplace of the Antichrist – a pilgrimage which, according to Dr Van Helsing, Count Dracula also undertook before becoming a vampire.)

A number of James's best stories are predicated on the discovery of ancient manuscripts or artefacts. 'Canon Alberic's Scrapbook' has a scholar on vacation in the South of France come upon a priceless collection of ancient manuscripts, including an illustration of 'The Dispute of Solomon with a demon of the night', with accompanying demon (James 1992: 10). In 'The Mezzotint', an antique print reveals an occult history of the abduction of children (a theme which recurs in 'Lost Hearts'), while 'The Tractate Middoth', set largely in the British Library, has the key to an inheritance in a mysterious manuscript, 'Talmud: Tractate Middoth, with the commentary of Nachmanides, Amsterdam, 1707' (ibid.: 114), guarded by the cobweb-covered ghost of a malevolent scholar. 'Casting the Runes', probably James's most celebrated story, has Karswell, an independent scholar, author of *The History of Witchcraft*, and self-proclaimed alchemist, revenge himself on a scornful academic establishment by apparently setting a demon on his reviewers! (If only ...) The demon's victim is whoever possesses, at a given hour, the mysterious runic parchment which Karswell passes on to Dunning, one of his reviewers, in the British Library. In an elaborate sting, Dunning and Harrington, the brother of one of Karswell's previous victims, return the parchment to Karswell on board a train to Dover. Two days later, at 'St. Wulfram's Church in Abbeville, then under extensive repair, [Karswell] was struck on the head and instantly killed by a stone falling from the scaffold erected round the north-western tower' (ibid.: 145).

'Casting the Runes', typically of James, maintains a studied ambiguity as to the nature of the agency responsible for Karswell's death – is he killed by his own conjured demon, by the power of suggestion, or by an unlucky accident? However, Jacques Tourneur's film-adaptation, *Night of the Demon*, aka *Curse of the Demon*, permits no such doubt while comprehensively improving on its source, for this is one of the very greatest of all horror movies. Here, the voice of scepticism is provided by Dr Holden (Dana Andrews), an American psychologist traveling to London to take part in a conference on occult beliefs, and clashing with 'Julian' Karswell (indelibly embodied by Niall McGinnis), here not only an alchemist but the head of a Satanic cult, and terrified by the powers he has unleashed, but over which he has no real control.

The film was much criticized, not least by its own creators, for the enforced inclusion by producer Hal E. Chester of a horned demon which, though terrifying in close-up, mostly just looks like a puppet:

'I had to sit by,' said Charles Bennett, author of the screenplay,
'while Chester made the biggest balls-up of a good script that
I've ever seen. ... [The demon's appearance] took a major
movie down to the level of crap. If Chester walked up my
driveway now I'd shoot him dead.'

(*Empire c.*2000: 27)[7]

Tourneur was an alumnus of producer Val Lewton's horror-studio at RKO
pictures, where movies such as *Cat People* and *I Walked with a Zombie*, both
directed by Tourneur, showcased a celebrated house-style of implied horror
based on the creation of an unsettling viewing-experience through the
virtuouso manipulation of shadow and sound. This technique Tourneur
displays again and again in *Night of the Demon* in a number of *tour-de-force*
scenes: Karswell in clown-costume conjuring up a storm at a children's party;
Holden's flight through the grounds of Lufford Abbey, ostensibly pursued by
a whistling cloud of smoke; his visit to the weird farmhouse of the Satan-
worshipping Hobart family at Stonehenge, and the subsequent hypnotism and
suicide of the catatonic Rand Hobart; a séance in the front parlour of a
suburban house which begins in comedy and ends in terror. As Carlos Clarens
writes, '*Night of the Demon* abounds in prosaic situations turning implacably
into nightmares' (1997: 144).[8] Certainly, then, this very unsubtle demon
undermines the subtle air of uncanniness which the film otherwise so
magnificently creates, and certainly it would seem to foreclose on the possibility
of any interpretation other than the supernatural one. Here, however, there is
a considerable distance between viewer and expert, for Holden is emphatically
not the ideal reader of *this* text. Indeed, part of the tension in this movie is
because the viewer realizes well in advance of Holden that his scepticism here
is more like materialist dogma, inadequate to account for the events in which
he is caught up, which *demand* a supernatural explanation, as his less-dogmatic
scientific colleagues, the Irish Dr O'Brien and the Indian Dr Kumar (both
hailing from cultures well versed in occultism and demonology), try to tell him.
However inept it may look, it is thematically entirely fitting that the demon
should appear at the end of the film to tear Karswell limb from limb, as by this
point *everyone* concerned, including Holden, knows that it must.

None of the occasional remarks made in this study about the perceived
cultural disreputability of its subject applies to the work of Jorge Luis
Borges, almost universally recognized as one of the most important writers
of the twentieth century. Borges's short metafictions – 'games with time and
infinity', as he was famously to call them[9] – brilliantly mix modes, but
almost invariably draw upon popular fictional models (detective, thriller,
war, horror) and precursors (Poe, Stevenson, Wells, Chesterton, Lovecraft),
deploying radical versions of the kinds of documentary techniques and
textual concerns which we saw in the early part of this chapter. Invariably,
too, Borges draws heavily upon familiar Gothic devices: the forbidden book
and the labyrinth which is both dungeon and library.

Thus, 'Tlön, Uqbar, Orbis Tertius' begins with 'a mirror and an encyclopaedia'. The encyclopedia is a rogue edition of volume XLVI of '*The Anglo-American Cyclopaedia* (New York, 1917) ... [which] is a literal but delinquent reprint of the *Encyclopaedia Britannica* of 1902' (Borges 1970: 27). This book has 921 instead of the regulation 917 pages, the difference being made up by an entry on the imaginary land of Uqbar and its own imagined world of Tlön, and its discovery leads in turn to the discovery of '*A First Encyclopaedia of Tlön. Vol. XI. Hlaer to Jangr*'. Tlön, the imaginative product of a secret society labouring across centuries to create a new world, is entirely governed by the precepts of idealist philosophy, which, following the thinking of George Berkeley, argues that reality does not exist independently from our perception of it: thus, it follows, for example, that you have no grounds for proving to me that you exist outside my perception of you; that when you walk out of the door and I can no longer see you, you are nevertheless still there. Borges writes in 'Tlön' that '[David] Hume noted for all time that Berkeley's arguments did not admit the slightest refutation nor did they cause the slightest conviction' (ibid.: 32). That is to say, the Berkeleian argument as stated here is a sophism, not referring to conditions outside of itself: following the thinking of Karl Popper, we should note that, not being empirically testable, and thus not subject even in theory to falsification, it is philosophically useless (Popper 1972). It is, however, for Borges, an *imaginatively* rich idea, as it has proven for many others: *The Matrix*, for example, working on the premise that our 'objective' reality is an elaborate fiction, and that we ourselves do not exist, at least not in the ways we imagine, is clearly a kind of pop-Borges (the conjunction here of Jorge Luis Borges and Keanu Reeves is truly a bizarre one, I can't help but think). Once the book is opened, the consequences are inevitable, and Tlön closes with the imaginary world replacing our own reality, and with the overthrowing of God:

> Manuals, anthologies, summaries, literal versions, authorized re-editions and pirated editions of the Greatest Work of Man flooded and still flood the earth. Almost immediately reality yielded on more than one account. The truth is that it longed to yield. Ten years ago any symmetry with a semblance of order – dialectical materialism, anti-Semitism, nazism – was sufficient to entrance the minds of men. How could one do other than submit to Tlön, to the minute and vast evidence of an orderly planet? It is useless to answer that reality is also orderly. Perhaps it is, but in accordance with divine laws – I translate: inhuman laws – which we never quite grasp. Tlön is surely a labyrinth, but it is a labyrinth devised by men, a labyrinth destined to be deciphered by men.
>
> (ibid.: 42)

This vision of creation as a system of signs, a code or book theoretically available for interpretation by a competent reader, but in practice, because

of its chaotic complexity, indecipherable or unreadable, recurs throughout
Borges's work. The labyrinth and the indecipherable book are thus recurring
and interconnected images in his stories. 'The Garden of Forking Paths' tells
of the polymathic Ts'ui Pên, who retires from public life 'in order to compose
a book and a maze' (ibid.: 49). The book turns out to be no more than an
incomprehensible jumble of chaotic fragments, while the maze is presumed
lost, until the Sinologist Stephen Albert deduces that the book and the maze
are one: in Ts'ui Pên's novel, *The Garden of Forking Paths*, every
conceivable outcome to every event happens simultaneously: thus linear time
(whose existence Borges elsewhere attempted to disprove) breaks down in
Ts'ui Pên's garden, and conventional narrative, unfolding as it ostensibly
does in linear time, is here an inadequate fiction.[10] 'The Book of Sand' posits
an infinite book, sold to the narrator by a Bible salesman, seemingly an
object of wonder, but actually an object of terror: 'I felt it was a nightmare
thing, an obscene thing, and that it defiled and corrupted reality. I considered
fire, but I feared that an infinite book might be similarly infinite, and
suffocate the planet in smoke' (Borges 1998: 483). Like Poe's Purloined
Letter, the Book of Sand is hidden in plain sight, placed uncatalogued on one
of the shelves of the Argentine National Library. 'The Aleph' features a poet
writing an endless epic exhaustively documenting the whole world, while in
his basement all of creation is compressed into one single point, and 'The
God's Script' has its protagonist, the imprisoned Mayan wizard Tzinacàn,
deciphering the divine writing encoded in the spots of a jaguar: 'It is a
formula of fourteen random words (they appear random) and to utter it in
a loud voice would suffice to make me all powerful' (Borges 1970: 207).

In what is for Borges a perfectly logical – indeed, an inevitable –
encapsulating symbol, 'The Library of Babel' posits the nature of the
universe as an interminable library, containing within its endlessly repeating
hexagonal chambers every conceivable book:

> The Library is total and ... its shelves register all the possible
> combinations of the twenty-odd orthographical symbols (a
> number which, though vast, is not infinite): in other words, all
> that is given to express, in all languages.
>
> (ibid.: 81)

Once again, Borges postulates reality as a code which is in principle decipherable,
but in practice chaotic: logically, the key to the Library, the catalogue or book
of books, must exist, though faced with such vastness any one person's chances
of discovering such a book can be computed as zero. Again logically, however,
someone must have discovered it: 'the Man of the Book. On some shelf in some
hexagon (men reasoned), there must exist a book which is the formula and
perfect compendium *of all the rest*: some librarian has gone through it and he
is analogous to a god' (ibid.: 83). The Library is therefore, and once again, a
labyrinth, impossible to navigate, and potentially endless.

Stephen King: writer's block

In his critical memoir, *On Writing*, Stephen King recalls an encounter which took place around 1961 with his school principal, Miss Hisler. The young King had made an early foray into the world of letters, writing, printing and selling his own novelized version of Roger Corman's *The Pit and the Pendulum*, 'Very Important Book #1':

> 'What I don't understand, Stevie,' she said, 'is why you'd write junk like this in the first place. You're talented. Why do you want to waste your abilities?' ... I have spent a good many years since – too many, I think – being ashamed about what I write. I think I was forty before I realized that almost every writer of fiction and poetry who has ever published a line has been accused by someone of wasting his or her God-given talent. ... But in my heart I stayed ashamed. I kept hearing Miss Hisler asking why I wanted to waste my talent, why I wanted to waste my time, why I wanted to write junk.
>
> (King 2000: 30–1)

This is King's primal scene, encapsulating in an adolescent encounter most of the themes which dominate his phenomenal body of work. First, there is the encounter between wise child and uncomprehending authority-figure: as a self-professed 'baby-boomer' growing up in the 1950s and 1960s, King's distrust of adult authority is understandable (born in 1947, he grew up through McCarthyism and the protests of the American Civil Rights movement, and made adulthood just in time for Vietnam and Watergate), giving him, as Nina Auerbach has noted, a 'passionate allegiance to pre-adulthood', which, she suggests, was instrumental in shifting the focus of horror towards adolescence in the 1980s, when 'horror will belong to the young' (1995: 159). King's work is saturated with narratives of children able to recognize long before their parents, guardians, or teachers the horror which confronts them and their communities. In *'Salem's Lot*, for example, it is young Mark Petrie, 'unhealthily' obsessed with horror movies, who is able to recognize the danger confronting the town in the form of an invasion of vampires, as he is able to provide what is for King the most lucid analysis of that danger: 'Understand death? Sure. That was when the monsters got you' (King 1976: 153). As a horror-writer, then, King's frames of cultural reference belong largely to his own pre-adulthood: *Invasion of the Body Snatchers*, and other alien-invasion movies of the 1950s; the stories of Ray Bradbury and Harlan Ellison; Forrest Ackerman's influential magazine *Famous Monsters of Filmland*; TV series such as *The Twilight Zone* and especially *The Outer Limits*.[11] King is, I would contend, perhaps the archetypal product of American post-war affluence, and the boom in consumerism and popular culture which it produced, and which he himself, not untypically, is eager to mythologize. In Stephen King's cultural imagination, it is forever about 1961, or should be, and he is very aware of his own propensity for both anti-authoritarianism and nostalgia: 'In my character, a kind of wildness and a deep conservatism are wound together like hair in a braid' (King 2000: 34).

For King, the adult best able to preserve the lessons of childhood is the writer:

> Kids are bent. They think around corners. . . . The imagination
> is an eye, a marvelous third eye that floats free. As children,
> that eye sees with 20/20 clarity. As we grow older, its vision
> begins to dim . . . The job of the fantasy-horror writer is to
> make you, for a little while, a child again.
>
> (King 1982: 456)

In this, the writer's enemy, the representative of adult authority in the world of letters, is the critic, whom King understands as the custodian of an outmoded vision of an elite culture (itself, I would say, a vision of 'the critic' which belongs most comfortably in the 1950s and 1960s):

> a good deal of literary criticism serves only to reinforce a caste-
> system that's as old as the intellectual snobbery which
> nurtured it. . . . Critics and scholars have always been
> suspicious of popular success. Often their suspicions are
> justified. In other cases, these suspicions are used as an excuse
> not to think. No one can be as intellectually slothful as a really
> smart person.
>
> (King 2000: 110–11)

King's public stance as a writer is selfconsciously unstuffy and fearful of 'pretension', and thus defensively anti-intellectual: 'This is a short book because most books about writing are filled with bullshit' (King 2000: xiii), King writes at the very beginning of *On Writing*. For King, scornful of an academic 'country club', writing is a defiantly blue-collar activity: he keeps regular working hours, driving every morning to a Portakabin on an industrial estate on the outskirts of town, and writing to the constant accompaniment of heavy metal music. In *'Salem's Lot*, Ben Mears offers similar advice: 'Strip to the waist, turn up the radio, and drink a gallon of beer. I've been putting out ten pages a day, fresh copy' (King 1976: 37; see also King 2000: 122). His genre, the range of narrative and grammatical devices upon which he draws, he likens to a toolbox, which – again drawing on his childhood – reminds him of his Uncle Oren's: 'You never saw a toolbox like this for sale at Wal-Mart or Western Auto, believe me' (King 2000: 84). He is understandably scornful of Romantic views of poetry as stemming from divine inspiration:

there was a view among the student writers I knew that good writing came spontaneously, in an uprush of feeling that had to be caught at once: when you were building that all-important stairway to heaven, you couldn't just stand around with your hammer in your hand.

(ibid.: 41–2)

But King *is*, if course, the man with a hammer in his hand, and *On Writing* is subtitled 'A Memoir of the Craft'. His craft is also, need it be said, a very masculine pursuit, most definitely not for sissies: 'Traditionally, the muses were women, but mine's a guy; I'm afraid we'll just have to live with that' (ibid.: 111).

Time and again, King's novels foreground his truest subject: himself, or more specifically his calling and career as a writer, for King writes compulsively, and writes compulsively about writing, and many of his protagonists are writers: Ben Mears in *'Salem's Lot*, Jack Torrance in *The Shining*, Paul Sheldon in *Misery*, Thad Beaumont in *The Dark Half*, Gordon Lachance in 'The Body', and others. They are all the same. King is a relentlessly monologic writer. That is to say that whether he is writing dialogue or third-person narrative, prose-treatise or memoir, or even, as in *Carrie*, presenting what purports to be a series of authentic documents and testimony, King always writes in the same voice, an instantly identifiable mixture of straight-talking, heavy sarcasm, hectoring diatribe, and a fondness for pop-cultural imagery which is often mystifying for those of us who do not share his own subject-position as a male baby-boomer steeped (or trapped) in the American popular culture of his period. Thus, when King goes out of his way to create a character who habitually speaks idiomatically, such as *The Dark Half*'s Trooper Hamilton – 'Safe is safe, sorry is sorry, and that's all I know, by the great by-Gorry!' – it only serves to highlight the fact that *all* of King's characters talk like this. In the same novel, Dr Pritchard the brain surgeon, says things like 'The kid's father would make Piltdown Man look like one of the Quiz Kids'; Thad Beaumont answers Alan Pangborn's question, 'Do you read minds as well as write books, Mr Beaumont?' with 'Read minds, write books, but honey, I don't do windows' (a piece of homoerotica so apparently hilarious that it causes Pangborn effectively to wet himself, though in a very masculine way – he spits beer over his crotch); earlier, Pangborn describes Mrs. Gamache 'snoring like a Jimmy-Pete doing seventy on the turnpike' (King 1989: 66, 11, 106, 56). All of these in turn sound like, for example, *Carrie*'s David R. Congress, the apparently academic author of *The Shadow Exploded: Documented Facts and Specific Conclusions Derived from the Case of Carietta White* (Tulane University Press, 1981): 'The great tragedy is that we are now all Monday-morning quarterbacks'; or like *Misery*'s Paul Sheldon: 'Even in good shape the outcome of a fight between him and Annie would have been in doubt. As he was now it would be like Wally Cox taking on Boom Boom Mancini' (King 1992b: 322, 489). And this, finally, is King himself, on recent American political history: 'In Vietnam, Nixon was executing his plan to end the war, which seemed to consist of bombing most of Southeast Asia into Kibbles 'n Bits' (King 2000: 40). This in turn is largely indistinguishable from Gordon Lachance's take on the politics of the early 1960s (that is to say, the level of King's political sensibilities was and remains that of a 13-year-old boy): 'The news was a lot of happy horseshit about Kennedy and Nixon and Quemoy and Matsu and the missile gap and what a shit that Castro was turning out to be after all' (King 1992a: 328). One sometimes wonders what King's enormous global readership really makes of this covert American cultural imperialism, in which the world's best-selling novelist inhabits a milieu which, in its very specificity, must often be incomprehensible even to many Americans under the age of 40. One way in which King himself imaginatively circumscribes this potential problem is by compressing his vast readership into one figure, the perpetually present 'Constant Reader', the ideal reader who shares King's own frames of reference, history, background, interests – who is, in effect, indistinguishable from Stephen King himself.

If *'Salem's Lot*'s Mark Petrie is a figure for the young Stephen King, then his adult counterpart in the novel is Ben Mears, returning to the town after many years away, with a mysterious compulsion to write about the old Marsden House which stems from a traumatic formative experience in which the young Ben, going into the derelict house on a dare, 'sees' the hanging corpse of the murderer Hubie Marsden. Ben is of course a novelist, whose book *Conway's Daughter* received mixed reviews, upon which Ben-King is only too ready to comment: 'most of the critics had clobbered it. Well, that was critics for you. Plot was out, masturbation in' (King 1976: 23). It is Ben and Mark, together with the imaginative English teacher Jason Burke, who form the core of the group of vampire hunters, and it is only Ben and Mark who make it out of 'Salem's Lot alive. Similarly, in 'The Body', the young Gordon Lachance is at the very least an indistinguishable contemporary of King himself: 'I was twelve going on thirteen when I first saw a dead human being. It happened in 1960, a long time ago ... although it doesn't seem that long to me.' Interspersed with the story's narrative are instances of the adult Gordon's published fiction shaped by the events 'The Body' recounts. The first of these, 'Stud City', is described by its author as being 'too much 1960' (King 1992a: 321, 358) – an accusation which could, to reiterate, symbolically be made for all of King's fiction.

Gordon Lachance criticizes 'Stud City' in the following terms:

> It ought to have THIS IS A PRODUCE [sic] OF AN UNDERGRADUATE CREATIVE WRITING WORKSHOP stamped on every page ... because that's just what it was, at least up to a certain point. It seems both painfully derivative and painfully sophomoric to me now; style by Hemingway

(except we've got the whole thing in the present tense for some reason – how too fucking trendy), theme by Faulkner. Could anything be more *serious*? More *lit'ry*?

(ibid.: 357)

Again because of his fear of seeming pretentious, of 'lit'ryness', King is refreshingly eager to communicate the tricks of his trade (the contents of his toolbox), and fascinated by the mechanics of its production. Thus *Misery*'s many disquisitions on, for example, the problems of typing on Corrosable Bond paper, the function of editors, or the necessity of plausible resolutions to serial-fiction cliffhangers, or *The Dark Half*'s remarks on writing with Berol Black Beauty pencils, are indistinguishable from the various hints, lessons and anecdotes of the writing life King provides in *Danse Macabre* and especially *On Writing*.

As often as not, for King writing is itself a subject for horror. The terrifying events of *The Shining* are all essentially predicated on Jack Torrance's severe case of writer's block. Leaving aside the novel's supernaturalism, Jack goes mad because he is unable to write, and one can imagine how terrifying an idea this must be for a graphomaniac like Stephen King. Even more terrifyingly, *Misery* seems to articulate many of King's own writerly anxieties in its narrative of a writer imprisoned and forced to write by his psychopathic 'number one fan':

> And while [Annie Wilkes] might be crazy, was she so different in her evaluation of his work from the hundreds of thousands of other people across the country – ninety percent of them women – who could barely wait for each new five-hundred-page episode in the turbulent life of the foundling who had risen to marry a peer of the realm? No, not at all. They wanted Misery, Misery, Misery. Each time he had taken a year off to write one of the other novels – what he thought of as his 'serious' work with what was first certainty and then hope and finally a species of grim desperation – he had received a flood of protesting letters from these women, many of whom signed themselves 'your number one fan'. ... He could write a modern *Under the Volcano*, *Tess of the D'Urbervilles*, *The Sound and the Fury*; it wouldn't matter. They would still want Misery, Misery, Misery.

(King 1992b: 464)

Misery is a novel dominated by its own textuality, and in other hands it would be tempting to call its textual playfulness postmodern. Its interposed novel, *Misery's Return*, which Paul writes at Annie's command, in order to stay alive (he likens himself to Scheherazade, forced to tell stories in exchange for an extra day of life), intrudes and comments on *Misery* itself.

It serves, that is, as a commentary on its own production, being the product and the symbol of Paul's imprisonment, pain, torture, and eventual dismemberment – as the text itself is effectively dismembered, produced on a typewriter with a missing tooth, unable to write the letter n, which must be filled in by hand. The typewriter itself is anthropomorphized, embodied as an agent of Annie, collusive in his torture: 'The typewriter sat there smirking at him. "I hate you," Paul said morosely, and looked out the window' (ibid.: 523). At the end of the novel Paul kills Annie by feeding her the burning pages of his manuscript after she falls over the typewriter.

One of the most terrifying things about Annie Wilkes is that she is oblivious to Paul-King's concerns with the act of writing, and that she therefore provides an interpretive model of the 'Constant Reader' distant from his own, and beyond his authorial control:

> He saw she was barely listening. This was the second time she'd shown not the slightest interest in a trick of the trade that would have held a class of would-be writers spellbound. The reason, he thought, was simplicity itself. Annie Wilkes was the perfect audience, a woman who loved stories without having the slightest interest in the mechanics of making them. She was the embodiment of that Victorian archetype, the Constant Reader.
>
> (ibid.: 488)

More disturbingly still, this child-murdering psycho *does* turn out to be Paul's ideal reader – steeped in the conventions of her chosen genre (the historical romance), she is a highly effective commentator on *Misery's Return*: 'Constant Reader had just become Merciless Editor. ... She really was Constant Reader, but Constant Reader did not mean Constant Sap' (ibid.: 517–18). Annie is right about one thing in particular, which is that Paul is a far better genre novelist than he is a writer of 'serious' fiction. Paul has killed off his heroine Misery Chastain in order to concentrate on his Great American Novel, *Fast Cars*, a novel which is, on the evidence we get, woeful. This is surely intentional on King's part, since he himself is an untiring champion of popular literature, and *Misery* is ultimately a vindication of genre fiction, with Paul learning the (very) hard way that it is *Misery's Return* and not *Fast Cars* which will be his masterwork.

This perceived duality of genre fiction and literary fiction, of which King is acutely aware, is explored even more radically in *The Dark Half*. Here, Thad Beaumont, a penurious writer of serious fiction, literally splits himself in two. His pseudonym and monstrous *alter ego*, George Stark, is a two-fisted writer of a series of bestselling pulp thrillers featuring the exploits of his brutal anti-hero, Alexis Machine (!). The novel begins with Beaumont, recently tenured and thus now financially secure, killing Stark off to concentrate on his 'real' writing – but Stark refuses to die, rising from his fake grave ('George Stark 1975–1988 Not a Very Nice Guy') (King 1989:

18) to wreak Alexis Machine-type havoc on Beaumont's life. King's 'Author's Note' to *The Dark Half* reads as follows: 'I'm indebted to the late Richard Bachman for his help and inspiration. This novel could not have been written without him.' If Thad Beaumont is Stephen King, then the late George Stark can only be the late Richard Bachman, who is of course Stephen King's own pseudonymous alter-ego, author of *Thinner*, *The Running Man*, and other books. Not a very nice guy ...

'If you go down to the woods today ...'

In October of 1994, three student film-makers disappeared in the woods near Burkittsville, Maryland while shooting a documentary.
A year later their footage was found.

Thus opens the cinema phenomenon of 1999, *The Blair Witch Project*. Directed by a pair of Florida film-school graduates, Daniel Meyrick and Eduardo Sanchez, and given extraordinary advance publicity by an imaginative Internet campaign, this tale of three film students, Heather, Josh and Mike, lost in the woods of Maryland and seemingly menaced by supernatural forces, was a runaway success because it apparently managed to convince large sections of the viewing public that what they were watching was not fiction but documentary reality. *The Blair Witch Project*'s claim to veracity was absolute and, it would seem, absolutely successful.

What *Blair Witch* really capitalized on was its audience's collective *desire* to believe in the reality of what they saw. Any kind of reflection on the object in front of their eyes would surely have dispelled the film's claims. For one thing, it is a film which closes with the deaths of all three film-makers, and thus a kind of 'snuff-movie'. Whether snuff-movies actually exist or are urban myths is a subject of considerable debate, but one thing is certain: if they do exist, they are highly illegal, and do not get screenings in every cinema in the country (see Kerekes and Slater 1995). It is massively unlikely that you have ever seen a genuine snuff-movie, whereas you may well have seen *Blair Witch*. Rather, what the audience was responding to was a series of cinematic cues and devices which traditionally signify 'reality': shooting on video rather than film (though *Blair Witch* alternates these two media); blurry, jerky, 'hand-held' camera-work; the lack of a 'classic' three-act cinematic structure; the presence of amateur or semiprofessional actors (heightened in this instance by the fact that the actors themselves had little idea what they were letting themselves in for, and *were* being terrorized in the woods by the directors).

The documentary style of *Blair Witch* serves, indeed, to draw attention to its own fictionality and artfulness in ways in which the 'neutral' style of classic American cinema, though ostensibly more formalized, does not. This it does both stylistically and by self-consciously foregrounding a number of generic conventions. First, *Blair Witch* is in essence an updating of one of the oldest of all Gothic devices – here, the found manuscript of *The Castle of Otranto* is technologically updated as the found videotape. This device also occurs on film in, for example, *Ring*, in which a 'curse video', recorded from a TV channel which isn't there, portends death to whoever watches ('You will die in one week,' says the woman on the tape, which attains the status of urban legend), and in fiction in Mark Z. Danielewski's brilliant, encyclopaedic, infuriating *House of Leaves* (2000). This is purportedly the account by Zampanó, a blind polymath (Borges, obviously) of *The Navidson Record*, a celebrated photographer's documentary film of his exploration of a terrifying, other-dimensional labyrinth (with its own minotaur-like monster) which mysteriously appears in his own house (Danielewski 2000). As such, it is tempting to read Danielewski's novel as a gargantuan extension of Borges's 'The House of Asterion', a tale set in a labyrinth which is likened to infinity, narrated by the minotaur himself.

Second, *Blair Witch* is generically a work of regional Gothic (another 'city slicker' narrative of urban folks in trouble in the country), and thus it opens with a series of mock-interviews with locals, who tell of local legends and atrocities. The film's generic status is itself frequently commented upon: when they first come upon the weird piles of stones which dot the woods, Josh asks, 'You ever seen *Deliverance*?'; later, on coming upon the glade of stick-men hanging from the trees, he notes: 'No redneck is this creative.' It seems that the film-makers meet their sticky end because they have disturbed an Indian burial ground. As *The Shining*, *Poltergeist*, *From Dusk Till Dawn* and numerous other films testify, the Disturbed Indian Burial Ground is such a Usual Suspect in horror narratives that it is almost a generic archetype itself.

The 'official' documentary which Heather, Josh and Mike set out to make, shot in black and white and on film, is inter-cut with the footage of the making of the movie, on video. In this, *Blair Witch*'s unacknowledged source is a far more notorious (and far more effective) quasi-snuff-movie, Deodato's *Cannibal Holocaust* (Kerekes and Slater quite accurately describe *Blair Witch* as '*Cannibal Holocaust*-Lite') (2000: 113). Like the film-makers in *Cannibal Holocaust*, Josh, Heather and Mike perpetually film each other, and film each other filming, consistently foregrounding what they, and the film, are setting out to do. Shortly before his disappearance, Josh apparently loses control and screams at Heather, but what he screams when out of control is the rhetoric of film-directing:

> OK, here's your motivation. You're lost. You're angry in the woods and no one here is here to help you. There's a fucking witch and she keeps leaving shit outside the door. There's no one here to help you. She left little trinkets. You fucking took one of them. She ran after you. There's no one here to help you. We walked for fifteen hours today – we ended up in the

same place. That's your motivation! That's your motivation!
... No, she's still making movies, man. That's my point.

At one point, Mike even says to Heather, encapsulating the ideas behind
Blair Witch itself, and many of the works discussed in this chapter: 'I see
why you like this video camera so much. ... It's not quite reality. ... It's
totally, like, filtered reality, man. It's like you can pretend everything's not
quite the way it is.'

Notes

1. Victor Fargas (Jack Taylor), in *The Ninth Gate*, an adaptation of Arturo Pérez-
   Reverte's novel *The Dumas Club* (Pérez-Reverte 1999), which posits an all
   powerful *grimoire*, the *Delomelonicon*, as old as human civilization, of which
   all subsequent *grimoires*, including the novel's own *The Book of Nine Doors*
   and, presumably, the *Necronomicon* itself, form a subset. See Chapter 8 for a
   fuller discussion of *The Ninth Gate*.
2. For an account of the anti-modernity and racist ideologies which motivated
   many High Modernist writers, see Carey (1992). For the anti-modernity of
   modernism, see Harvey (1989: 10–38).
3. Reproduced in Barker (1997: 54). The film features Dean Stockwell as a dashing,
   white-suited Wilbur Whately, far removed from the gigantic goat-octopus of
   Lovecraft's original. Unquestionably, this is partly because the film is a product
   of James H. Nicholson and Samuel Z. Arkoff's celebrated low-budget
   exploitation studios, American International Pictures (the studio responsible for
   many of Roger Corman's films), and thus had a non-existent effects budget.
4. Borges's scepticism notwithstanding, the influence of Lovecraft on his own
   writing is, in places, palpable: the mad city of 'The Immortal', for example, in
   which conventional scale and geometry break down, seems to me to have been
   lifted directly from Lovecraft's 'non-Euclidean' city of R'lyeh in 'The Call of
   Cthulhu'.
5. For a brief account of the *Necronomicon*'s afterlife, on which I draw here, see
   Newman (1996: 231). Lovecraft's novel *The Case of Charles Dexter Ward*
   (1927–8) is reprinted in Lovecraft (1993: 141–301).
6. Newman (1996: 231) credits authorship to George Hay.
7. The same piece quotes Dana Andrews: Hal was a real little schmuck. ... He
   would come up and start telling Jacques how to direct the picture. Jacques
   would say, 'Now, now, Hal' and try to be nice. But I just said, 'Look, you little
   son-of-a-bitch, you want me to walk off the picture? I didn't come all the way
   over here to have the producer tell me what he thinks about directing the
   picture. Let the director direct the picture!'
8. Like most commentators, Clarens considers the demon's inclusion 'atrocious',
   suggesting that 'It is a tribute to the director's skill that his movie survives such
   a monumental blunder' (1997: 145).
9. Borges (1970: 282). Although this volume, *Labyrinths*, has been superseded by
   the *Collected Fictions* (Borges 1998), its translations are more accomplished
   (though not necessarily more faithful), and thus the translations I cite will be
   from *Labyrinths*, except in those instances of works which only appear in the
   Collected Fictions.
10. For Borges on linear time, see 'A New Refutation of Time' (Borges 1970:
    252–70).
11. King gives a clear account of his own sources and interests in King (1982). See,
    for example, pp. 260–2 for his thoughts on *The Twilight Zone* and *The Outer
    Limits*.

|6|

Them!

Narratives of pestilence and invasion

In a televised debate on horror broadcast for Halloween 1991, the director John Carpenter theorized that all horror narratives were fundamentally divisible into two groups, which he called 'left-wing' and right-wing' horror.[1] In 'left-wing' horror narratives, the source of the threat is within. That is, it posits an internal agency of horror: that which we have to fear is located within ourselves, in the human mind and its potential for creation or destruction, and in the human body and its potential for metamorphosis or mutilation. *Frankenstein* might be said to be the archetype for this kind of horror. Conversely, in 'right-wing' horror, the threat comes from without, something other, alien and external to humanity, which is coming to get 'us' remorselessly, and against which we must guard if we can. The archetype for *this* kind of horror would then be *Dracula*, and its set of fears and attitudes are given notable articulation by Reese (Michael Biehn) in James Cameron's *The Terminator* (1984): 'Listen, and understand! That Terminator is out there! It can't be bargained with. It can't be reasoned with. It doesn't feel pity, or remorse, or fear. And it absolutely will not stop, ever, until you are dead!'

Obviously, this division of Carpenter's is provisional and somewhat crude, and yet it does provide a useful starting-point for the analysis of many of the subjects of this book. By this reading, for example, the mad scientists of Chapter 2 and the psychos of Chapter 3 are obviously examples of the genre's 'left-wing' tendencies, while the questionable foreigners of Chapter 1 and the vampires of Chapter 3 give rise to 'right-wing' fears – as also they give symbolic articulation to a set of fears commonly associated with the actual political right, fears of invasion from without, of immigration and immigrants, of the pollution or swamping of an indigenous national culture by mysterious, oriental, uncivilized or otherwise alien peoples. These, too, are to be the subjects of this chapter. Given many of the recent pronouncements and concerns of, for example, the British political right, both 'mainstream' and extreme, it is tempting, and not entirely inaccurate, to suggest that these narratives articulate or comment upon, through their images of threats from monstrous aliens, relentless supernatural forces, or seemingly unstoppable killer diseases, fears of what we would now call multiculturalism. Their condition, then, is one of *paranoia*.

In using this term, Andrew Tudor's fundamental distinction in horror narratives between 'security' and 'paranoia', while surely broadly correct, is too narrowly defined (1989: 211–24). For Tudor, this distinction is dependent on a film's closure: closed narratives, films which conclude with the unambiguous destruction of the threat, are secure, while open narratives, which avoid resolution and close with the threatening agency undestroyed or even triumphant, are paranoid. However, it seems to me that security and paranoia are as much cultural conditions here as they are narrative tropes. Thus, those narratives in which a threat is used to define or shore up a dominant or indigenous culture (*The Monk*, for example, or in this chapter the novels of James Herbert) might be called 'secure', while those narratives in which cultural norms are relativized or problematized (*The Wicker Man*, *Night of the Living Dead*) are paranoid. This distinction is apparent in the radically differing ideologies of two versions of the same narrative – in the 'paranoid' British imperial disquiet of H.G. Wells's *The War of the Worlds*, and in the 'secure' American imperial triumphalism of *Independence Day*.

In the 1890s, at the height of British imperial expansion and confidence, a number of lastingly influential paranoid narratives appeared, foremost amongst them *Dracula* (1897) and *The War of the Worlds* (1898). Such visions of an imperilled Victorian England were not in themselves new. The year 1871 saw the publication of Sir George Tomkyns Chesney's *The Battle of Dorking: Reminiscences of a Volunteer*, which, with its vision of a German invasion and conquest of England beginning in the Home Counties, was a great popular success and led directly to a cottage industry of sequels, spin-offs and rip-offs: Charles Stone's *What Happened After the Battle of Dorking; or, The Victory in Tunbridge Wells* (1871); M. Moltruhn's *The Other Side at the Battle of Dorking* (1871); Arthur Sketchley's *Mrs. Brown at the Battle of Dorking* (1871); *The Battle off Worthing; or, Why the Invaders Never Got to Dorking* (1887), by 'A Captain of the Royal Navy'; and, written after Stoker and Wells, Col. Fredric Nautsch's *The New Battle of Dorking* (1900). Wells himself imagined a successful German war on England in *The War in the Air* (1908) (this war is hugely destructive, its mass slaughter compounded by the spread of the devastating plague, the Purple Death), while Saki's *When William Came* (1913) envisages, on the eve of the First World War, an England already under German rule.[2]

But the most successful *Mitteleuropean* invader of Victorian England was not Count Bismarck but Count Dracula. In his essay 'The Occidental Tourist: *Dracula* and the Anxiety of Reverse Colonization', Stephen D. Arata writes:

Transylvania was known primarily as part of the vexed 'Eastern Question' that so obsessed Britain's foreign policy in the 1880s and 90s. The region was first and foremost the site, not of superstition and Gothic romance, but of political turbulence and racial strife. Victorian readers knew the Carpathians largely for its [*sic*] endemic cultural upheaval and its fostering of a dizzying succession of empires. By moving Castle Dracula there, Stoker gives distinctly political overtones to his Gothic narrative. In Stoker's version of the myth, vampires are intimately linked to military conquest and to the rise and fall of empires.

(1997: 462–3)

Count Dracula himself says to Jonathan Harker that 'we [the Szekelys] were a conquering race' (Stoker 1997: 34), and this eastern conqueror, with his hordes of rats and other vermin, including the undead themselves, is heading like Chesney's Hun or Wells's Martians for the heart of the British empire, suburban London and the Home Counties.

The War of the Worlds opens with what was, for 1898, with the Boer War raging, an unimaginable statement of cultural relativism, positing a culture sufficiently technologically advanced as to render the English not only their colonial subjects, but their evolutionary inferiors and indeed their food – to be treated like livestock, or the subjects of vivisection or biological experimentation:

No one would have believed in the last years of the nineteenth century that this world was being watched, keenly and closely by intelligences greater than man's and yet as mortal as his own; that as men busied themselves about their various concerns they were being scrutinized and studied, perhaps almost as narrowly as a man with a microscope might scrutinise the transient creatures that swarm and multiply in a drop of water. ... Yet across the gulf of space, minds that are to our minds as ours are to those of the beasts that perish, intellects vast and cool and unsympathetic, regarded this earth with envious eyes, and slowly and surely drew their plans against us.

(Wells 1995b: 185)

Wells was a trained biologist, and the novel continually returns to this comparison of humanity to 'lesser' animals: 'The Martians took as much notice of such advances as we should of the lowing of a cow'; 'the Martian machine took no more notice for the moment of the people running this way and that than a man would of the confusion of ants in a nest which his foot had kicked'; 'did they interpret our spurts of fire ... as we should the furious unanimity of onslaught in a disturbed hive of bees'; 'It never was a war, any more than there's a war between men and ants. ... We're eatable ants'; and, most significantly, 'So some respectable dodo in the Mauritius might have lorded it in his nest, and discussed the arrival of a shipful of pitiless sailors in want of animal food. "We will peck them to death tomorrow, my dear."' (ibid.: 213, 230, 247, 299, 207). One of the things this does is effectively to reverse many of the (spurious) claims of Social Darwinist thinkers of the time, which constructed an inherently superior ideal of Englishness on evolutionary grounds: other races, or the working class, or criminals were simply an inferior evolutionary type to the modern, upper-middle-class Englishman. Here, that very Englishman is himself a species of cattle. As John Carey has argued, Wells could be wildly self-contradictory in his beliefs, particularly about the desirable future for humanity: like many intellectuals of his time (Yeats, Shaw, Lawrence) he *was* drawn to the eugenics movement, at least in theory (though he considered its aims impractical), and his fears about an overpopulated world did lead him to advocate the compulsory sterilization of certain groups (Carey 1992: 118–51). In practice, though, much of his fiction tended to undermine his pronouncements, and in *The War of the Worlds*, the advocate of a new Utopian human society based on selective breeding, the Putney artilleryman, is finally dismissed by the narrator as a 'strange undisciplined dreamer of great things' (Wells 1995b: 306).

Giving them, as it were, a taste of their own medicine, Wells presents the English as helpless in the face of a technologically superior colonizing power, and completely unprepared for any threat to their own status as global superpower: 'They've ... crippled the greatest power in the world. They've walked over us' (ibid.: 299). Thus, while the Martian conquest is certainly facilitated by, for example, poor communications between Weybridge and London, it is also helped immeasurably by complacency, a refusal to take the threat seriously, to believe that English military superiority could be compromised – in spite of the fact that it was *already* showing signs of compromise during the Boer War, and would be effectively brought to an end by the First World War, where mass slaughter in the trenches was in part a consequence of this military complacency – a future spookily anticipated in Wells's famous description of the Martian Conquest: 'It was the beginning of the rout of civilisation, of the massacre of mankind' (ibid.: 260). Initially, though, the arrival of the Martians is subordinated to traditional European political concerns: 'Many people had heard of the cylinder, of course, but it certainly did not make the sensation that an ultimatum to Germany would have done' (ibid.: 208).

'What are these Martians?' the narrator is asked by the crazed curate, who can only interpret their presence as the punishment of a vengeful God for humanity's sins. 'What are we?' is the narrator's answer (Wells 1995b: 235). If the Martians in *The War of the Worlds* are, symbolically, the English, then who are the actual English in the novel? The answer, it seems to me, is something very like the Irish. For one thing, the novel effectively reverses the terms of Swift's *A Modest Proposal* by presenting the *English* as livestock – Mars, more ancient than the Earth, has run out of food; the Martians are here in part to breed and farm people in order to eat them (more specifically, like Count Dracula, they've come to drink the blood of Englishmen).[3] More seriously, though, the English are here like the Irish in that they become a nation of enforced émigrés, driven from their homeland by starvation and oppressive colonization. In one of the novel's most telling scenes, the narrator's brother and his companions, fleeing as part of 'The Exodus from London' (as the title of one chapter has it), arrive at the Essex coast, where they come upon a vast crowd, what survives of six million Londoners, all desperate to get out of the country:

> For after the sailors could no longer come up the Thames, they came on to the Essex coast, to Harwich and Walton and Clacton, and afterwards to Foulness and Shoebury, to bring off the people. They lay in a huge sickle-shaped curve that vanished into the mist at last towards the Naze. Close inshore was a multitude of fishing-smacks – English, Scotch, French, Dutch, and Swedish; steam-launches from the Thames, yachts, electric boats; and beyond were ships of large burden, a multitude of filthy colliers, trim merchantmen, cattle-ships, passenger-boats, petroleum-tanks, ocean tramps, an old white transport even, neat white and grey liners from Southampton and Hamburg; and along the blue coast across the Blackwater my brother could make out dimly a dense swarm of boats chaffering with the people on the beach, a swarm which also extended up the Blackwater almost to Maldon.
>
> (ibid.: 262)

Wells was a brilliant reader of his own times, and thus could seem uncannily prescient: the novel's vision of mass evacuations, of a displaced populace fleeing for its life from a terrifying enemy, is one which has any number of resonances across the twentieth century, not least with events in Nazi Germany (as of course does his comment about 'the rout of civilisation ... the massacre of mankind'). In the *nineteenth* century, however, the readiest local model for the creation of this kind of enforced diaspora would have come from Ireland.

As the twentieth century wore on, paranoid English imperial fantasies of invasion were forced to give way to the post-imperial realities of multicultural life, particularly in urban centres. These in turn produced their own fears. In 1968, the Conservative Cabinet Minister Enoch Powell delivered his noxious 'Rivers of Blood' speech, prophesying a dire future of an England swamped by immigrants, and consequently riven by strife and violence. As ever, what was really being articulated here was a fear of *black* immigrants, particularly of Afro-Caribbean and Indian subcontinent immigration, and Powell's speech (which quite rightly spelled the end of his career as a mainstream politician) led directly to the rise of the racist National Front in the 1970s, a neo-Nazi organization determined to keep England 'white' and which enjoyed some measure of support, particularly among the white working class of the inner cities.

It is in this context that the publication in 1974 of James Herbert's *The Rats* must be understood. Unfortunately, the time was ripe for Herbert's best-selling tale of London under siege, invaded by a horde of plague-bearing black rats. You are never more than five feet away from a rat, and rats have thus become potent symbolic vehicles for the articulation of fears of secret, deadly invasion, as well as being genuine objects of terror in themselves, as they are for Winston Smith in George Orwell's *1984*, itself another novel of dystopian London. Just as the scene in Murnau's *Nosferatu* where Max Schreck's semitic Graf Orlock gets off the death-ship at Bremen bringing with him a plague of rats has clear and tragic resonances for Weimar Germany[4] – fears of invasion by Jews, who must, like vermin, be eradicated – so Herbert's agenda is sufficiently clear and crude as to warrant a clear, crude statement: for black rats, read black *people*. And the rats *are* immigrants, brought back from New Guinea by a zoologist, the suspiciously Germanic-sounding Professor Schiller; they interbreed with the local population to produce a deadly mutant strain. The social agenda here seems hardly to require comment.

The National Front and later the British National Party made political capital from genuine working-class feelings of abandonment and disenfranchisement, particularly in inner London, in places like Millwall and the Isle of Dogs (where, in 1993, Derek Beacon was elected as a local councillor – so far the only BNP candidate to receive a popular mandate). So too does *The Rats* identify a genuine sense of social crisis, repeatedly commenting on living conditions in the East End, on slum-clearance and the catastrophic mistakes of town-planners, which create the circumstances under which the rats can breed:

> Civilized London. Swinging London. Dirty bloody London! ...
>
> But what disgusted him more? The vermin themselves, or the fact that it could only happen in East London? Not Hampstead or Kensington, but Poplar. Was it the old prejudices against the middle and upper classes, the councils that took the working class from their slums and put them into tall, remote concrete towers, telling them they'd never been better off, but never realizing that forty homes in a block of flats become forty separate cells for people, communication between them confined to conversation in the lift, was it this that really angered him? That these same councils could allow the filth that could produce vermin such as the black rats.
>
> (Herbert 1999: 61–2)

The novel's protagonist (and Herbert's mouthpiece), Harris, is, like Herbert himself, a product of the East End made (relatively) good, an old-school working-class socialist (which political stance certainly need not preclude racism) and vigorous quasi-intellectual. He is an art teacher in an inner-city comprehensive, thus sensitive and socially concerned, who distinguishes himself from his colleagues in his insistence on reading *The Daily Mirror* rather that *The Guardian*: so, no wet liberal he:

> He'd come from the same area: the East End had no mystery for him. . . . At thirty-two he was back, teaching little facsimiles of his former self. They'd tried to give him a rough time of it at first, the little bastards, because art, to them, was playtime, and anyone who taught it was queer anyway.
>
> (ibid.: 12)

Not Harris, who operates according to what might charitably be termed an outmoded discourse of masculinity: seeing in his school 'Two giggling girls, both in short skirts. Both with bouncing breasts, both about fourteen years old', he remarks to himself, 'the crumpet's good' (ibid.: 12–13). (Outmoded, yes, and professionally unethical – not to mention here actually illegal.)

Harris is 'embittered' by 'The incompetence of "authority" . . . He was still a student at heart, a rebel against the powers that be' (ibid.: 62–3). Like Harris, the novel itself is consistently scornful of 'authority' – government, civil servants, head teachers, academics, committee-men – as impotent, self-interested, and weak. Set against this is a rugged right-wing individualism embodied by natural leaders and men of action such as Harris himself. The novel's social mechanics are played out in microcosm when the rats attack London Zoo: 'The prouder [animals] stayed to fight, and killed many vermin before they themselves fell, but the majority chose to flee.' Proudest of all is the gorilla, 'the old man of the zoo' (that is, its representative of traditional masculinity), who, though heavily outnumbered, goes down fighting, 'recapturing its ancient primitive majesty, pulling the rats apart with its great hands, crushing their bones with its immense strength, tossing them away like limp rags' (ibid.: 165–6).

Along with (coexistent with) the novel's version of the 'ancient primitive majesty' of masculinity under threat comes a vision of traditional, but vanishing, Englishness. Escaping embattled London for a cultural visit to Stratford-upon-Avon, 'he expected to find quaint, olde-worlde, oak-beamed houses in cobbled streets', but is disappointed instead to find pubs with fake wooden beams made of plastic (later in the novel, he finds himself in a pub drinking keg bitter on imitation leather seats with Foskins, the man from the ministry). But not even Shakespeare's birthplace is safe from the hordes of foreign invaders: 'Walking towards the Royal Shakespeare Theatre he saw that many of the streets had managed to retain their old charm, after all, but it was the throngs of people, *multi-racial accents*, that destroyed any hope of atmosphere' (ibid.: 69, my emphasis).

The novel is structured around a series of set pieces, in which the rats attack a number of institutions (the London Underground, London Zoo, Harris's school), interspersed with scenes of individual carnage. Here, as throughout his entire *œuvre*, Herbert deploys a startling narrative technique, which is to give the reader mini-biographies of characters who are then bloodily despatched. Often, these narratives fall within Herbert's strict moral compass, presenting characters who transgress the norms of his social and sexual agenda and thus, it is strongly implied, somehow deserve their fates – because of their blackness or un-Englishness, their inability to survive in the social-Darwinist world of the modern city (he has a particular fondness for doing away with homeless people), their sexual deviance, lack of masculinity, or (in women) promiscuity. *The Rats* opens with Henry Guilfoyle (even his un-Saxon name suggestive for Herbert, I suspect, of effeteness), a gay salesman who, tortured by the heteronormative demands of the milieu in which he operates, takes to the bottle and ends up as a down-and-out. In other hands, Guilfoyle's life might have been the subject for tragedy, or at least pathos, but here he's just rat-food. As is Mary Kelly, another homeless person – an Irishwoman driven mad by sex and Catholicism (so, no stereotyping here, then), who, after the death of her prodigious lover Timothy Patrick (crushed by a tank!), 'went to live with a group of Pakistani immigrants in Brick Lane and stayed there for several years, being used by all the men either collectively or singly', and who ends up masturbating with a liquor bottle (ibid.: 34). As is Errol Johnson, 'that daft ape Errol', according to his supervisor, a 'coloured' subway worker who, on seeing the rats swarming into the station, panics and throws himself in front of a train (ibid.: 78–9).

'Keep watching the sky!'

'Vampires,' Nina Auerbach notes, 'go where power is' (1995: 6). So too, and for the same reasons, do alien invaders, and as the twentieth century progressed America took over from England as the primary site of invasion narratives. And so it was that on the evening of 30 October 1938, a programme of music by Ramon Raquello and his orchestra, broadcast from the Park Plaza Hotel, New York, was interrupted by the following announcement:

> Ladies and gentlemen, we interrupt our program of dance music to bring you a special bulletin from the Intercontinental Radio News. At twenty minutes before eight, central time, Professor Farrell of the Mount Jennings Observatory, Chicago,

Illinois, reports observing several explosions of incandescent gas, occurring at regular intervals on the planet Mars.

(Higham 1986: 125)

The broadcast returned to Ramon Raquello, only to be interrupted again shortly afterwards by a newsflash from Wilmuth Farm, Grovers Mill, where reporter Carl Phillips, along with Professor Pierson of Princeton University, described the landing of a flaming object, 'about thirty yards' in diameter, made of yellowish-white metal: Phillips informed listeners:

> This end of the thing is beginning to flake off! The top is beginning to rotate like a screw! The thing must be hollow! ... I can see peering out of that black hole two luminous disks ... Are they eyes? It might be a face ... It might be ... Good heavens, something's wriggling out of the shadow like a grey snake.

The Martians had landed!

Many listeners, switching over after the end of the popular ventriloquist programme, *The Edgar Bergen and Charlie McCarthy Show*, has missed the beginning of the broadcast, and thus did not realize that they were listening to Orson Welles's Mercury Theatre adaptation of *The War of the Worlds*, a classic (perhaps *the* classic) instance of the kinds of technique for documentary veracity discussed in Chapter 5. Panic ensued, with rioting, looting and violence across the United States as the terror-stricken population sought to protect themselves from the invading Martians. But, as Charles Higham notes, what was genuinely disturbing about Welles's broadcast was what it revealed about the state of the nation in 1938, on the eve of the Second World War:

> Far from marshalling, or even attempting to marshal, a coherent response to what they believed were invading forces, red-blooded Americans had fled like children before Welles's Halloween gimmick. What would happen if there were a real invasion? What would happen if long-distance aircraft allowed the German airforce to bomb New York?

(ibid.: 128)

War of the Worlds was filmed in 1953 by special effects maestro George Pal who, like Orson Welles, shifted the location of invasion to what was by then the great post-war superpower, the USA. Pal's is one of a famous series of movies from the 1950s depicting alien invasions of America (or still, on occasion, Britain), all of which reflect or articulate a sense of Cold War paranoia. Here, America and its values are consistently presented as under threat of invasion from enemies Without, or infiltration from Within. Indeed, the 'baby-boom horror' milieu which produced a generation of notable American horror writers and directors – Stephen King, but also Wes Craven,

John Carpenter, Tobe Hooper and, most importantly for our purposes here, George A. Romero – is best viewed as itself a product of these early years of the Cold War. Thus, throughout the 1950s, these future *auteurs* and their contemporaries thrilled to such visions of an imperilled Earth/America (the two are essentially indistinguishable) as *The Thing*, *The Man From Planet X* (where the invasion takes place on a remote Scottish island), *The Day the Earth Stood Still* (where a benign alien, Klaatu, comes with a warning about humanity's capacity for self-destruction – he wants to put an end to nuclear testing), *Red Planet Mars*, *It Came From Outer Space*, *Invaders From Mars*, *Phantom From Space* and *Killers From Space*, *This Island Earth*, *The Quatermass Experiment* (the first in a successful series), and numerous others. While these films do vary ideologically, from the liberal pacifism of *The Day the Earth Stood Still* to the hawkish McCarthyism of *Red Planet Mars*, nevertheless they are best understood as a group, reflective of the concerns of the society and the times which produced them.

The best and most interesting of these films, and one worth studying at some length, is Don Siegel's great *Invasion of the Body Snatchers*. Like *The Thing*, *Body Snatchers* has as its hostile aliens a vegetable lifeform (growing in seedpods), soulless and unindividuated. What is most interesting about Siegel's film is that it works simultaneously on two ostensibly opposing levels, as a document of Cold War paranoia (for soulless vegetables, read Communists), and as a startling parable of 1950s' conformity, where the aim is to make everyone exactly the same. It is this interpretive doubleness, I think, which has allowed for the film's two impressively self-standing remakes: Philip Kaufman's (1978) *Body Snatchers* is best viewed along with *All the President's Men*, *Three Days of the Condor*, *The Parallax View* and others, as part of a series of 1970s' films concerned with (post-)Watergate conspiracy theories and the rottenness of American political institutions; while Abel Ferrara's visceral (1994) *Body Snatchers* continues its director's interest, from *The Driller Killer* onwards, with the problems of radical individualism in a conformist (American) modernity.

In Siegel's *Body Snatchers*, Dr Miles Bennell (Kevin McCarthy) returns to his hometown of Santa Mira, California, with the mounting suspicion that 'Something evil had taken over the town.' The film begins with an accumulation of seemingly banal details. Miles has a townful of patients, none of whom will say what's the matter with them. The Grimaldis' vegetable stand is closed and derelict, whereas a month earlier it had been the cleanest stall in town; little Jimmy Grimaldi runs away because he thinks his mother isn't his mother. The restaurant has been empty for the last three weeks. Wilma suspects that her Uncle Ira is an impostor:

> There's something missing. He's been a father to me since I was a baby. Always when he looked at me there was a special look in his eye – that look's gone. ... There's no emotion, none. Just the pretence of it.

'The trouble is inside *you*,' Miles says to Wilma, and refers her to a psychiatrist, Dr Kaufman, the film's embodiment of rational scepticism, who detects 'an epidemic of mass hysteria' caused by 'worry about what's going on in the world, probably'. Just such a worry is voiced by Miles himself, who wonders whether the alien pods are the mutant products of nuclear testing.

The family is the greatest site of vulnerability in *Body Snatchers*, as it was later to be in *Village of the Damned*, based on John Wyndham's *The Midwich Cuckoos*, where a series of women are impregnated by an alien force and give birth to a group of evil telepaths. Miles's friend Jack Belicec finds a pod version of himself and his own family growing in his greenhouse; a mother takes a pod to her child's room, telling him, 'There'll be no more tears'; Miles's girlfriend Becky is turned in front of his eyes: 'A moment's sleep and the girl I loved was an inhuman enemy, bent on my destruction.' Normal affective bonds have broken down, no guarantee against the threat from the pods: 'I wasn't sure now there was anyone I could trust,' Miles says, and looks out at the town, all changed, 'people I've known all my life'. It is Miles who makes the film's central plea for a restoration of these affective bonds:

> In my practice, I've seen how people allow their humanity to drain away. Only it happens slowly instead of all at once – they didn't seem to mind. ... We harden our hearts, grow callous – only when we have to fight to remain human do we know how precious it is, how dear.

As the film draws to a close, *all* its authority figures – parents, police, Dr Kaufman, the FBI, even, it is implied, the governor's office in Sacramento (unfortunately not occupied by Ronald Reagan in 1956) – have become pods, and Miles's narrative closes with the justly celebrated scene where he frantically attempts to stop traffic on the highway – a lone, apparently crazy figure – which closes with an extreme close-up on Miles's face as he addresses the viewer directly: 'They're here already! *You're next!*'

Last Men and killer diseases

The scientific endeavour of the Enlightenment had produced a new interest in the possibility of greatly extending the span of human life. The third book of Jonathan Swift's *Gulliver's Travels* (which, remember, Shelley's Roger Dodsworth claimed to have read), the voyage to Laputa, is in part a Menippean satire – that is, a satire on the follies of knowledge. On the island of Luggnagg, you'll remember, Gulliver encounters 'the *struldbruggs* or *immortals*', doomed perpetually to age, but never to die: 'They were the most mortifying sight I ever beheld', Gulliver says (Swift 1976: 168–73).

Gulliver's remark, before meeting the *struldbruggs*, that gifted with immortality he should become 'the oracle of the nation', should remind us that the archetype for the *struldbruggs* is surely the Sibyl of Cumae, who, in asking for eternal life, neglected to ask also for perpetual youth.

But it is the interest in the beneficial possibilities for humanity of a greatly extended lifespan which is characteristic of what George Sebastian Rousseau has called 'The Geriatric Enlightenment' (Rousseau *c*.2002). Rousseau enumerates literally hundreds of the eighteenth century's prodigious long-livers, whose very fact was understood as an indicator of the progressive nature of humanity – as we progress towards enlightenment, our lifespan increases drastically. Death is, in principle, defeatable; we can live forever. Rousseau does not, however, mention one instance of this kind of thinking which is particularly important to me in this context. At the very end of *Enquiry Concerning Political Justice*, Godwin notes that, were his Enlightenment-anarchist system to be adopted, it would inevitably lead to 'Health and the Prolongation of Human Life' (Godwin 1985: 770–7). It was in part this idea of Godwin's which inspired Thomas Malthus to write his *Essay on the Principles of Population* (1798), subtitled 'On the Speculations of Mr. Godwin, M. Condorcet, and Others'. With population doubling and redoubling, perpetually draining the world's resources, Malthus believed, then a greatly extended human lifespan would be devastating: people needed to die in large numbers to check the problem of runaway population. Thus began a small but significant paper war between Godwin and Malthus. Godwin replied to Malthus in *Of Population: An Enquiry Concerning the Power of Increase in the Numbers of Mankind, being an answer to Mr Malthus's Essay on that Subject* (1820): far from being over-populated, Godwin argued that 'the earth is not peopled'; humanity is 'a little remnant widely scattered over a fruitful and prolific surface' (Godwin 1820: 15–16).

It is this Godwinian view of an under-populated, and of a potentially depopulated world, that informs Mary Shelley's (1826) novel, *The Last Man*, the narrative of Lionel Verney, the sole surviving human being in a world destroyed by plague. The novel's framing narrative has Mary Shelley herself, in 1818, the year of *Frankenstein*'s publication, discovering the cave of the Sibyl (it's near Naples, if you're interested), where she discovers a manuscript from the future – this overturns the standard Gothic trope of the found manuscript, which is usually venerable, signifying the irruption of the past into the present: here it is the irruption of the future into the present.

By the time Shelley gets to it in 1826, the trope of the Last Man was a common or even a hackneyed one. The first Romantic 'Last Man' was Jean-Baptiste François Xavier Cousin de Grainville's *Le Dernier Homme* of 1795, which had been translated anonymously into English as *The Last Man, or Omegarus and Syderia: A Romance in Futurity* in 1806. Shelley had almost certainly read this translation: in it, a man, travelling in Syria, comes upon a cave, 'The Cave of Death', where a ghostly figure – analogous to the Sybil – tells him 'I am the Celestial Spirit to whom eternal futurity is known. All events are to me as if they were passed' (Grainville 1806: 5). He is shown a mirror, in which he sees reflected his own destiny as 'Omegarus', the last man on a world which has been depopulated by a plague which renders humanity sterile – no more children are being born. In 1823, the Scottish poet Thomas Campbell had published his poem 'The Last Man', itself a dream-vision, which images forth the last human being surrounded by skeletons, and rounds up the usual suspects – death, war, famine and pestilence:

> The skeletons of nations were
> Around that lonely man!
> Some had expired in fight – the brands
> Still rusted in their bony hands;
> In plague and famine some!
> Earth's cities had no sound nor tread;
> All ships were drifting with the dead.
> (Campbell 1840: 120–4)

Campbell was the editor of the *New Monthly Magazine*, which published several of Shelley's works, but which declined to publish 'Roger Dodsworth' in 1826. Contemporary reviewers noted similarities between Campbell's poem and Byron's apocalyptic dream-vision, 'Darkness' (and they are very similar, and share with several other Romantic texts, including *Frankenstein* – and, most famously, 'The Rime of the Ancient Mariner' – the image of a ghost- or death-ship). Thomas Lovell Beddoes had himself been planning a drama on this very subject, but gave it up, feeling that the market was already glutted with Last Men. As indeed it was: the *Monthly Magazine* satirized this familiar trope in 1826, with an essay entitled 'The Last Book: with a dissertation on Last Things in General' (Paley 1993: 107).

Into futurity. The name Omegarus might remind us that in 1971, the film *The Omega Man* was released – a Last Man narrative, the story of the last surviving human being after a plague has turned humanity into albino zombies. Following the lead of Shelley and her contemporaries, apocalyptic plague-narratives proliferated during the twentieth century, from Jack London's *The Scarlet Plague* (1915), with its titular overtones of Poe's plague-story 'The Masque of the Red Death', to Stephen King's *The Stand* (1978) in fiction (where the plague is created by military research, and the post-apocalyptic forces of darkness muster in Las Vegas under a Satan-figure called Randall Flagg), and on film *The Andromeda Strain* (a paranoid product of the space race and moon landings, in which a deadly inter-stellar virus hitches a ride to earth on board a satellite, a premise lifted from *Quatermass* and *Night of the Living Dead*) and *Outbreak*, in which an Ebola-type virus threatens to wipe out the USA.[5] *Outbreak* stemmed in part from concerns amongst virologists in the 1990s about the human immune system's increasing inability to cope with rapidly mutating diseases, a series of dire warnings gathered together in Laurie Garrett's acclaimed bestseller *The Coming Plague: Newly Emerging Diseases in a World out of Balance* (1994), with its compelling narratives of the Marburg, Lassa and Ebola viruses, each more deadly then the last (Garrett herself had won a Pulitzer Prize for reporting on Ebola). Apocalyptic, too, was the rhetoric of moral outrage accompanying the discovery and spread of AIDS in the 1980s. With its origins, like Lassa and Ebola, in Africa, and thus carrying more than a whiff of postcolonial anxiety (symbolically, the disease was immigration by another means), and with its exclusive association in the popular imagination with gay sex and thus with deviancy, the disease afforded certain conservative commentators what appeared to be a legitimate opportunity to voice otherwise unacceptable prejudices, seeing AIDS simultaneously as a consequence of sexual deviance and a vehicle for divine retribution. This, for example, is Ray Mills, a columnist for the *Daily Star* newspaper, writing in 1986:

> Hang 'em, flog 'em, castrate 'em and send 'em home. ... The freaks proclaim their twisted morality nightly on TV. ... Where it may end of course is by natural causes. The woofters have had a dreadful plague visited upon them, which we call AIDS. ... Since the perverts offend the laws of God and nature, is it fanciful to suggest that one or both is striking back?
>
> (Davenport-Hines 1990: 336–7)

Almost invisible in this astounding outburst of bile, the exhortation to 'send 'em home' is a return to Powellite rhetoric, a call for the enforced repatriation of an immigrant community, who bring to England deviancy and death.

The Omega Man was based on Richard Matheson's (1954) Last Man novel, *I Am Legend*, and starred Charlton Heston, who was for a brief period in the late 1960s and early 1970s, with this film, plus *Planet of the Apes* and *Soylent Green*, Hollywood's professional Last Man, our official representative at the end of time. In Matheson's original novel, the protagonist Robert Neville is the sole survivor in a world of vampires created by an irradiated virus, the product of nuclear testing, making *I Am Legend* a characteristic 1950s' document. Like many others, Matheson used his invading force as a vehicle to comment on immigration, discrimination, here with a proto-Civil Rights element:

> Friends, I come before you to discuss the vampire; a minority element if ever there was one, and there was one.
>
> But to concision: I will sketch out the basis of my thesis, which thesis is this: Vampires are prejudiced against.

> The keynote of minority prejudice is this: They are loathed
> because they are feared. . . .
>   Robert Neville grunted a surly grunt. Sure, sure, he thought,
> but would you let your sister marry one?
>
> (Matheson 1995: 31–2)

The novel closes on a relativist note with Neville's realization that, as the Last Man, *he*, and not the vampires, is the ethnic minority, and that given his vampire-hunting existence *he* is the ruthless predator, or even the mass-murderer, who deserves to be hunted and killed. The vampires are the victims of a plague, not the embodiments of evil. The monstrosity is his.

But it is surely the *Terminator* movies, our truest modern Frankensteins, that are the legatees of Shelley and her Last Men. Imaging forth a future where humanity is destroyed by its own creation (memorably embodied by Arnold Schwarzenegger), the first *Terminator* movie is the narrative of a man, Reese, who returns from the future, with a warning for mankind, and to save humanity. Whatever the poet's intentions, the illustrator to Thomas Campbell's *Poetical Works* was convinced that the Last Man was Jesus Christ: his poem was accompanied by a woodcut depicting the second coming, with Christ at the end of time surrounded by a valley of dry bones. *Terminator*, too, brings this Christological interpretation to the Last Man. Sarah Connor is impregnated by Reese, giving birth to young John Connor (note the initials), who grows up to be the saviour of humanity, leading the counter-revolution against the machines. It is strongly implicit, I think, that Reese *is* John Connor himself, and not simply his emissary (he bears the photograph of Sarah taken as she flees with John south over the Mexican border, a storm brewing): thus, like Christ, he is simultaneously himself and his own father. *Terminator 2* is subtitled 'Judgement Day', the day of Christian apocalypse here understood as being the day when the machines take over, triggering a nuclear holocaust which destroys much of humanity. Judgement Day, we are told, is 30 August 1997. 30 August 1997 is the two hundredth anniversary, to the day, of the birth of Mary Shelley.

'The Dead Walk!'

In 1968, the year of the assassinations of Martin Luther King and Robert Kennedy and the election of Richard Nixon, and with America mired in an unpopular and unwinnable war in Vietnam, George A. Romero, an independent film-maker from Pittsburgh of great political intelligence, presented audiences with an enduring metaphor for the parlous state of his nation. A satellite probe returns from Venus bringing with it a mysterious form of radiation which causes the dead to rise from their graves and walk as an army, consumed by a mindless craving for human flesh. Thus was born the modern zombie movie, and the modern horror movie: *Night of the Living Dead.*

From the beginning, zombification had provided a ready political metaphor due to its connections with Haitian voodoo and thus with colonialism and particularly slavery. In the first zombie movie, *White Zombie*, Murder Legendre (Bela Lugosi), a slaver by other means, creates an army of zombies to work on his sugar plantation, perpetually turning a giant grinding-wheel in his sugar-mill, a lasting image of dehumanized labour. *I Walked with a Zombie*, based on *Jane Eyre*, anticipates Jean Rhys's *Wide Sargasso Sea* as a West Indian re-vision of a Brontë novel. Betsy Connell (Frances Dee) goes to work as a nurse on a plantation in St Sebastian, caring for Jessica Holland (Christine Gordon), who has become 'a woman without any willpower, unable to speak, or even act by herself – though she will obey simple commands', and becomes embroiled with a zombified slave, Carrefour (Darby Jones). *Plague of the Zombies* has Cornish squire Clive Hamilton (John Carson) returning from Haiti and using the knowledge he has acquired there to create an army of zombie slaves to work in his tin mine. *The Serpent and the Rainbow*, a rare post-Romero voodoo zombie movie, is set in Duvalier-era Haiti (and the Duvaliers *were* said to have used voodoo to cement their brutal regime), and examines the possible medical basis for zombification – though nothing in the movie compares to the altogether more secular horror of Duvalier henchman Zakes Mokae nailing Bill Pullman's scrotum to a chair.

In *Night of the Living Dead* and its two equally impressive sequels, *Dawn of the Dead* and *Day of the Dead*, Romero develops on *The Plague of the Zombies*'s vision of the walking dead as corpses in various stages of decomposition, dispenses with voodoo in favour of a mad-scientific cause of zombification, and adds cannibalism and a wholly new apocalyptic political element. More than anything, it is this combination of nihilism and gore which inaugurates and characterizes much modern horror: one of *Night*'s financial backers was a local butcher whose contribution to the film, as many commentators have noted, is right up there on the screen for all to see. By the closing sequence of *Day*, the cast and crew found themselves vomiting between takes because of the stench of rotting pig's entrails on set.

Night opens with brother and sister Johnny and Barbara arriving at a rural Pennsylvanian cemetery to visit their father's grave. As Johnny clowns and bickers with his sister, a shabbily dressed man staggers towards them, unnoticed until he attacks Johnny, who hits his head on a gravestone and is killed. Barbara (Judith O'Dea) flees to an abandoned farmhouse, where she finds a group of survivors led by Ben (Duane Jones), the first of the series's three heroic black characters (as the last two films also feature strong, self-authorizing female leads, though here Barbara spends most of the film in a catatonic state – Tom Savini's (1990) remake remedies this by featuring Patricia Tallman as a pistol-packing Barbara); these in turn are joined by the Cooper family, led by Karl Hardman's venal, bullying patriarch. Romero's films are as much a study of group dynamics as they are of flesh-eating zombies, and here it is unclear which will prove the more dangerous, the tensions inside the farmhouse or the zombies outside.

Night questions and undermines established American structures of authority on a number of levels. The collapsing family is here figured as a locus of horror. The home becomes a fortress, a site of hostility, claustrophobia and paranoia, boarded up against the unstoppable threats outside, and also, finally, a prison, which affords the survivors scant protection and no escape. As in *Invasion of the Body Snatchers*, traditional familial affective bonds and relationships no longer hold. The film opens with a depiction of Johnny and Barbara's edgy relationship: later, he will return in zombie form to attack her, bent on eating her. The Coopers are a dysfunctional family nominally held together by overbearing patriarchal authority. Their young daughter, bitten by a zombie, responds to her mother's attempts at comfort by attacking and biting her, as she later devours her own father: a memorably grotesque emblem of 1960s' youth revolt against parental values.

Meanwhile, TV and radio stations relay here and in *Dawn of the Dead* a series of confused and misleading broadcasts from an incompetent central government and their impotent scientific authorities, and outside the army of the dead marches relentlessly on. Peter Dendle quite rightly identifies zombies as a species of 'blue-collar undead', whether actual West Indian slaves or dehumanized American wage-slaves (a point *Dawn of the Dead* explores brilliantly), or drafted grunts sent in for slaughter (or even the Viet Cong themselves: an unstoppable enemy willing to face destruction in huge numbers without caving in). Coercive authority here is represented by the sheriff and his posse of drunken rednecks, who are almost certainly more disturbing than the zombies themselves, and Dendle further notes that zombie movies tend to be set away from centres of population or culture – here in rural Pennsylvania, and elsewhere in Louisiana, Kentucky, Alabama, Tennessee, Maryland, Missouri, or the Florida swamps (Dendle 2001: 11). American zombie movies are therefore clearly a part of the regional Gothic tradition identified throughout this study. Ben, the only survivor of the attack on the farmhouse, stumbles out exhausted only to be shot by the authorities – an innocent black man shot by the forces of American law and order, in a telling image of its time. The film closes with shots of Ben's body being lifted with a meathook onto an enormous pyre of corpses.

Tom Savini was unable to collaborate with his friend Romero on *Night of the Living Dead* because in 1968 he was seeing active service as a combat photographer in Vietnam. Enlisting in the army's 'Hold' programme as a way of avoiding the draft, Savini trained as a photographer in Fort Monmouth, and found himself photographing the fighting in Vietnam. These experiences were to inform Savini's vocation as one of the most creative figures in modern cinema, an unparalleled make-up artist whose vision of the human body as a combination of detachable parts and exploding viscera was a direct product of his military service and the psychological damage it caused him and so many of his contemporaries. Interviewed in 1982, Savini said:

> I saw a lot of bloodshed there, and my job was to photograph it. ... [I] walked around and nearly stepped on a human arm, one end of it jagged and torn, its fist clenched and grabbing the ground ... [soldiers with] certain private parts of their bodies blown off. ... Perhaps my mind was seeing it as special effects to protect me. ...
>
> It's a funny thing. Your mind just takes care of itself under extreme conditions. It shuts off. But it caught up with me later on. Like everyone else who went to Vietnam, I was really screwed up when I got back. My marriage went instantly into the toilet. ... Vietnam changed my life; it made me want to escape from reality forever.
>
> (Skal 1994: 308)

Savini's unique talents are strongly in evidence throughout *Dawn of the Dead*, with its eye-catching hordes of electric blue zombies (by *Day of the Dead*, they will have turned a dull grey-green). The film opens on a characteristically political note with a SWAT team, which includes at least one trigger-happy racist cop, storming a Hispanic housing project whose residents refuse to give up their dead. It is a scene of apparently undiscriminating carnage, accompanied by an apocalyptic warning from an elderly priest. The body (meat, substance, corpus) of the film, no less directly politically engaged, takes place in a gigantic shopping mall, where a group of survivors are holed up and, as in *Night*, under constant threat from an army of zombies, affording Romero the opportunity for an extraordinary satire on modern American consumerism, where the dehumanizing politics of commercial desire conspire to create a mindless army of ravening wage-slaves. One of the characters muses on why the zombies should head for the mall in such numbers – 'instinct – memory, it's part of what they were. This was an important place in their lives.' Indeed. And it's Romero's point that, in the mall, the survivors and the zombies go about their daily business in essentially the same way, performing the same functions – browsing through the mall, going to shops, riding the escalators, skating on the ice-rink, killing. Here and in *Day of the Dead*, the zombies also provide a representative demographic cross-section: businessmen, housewives, builders, cops, even a clown and a Hare Krishna zombie. 'They're us!' says Peter (Ken Foree), the SWAT officer, and the film targets what is for Romero the putrid essence of modern America, in 1979 or 2002, a toxic combination of consumerism and violence.

By 1985's *Day of the Dead*, the constant radio and television broadcasts by the authorities which accompanied the first two films have all fallen silent

– all that remains of the media is a newspaper blowing through a deserted city street, its headline, 'The Dead Walk!' Indeed, all that remains of authority, if not of humanity altogether, is an ever-diminishing group of soldiers and scientists under siege in a government storage facility in the Florida everglades, surrounded by a cave full of useless documents, official statistics, the records of government surveillance, all mouldering.

Like *Night of the Living Dead*, the film essentially dramatizes a power struggle between survivors, mostly far more mutually dangerous and individually unpleasant than the zombies themselves. The power-struggle is embodied by representatives of two competing types of authority, coercive and scientific, the hawkish Captain Rhodes (Joe Pilato), the military commander perpetually threatening to courtmartial and execute the few remaining survivors for imagined breaches of security and violations of command, and the team of scientists researching zombification, led by Dr Logan (Richard Liberty). Logan is a classic cinematic mad scientist, habitually referred to as 'Dr Frankenstein' though actually closer in method to a combination of Drs Moreau and Pavlov, perpetually covered in blood, performing meatball surgery on the captive zombies, and attempting to socialize a trained zombie, 'Bub' (Howard Sherman). Caught between the fascistic Rhodes and the deranged Logan are John (Terry Alexander), a heroic West Indian pilot, McDermott (Jarlath Conroy), a boozy Irish radio engineer, and Sarah (Lori Cardille), the sole remaining rational scientist. Perhaps the only valid discovery which Logan makes is that zombies die naturally with the decomposition of the brain in about 18 months, which means that the epidemic, although total, will be relatively short-lived. The film, and the trilogy, thus end on a strangely hopeful, Edenic note, with John, McDermott and Sarah escaping the storage facility and flying off to a deserted tropical island, presumably to start over again, repopulating humanity. Earlier in the film, John wonders aloud whether the plague of zombies might not be a punishment from God for creating the Bomb. In Romero's trilogy, as in invasion narratives generally, we tend to get what we deserve.

Notes

1. The discussion was broadcast on Channel 4, 31 October 1991. Other participants included Clive Barker and Ramsay Campbell.
2. See Chesney and Saki (1997). For the definitive account of this subject, see Clarke (1966: 30–63).
3. This version of the 'colonial cannibalism' discussed in Chapter 1 is revisited in Peter Jackson's *Bad Taste*, where an intergalactic fast-food conglomerate invades New Zealand, another former subject of the British Empire, in search of tasty human flesh.
4. Orlock is also being blamed for, or symbolically associated with, the actual Bremen plague of 1838: see Clarens (1997: 22).
5. For a comprehensive study of apocalyptic cinema – from plagues to nuclear holocausts to alien invasions – see Newman (1999).

|7|

Transformations
Body horror

He's the hairy-handed gent
Who ran amok in Kent

Warren Zevon[1]

'It's the Wolf!'

In the middle of the nineteenth century, the Reverend Sabine Baring-Gould, an English clergyman on a walking holiday in western France, injured himself while exploring a cromlech near Champigné. As the sun was about to set, Baring-Gould hobbled to a nearby hamlet, hoping to hire a trap back to town. These being the provinces, and furthermore the *Celtic* provinces, it was only with difficulty that Baring-Gould made himself understood to the villagers, who spoke only Breton. He sought out the priest, who in turn led him to the mayor:

> 'Monsieur can never go back to-night across the flats because of the – the –' and his voice dropped; 'the loups-garoux. ... If the loup-garou were *only* a natural wolf, why, then, you see' – the mayor cleared his throat – 'you see we should think nothing of it; *but*, M. le Curé, it is a fiend, a worse than fiend, a man-fiend, – a worse than man-fiend, a man-wolf-fiend.'
> (Baring-Gould 1995: 2–4)

With true English resolve, Baring-Gould decides to brave the walk alone, regardless of the *loup-garou* ...

In the early 1980s, two American students, David Kessler and Jack Goodman, on a backpacking holiday in the North Yorkshire Moors, happened upon a secluded pub, the Slaughtered Lamb, in the village of East Proctor. With night falling and the weather worsening, they went inside.

Immediately, the pub fell silent – the locals stopped playing their games of darts and chess and stared at the two visitors, who were clearly not welcome, especially when they asked about the strange symbol painted on the wall, apparently in blood – a pentangle. Making their excuses, they left quickly, accompanied by warnings to stick to the roads and stay off the moors, and, ominously, 'Beware the moon, lads!' Shortly afterwards, they were attacked by a ferocious beast, which killed Jack and left David badly wounded. The villagers shot the beast which, on dying, assumed the shape of a man.

The stories are remarkably similar. Though separated by over a hundred years, they share a number of familiar elements: the remote locale, away from centres of civilization and modernity; the cultured representative of that modernity as needy, lost or stricken traveller, coming upon a village at nightfall; the hostile or frightened locals, who decline to help but utter dark warnings; the terrible local secret of the wild beast who is also a man. One of these stories is scholarship, the other cinema: the first is from Sabine Baring-Gould's Victorian study of lycanthropy, *The Book of Werewolves* (1865) (the Reverend obviously survived to tell the tale!); the second is the opening scene of *An American Werewolf in London*. Here, in essence, we have the werewolf story, that most common of transformation or metamorphosis narratives in the horror genre.

Lycanthropes, *loups-garoux*, werewolves, changelings, beast-men, feral children, wodwos, and various other wild-men, positioned halfway between civilized humanity and savage bestiality, are recurring characters in folklore, fairytale, and modern horror, as well as providing an irresistible image for twentieth-century psychoanalysis ('the beast within'), particularly in the work of Freud himself. Baring-Gould traces their history back to a number of sources, including that of the Scandinavian Berserkers, terrifying warriors clad in the skins of beasts, and said to be possessed by their ferocious spirits (Baring-Gould 1995: 35–52). In the Old English epic *Beowulf*, the hero's name translates as 'bee-wolf', meaning bear: the mighty Norse warrior of this foundational text of English literature is a lycanthrope, a were-bear. Margaret Robson has argued that the numerous medieval accounts of wild men, such as the romance of *Sir Gowther* with its dog-man protagonist, may be the articulation of a pre-scientific culture's understanding of what have in modernity been codified as recognizable medical conditions, such as autism (Robson 1992). More directly to our purposes, Berserker (or 'Bersicker') is the name of the gigantic wolf which Count Dracula frees from London Zoo and gets to do his bidding. Not only can Dracula command wolves ('the children of the night'), but he himself is a lycanthrope, able to transform at will into a gigantic dog (or wolf), as he does when disembarking at Whitby – an episode which also partakes of numerous folktales of ghost or black dogs, the padfoot, barguest, shrike, or Black Shuck, given even more famous *fin-de-siècle* expression in Arthur Conan Doyle's *The Hound of the Baskervilles* (1902).[2]

Voyages of discovery and colonial explorations, contacts between Europeans and Amerindian and other 'savages', led in the seventeenth and eighteenth centuries to an explosion of interest in ideas of 'natural' humanity, ideas famously embodied in Rousseau's Noble Savage. As suggested in Chapter 1, this accounts for modernity's interest in cannibalism and other barbaric practices among (proto-)colonial subjects, though it also led to a renewed interest in the domestic versions, the European wild men living among us. In 1735 the Swedish biologist Carolus Linnaeus published his great work of taxonomy *Systema Naturae* (*The System of Nature*, whose definitive edition appeared in 1758); it was in this volume that creatures were given their classification, and Linnaeus's method was to categorize binomially. What this entailed was a categorization composed of two names, representing the genus (which could be shared with other closely related species), and the second, or 'trivial' name, which formed the distinctive marker of a species. Thus both dogs and wolves belong to the genus *canis*, but each has a particular trivial name to designate the species; dogs are classified as *canis familiaris* and wolves as *canis lupus* (Gould 1997a: 421–2). It was in fact Linnaeus who gave mankind their scientific name, *homo sapiens*. This classification, in honour of our supposed wisdom, also, however, contained a sub-species, not *homo sapiens* but *homo ferus* – wild men. According to Linnaeus, this species of humanity 'Walk on all fours, are dumb, and covered with hair', and he listed nine recorded instances from 1544 (Newton 2002: 38).

The most celebrated eighteenth-century instance of *homo ferus*, however, post-dated Linnaeus. This was the famous case of Victor, the 'Wild Boy of Aveyron' (1797–1800), a case which, as Marilyn Butler argues, may have contributed directly to some of the animating ideas of *Frankenstein*, whose Monster lives for a long period essentially as a wild man in the woods. *Frankenstein* also articulates Enlightenment theories of language acquisition, as the Monster hides in the bushes overhearing the Arab girl Safie being taught English. The Wild Boy of Aveyron himself became a test case for theories of nurture based on language-acquisition: he was put under the care of the physician Jean-Marc Gaspard Itard at the Paris institution for deaf-mutes. Examining this and other cases of feral children, in which he took a particular interest, the Scottish linguist Lord Monboddo suggested that, in Butler's words, they 'represented a sub-species between mankind and the primates' (Butler 1996: 308).[3]

If the episodes from *The Book of Werewolves* and *An American Werewolf in London* closely resemble each other, then what they both in turn resemble is that *locus classicus* of regional Gothic, *Wuthering Heights*. There, Lockwood, our man in the novel, its representative of cultured modernity (or 'city slicker') travels away from centres of civilization and symbolically backwards in time to a world of superstition, a world seemingly governed by supernatural forces, and a world of astonishing violence and brutality. There, like Baring-Gould, he encounters both linguistic difference and separatism (the incomprehensible Joseph), and, in the person of Heathcliff, a feral child grown into a savage man, living beyond the pale of community. Heathcliff is also given, at least rhetorically, to cannibalism, the language of devouring:

> I never would have banished [Edgar] from [Catherine's] society as long as she desired his. The moment her regard ceased, I would have torn his heart out, and drunk his blood! ... I have no pity! I have no pity! The more the worms writhe, the more I yearn to crush out their entrails. It is a moral teething, and I grind with greater energy, in proportion to the increase of pain.
>
> (Brontë 1991: 170, 174)

The publication in 1859 of Charles Darwin's *The Origin of Species*, and the cultural anxieties to which it contributed, obviously stands as a watershed in the production of beast-men narratives. As noted in Chapter 2, the years 1860–1950 were a boom-time for Darwinist (or more properly pseudo-Darwinist) horrors, and the late nineteenth century in particular saw a proliferation of beast men. *Dr Jekyll and Mr. Hyde*, that compendium of late Victorian anxieties, mingles Darwinist fears of atavism with class anxieties to produce in the figure of Hyde a working-class beast-man, less evolved than the middle-class professionals he so fascinates and terrifies (a similar case could be made, incidentally, for the provenance of that very real late Victorian London beast-man, John Merrick, the Elephant Man).[4] In *The Island of Dr Moreau*, Wells's mad vivisectionist attempts to create a race of super-evolved beast-men through a combination of selective breeding and surgery, but finds to his dismay that evolution is Darwinist, not Lamarckian – that is to say, the beast-men's offspring do not inherit acquired characteristics, but are born as beasts: 'Moreau took them and stamped the human form upon them.' Furthermore, without Moreau's constant, aggressive surgery, the beast-men revert to animals, as they do towards the close when they turn on their sadistic creator: 'As soon as my hand is taken from them, the beast begins to creep back, begins to assert itself again.' For Wells, Moreau's endeavour is animated by a racial theory of evolution which parallels the author's own interest in eugenics: Moreau's Ape Man, a surgically altered gorilla, is 'a fair specimen of the negroid type', while his 'Satanic' Satyr, a goat-man, has an 'ovine' face, 'like the coarser Hebrew type' (Wells 1995b: 139, 136, 134, 142). Similarly, H. Rider Haggard's *She* (1887) closes with the set-piece death of Ayesha, 'She Who Must Be Obeyed', a classic case of late Victorian reversion, down the evolutionary ladder, as the image has it (but see below for why this image is wrong):

> '*Look! – look! – look!* she's shrivelling up! she's turning into a monkey!' ... She ... lay before us, near the masses of her own dark hair, no larger than a big monkey, and hideous – ah, too hideous for words. ... There ... lay the hideous little monkey

frame, covered with crinkled yellow parchment, that had once been the glorious *She*.

(Haggard 1991: 293–5)

The Welsh occultist Arthur Machen's brilliant, incoherent novella *The Great God Pan* (1894) closes with much the same image. The novella opens with mad scientist Dr Raymond performing brain surgery on a subject, 'Mary', in an attempt to open her mind to the true reality masked by our everyday life (Machen, like Yeats, was a member of the Order of the Golden Dawn): 'the ancients knew what lifting the veil means. They called it seeing the God Pan' (Machen 1993: 32). This experience leaves Mary catatonic (we are to assume it was the revelation that led to the catatonia, not Raymond's surgical procedures) but pregnant. She gives birth to a girl, Helen Vaughan (born, we are told, in the Red House, Breconshire – so, more Celtic Gothic here, then) whose father is none other than the Great God Pan himself (the influence of Machen on Lovecraft, here as everywhere else, is palpable and acknowledged), and who grows up a deadly seductress, sexually irresistible. Her eventual dissolution and death are recorded by the physician Dr Matheson:

> I saw the form waver from sex to sex, dividing itself from itself, and then again reunited. Then I saw the body descend to the beasts whence it ascended, and that which was on the heights go down to the depths, even to the abyss of all being.
>
> (Machen 1993: 114)

The examples from Wells and Haggard provide a familiar colonial spin on Darwinism, as does that most celebrated of all late-Victorian feral children, Mowgli in Rudyard Kipling's *Jungle Books* (1894), raised by the wolves. Colonial subjects are a related but *lower* lifeform to white, Western humanity: like *homo ferus*, they are scientifically to be positioned midway between man and beast, and thus require subjugation. The evolutionary biologist Stephen Jay Gould begins his book *Wonderful Life* by showing how popular misconceptions about evolution have been conditioned by erroneous but powerful metaphors, notably that of the 'evolutionary ladder', which figures, as here, certain species as less evolved versions of other species, a misconception which can then easily be mapped onto theories of racial difference and superiority/inferiority (Gould 1991: 23–52). Furthermore, as Gould has shown in *The Mismeasure of Man*, his study of the fundamental errors made by *all* attempts to provide a scientific, quantifiable basis for inherent racial differences (and Gould's particular target here is the IQ test, 'the argument that intelligence can be meaningfully abstracted as a single number capable of ranking all people on a linear scale of intrinsic and unalterable mental worth') (1992: 20), not only is the science of these endeavours erroneous, but they are invariably conditioned by the often unconscious biases of the scientists themselves, who usually end up 'confirming' what they set out to discover, which is that black people are inherently inferior to whites. Such pseudoscience, encompassing versions of evolutionary biology, craniometry and physiognomy, and intelligence-testing, has been used to justify, for example, the slave-trade, or more recently the denial of funding for education and welfare programs for black communities in America.

The Darwinist beast-men of late Victorian horrors were soon complemented by Freudian psychoanalysis, for which the lycanthropic image of the 'beast within' as a model for socialized repression was to prove irresistible. As ever, it seems, *Dr Jekyll and Mr. Hyde* anticipates these issues and images, and can quite easily be read as a Freudian parable of the dangers of repressed desire: 'My devil had been long caged, he came out roaring' (Stevenson 1994: 80). Of course, we can also look to Freud's own work for examples here, and particularly in this context his case history of the 'Wolf Man' (1914). Whether or not we accept the tenets of Freudian psychoanalysis, Freud himself remains one of the most influential figures in the study of horror, and also, I would contend, one of the genre's foremost practitioners. He is writing a kind of Gothic, an imaginative world of contorted and disfigured sexual-familial relations, in which the past (infancy) looms over the present (adulthood), exercising a monstrous, inescapable influence on individuals who are, as a consequence, necessarily driven beyond sanity by the unbearable burden of dark secrets. Except that, in the Freudian schema, this condition obtains for *all* of us!

The Wolf Man, officially entitled 'From the History of an Infantile Neurosis', recounts the case of a patient whose health deteriorated badly after a bout of gonorrhoea aged 18, and who had since infancy been afflicted by 'an anxiety-hysteria (in the shape of an animal phobia)' (Freud 1979: 234). Most particularly, this was a fear of wolves, encapsulated in a terrifying childhood dream in which the patient saw six or seven white wolves sitting silently in a tree outside his bedroom window. The fear of the wolf Freud interprets as the Wolf Man's fear of his own father, which, by a brilliant interpretive sleight of hand, Freud traces back to a primal scene in which the infant Wolf Man witnesses his parents having sex: '*coitus a tergo, more ferarum*' ('sex from behind, like the animals') (ibid.: 292). This position allows the infant Wolf Man simultaneously to see both parents' genitals, and to interpret his mother's vagina as lack, as a castrated bleeding wound. From this, claims Freud, comes the Wolf Man's repressed desire to be penetrated by his father – that is, to be his mother, to be castrated – which is in turn displaced onto the image of the fearsome wolf. It is this forbidden desire to be penetrated by his father which leads, as it would, to the Wolf Man's neurosis, which manifests itself as anal eroticism (symbolically viewing his own anus as a vagina, projected outwards onto an obsession with, for example, excrement), and in a masochistic desire to be beaten on the penis, as a symbolic act of castration. Furthermore, this neurotic adult is represented by Freud as having been a feral child: 'He had become discontented, irritable and violent, took offence of every possible occasion, and flew into a rage and screamed like a savage'. 'In this phase,' Freud writes, 'the sexual aim could only be cannibalism – devouring' (ibid.: 242, 347). We are in familiar territory.

Classic Hollywood horror movies offered werewolves of both the Darwinist (external invasion) and Freudian (internal neurosis) types. The former is exemplified by *The Werewolf of London*, in which English botanist Dr Wilfred Glendon (Henry Hull) is attacked by a ferocious beast while in Tibet searching for a specimen of *Marifasa Lupina*, a flower which blooms by moonlight, and returns to London an unwitting werewolf. A series of murders ensues, though it becomes apparent that there are not one but two werewolves loose in London – the other is revealed as Yogami (Warner Oland), the lycanthrope who attacked Glendon in Tibet and has followed him to London. Glendon kills Yogami, but is then himself shot by the police. *The Werewolf of London*, then, is a variant on the 'yellow peril' narratives of Sax Rohmer: it is, in fact, a strange amalgam of *Dracula* and *Fu Manchu*. Furthermore, since Henry Hull refused to sit for Jack Pierce's elaborate planned make-up (an all-over yak-hair job, which later graced Lon Chaney Jr.'s Wolf Man), his werewolf is far more man than beast – he looks like Eddie Munster, a far cry from the four-footed, mute, hairy beast of *An American Werewolf in London*.

Far more Freudian is *The Wolf Man*. Not only is Larry Talbot's lycanthropy here an outward projection of the obvious sexual frustration he feels in his relationship with Jenny Williams, but it is also a highly Freudian manifestation of his difficult, competitive relationship with his suspiciously young father, Sir John. In the film's great, Freudian climax, a riot of phallic symbolism, Sir John beats Larry to death with his (Larry's) own silver-topped cane, which he had bought to court Jenny Williams, and which breaks in the process. Thus the film offers a symbolic visualization of the fantasies of Freud's own Wolf Man, his desire to be penetrated by his own father, displaced onto a desire to be beaten on the penis until it breaks.

Cat People is even more programmatically Freudian, to the extent of featuring a Freudian psychoanalyst, the extraordinarily louche Dr Louis Judd (Tom Conway), an extract from whose *The Anatomy of Atavism* prefixes the film: 'Even as fog continues to lie in the valley, so does ancient sin cling to the low places, the depressions in the world consciousness.' One such 'depression in the world consciousness' is Serbia, birthplace of Irena (Simone Simon), haunted by local folklore, the legend of the purification of Serbia by King John: the people 'had become witches – they were evil'. Irena believes herself the descendent of these 'cat people' – at her wedding party in a Serbian restaurant, a feline women approaches her, saying, 'My sister! My sister!' – and therefore that sexual arousal or jealousy will turn her into a big cat, a black panther. Falling in love with 'Americano' shipbuilder Oliver Reed (Kent Smith), she is unable to kiss him: 'I've lived in dread of this moment.

I've never wanted to love you. I've stayed away from people. I've lived alone. ... I've fled from the past. Some things you could never know or understand. Evil things, evil.' Irena lives next to the zoo: the lions roar all night, which she finds 'natural and soothing' – but 'the panther, it screams like a woman. I don't like that.' This frigidity, a terror of sex and its consequences, continues after Irena and Oliver's marriage, which remains unconsummated, played out in silence across a number of scenes in their darkened, shadowy apartment: 'I want to be Mrs. Reed *really* ... but I can't,' she tells him. 'I envy women I see on the street. ... I envy them. They're happy. They make their husbands happy.' Oliver sends Irena to Dr Judd, who suggests that the origin of her neurosis lies in childhood trauma, the death of her father.

The film's thematic interests are given symbolic articulation in a series of recurring images of phalluses and penetration, and about two-thirds of the way through the film Irena has an astoundingly Freudian dream which, in a thirty-second sequence, encapsulates the whole film's concerns – another phallic riot of cats, a sword, a key. Irena and Oliver's sexless marriage is foreshadowed in the film's opening tableau, in which Irena repeatedly fails to throw scrunched-up paper into a bin, whereas Oliver gets it in first time. Irena, a fashion designer, stands at the panther's cage in the zoo, drawing: her picture is of a panther with a sword through it, an image which recurs in Irena's apartment, where she has a statuette of King John spearing a cat. In the zoo, the keeper habitually leaves the key in the lock of the panther's cage, a key which Irena eventually steals. Like King John in Irena's statue and her dream, Dr Judd carries a sword-stick which, in a prefiguring of his later attempted seduction of Irena, he hides under the cushions in her apartment, and then borrows Oliver's key to retrieve. When Dr Judd tries to kiss Irena, she attacks him, apparently in cat-form: he draws his sword-stick, which, like Larry Talbot's phallic cane, breaks, half of it lodged in Irena's shoulder. She staggers to the panther's cage at the zoo, and dies.

Like *The Wolf Man*, *Curse of the Werewolf* closes with its lycanthrope, Leon (Oliver Reed), killed by his own father – here actually his adopted father, Don Alfredo (Clifford Evans). The film features a risible transformation scene and a monster more teddy bear than wolf, but transcends its many faults because of a brilliant, unbearable opening scene. It is tempting to call *Curse of the Werewolf* a Marxist film. Like *Jekyll and Hyde*, it is underpinned by a social Darwinist agenda, examining the relationship between poverty and bestiality, though here the subject is anchored firmly in class hatred: the poor are *made* beastly by dehumanization at the hands of an immoral ruling class.

A beggar (Richard Wordsworth, giving a very moving performance) interrupts the wedding feast of the sadistic, tyrannical Marques Siniestro (Anthony Dawson). Siniestro's bride pleads with her husband to treat the beggar with compassion – 'He's a man, not an animal'; the Marquis proffers the starving beggar a chicken-leg, saying 'Here, dog! Here's your bone. Come on – come and get it like a good dog.' Like the Marxian class schema, the relationship between the Marques and the beggar is dialectical, mutually dependent. Imprisoned in a dungeon for many years, the beggar becomes bestial, hairy, gnawing on bones, while the syphilitic Marques grows mad, withered and pockmarked. The Marques attempts to rape the jailer's mute daughter: she bites him and is thrown into the dungeon, where she is raped by the beggar. The beggar dies, but not before impregnating her; let out of the dungeon, the girl goes to the Marques's chamber and kills him. She herself then dies in childbirth, having 'lived like an animal' in the forest before she is discovered by Don Alfredo. Her son, Leon, is born on Christmas Day, when 'an unwanted child is an insult to heaven'; instead of a baby's cry, Alfredo hears the howl of a wolf. At his baptism, a black shadow falls upon the church, the font bubbles, and a demon-face appears in the water, ostensibly the reflection of a gargoyle.

'What big teeth you have ...'

In *Cat People*, Irena is told that her psychological problems stem from a literal belief in fairytales. Fairytales, of course, abound with beast-men and talking animals – 'Beauty and the Beast', 'Little Red Riding Hood': this is a huge subject with an extensive scholarly literature of its own, and I can do little more here than gesture towards it. In *The Uses of Enchantment*, the psychoanalyst Bruno Bettelheim argues that fairytales have an educative function, dramatizing for children a series of psychological crises, usually of a sexual-familial nature. 'Little Red Riding Hood' explores 'the threat of being devoured', within an Oedipal conflict: 'But the wolf is not just the male seducer, he also represents all the asocial, animalistic tendencies within ourselves' (Bettelheim 1978: 169, 172). Bettelheim notes that, unlike 'Hansel and Gretel', which it otherwise resembles in its concerns with orality and fears of devouring, 'Little Red Riding Hood' marginalizes female monstrosity (the cannibalistic witch, the grandmother), foregrounding the masculine sexuality embodied by the wolf. Marina Warner suggests a deeper link between witch and wolf:

> The wolf is kin to the forest-dwelling witch, or crone; he offers us a male counterpart, a werewolf who swallows up grandmother and then granddaughter. In the witch-hunting fantasies of early modern Europe they are the kind of beings associated with marginal knowledge, who possess pagan secrets and are in turn possessed by them.
>
> (1995: 181)

Here, as ever it seems, the locus of horror is in marginality.

The modern writer most interested in humanity's essential wolfishness is also, and consequently, the modern writer most interested in fairytales,

Angela Carter. Transformations to or from beasts are recurring images in her work, and particularly in the reimagined fairytales that form her collection *The Bloody Chamber* (1979), which foregrounds numerous versions of both the 'Beauty and the Beast' and 'Little Red Riding Hood' stories. For Carter, the transformation from human to wolf, governed by the cycle of the moon, is connected to the menstrual cycle, also lunar. Thus, for Carter, transformation into beast-form is often used as an image for, or an accompaniment to, female puberty, the transformation of the body with its concomitant associations of both the shedding of blood (the vagina as 'bleeding wound') and the growing of hair, which signifies the coming of adult sexuality. 'Wolf-Alice', which tells of the relationship between a feral child (raised by wolves) and a vampire, pivots on Alice's first menstruation, which she associates with her lupine essence. 'The Company of Wolves', one of several Little Red Riding Hoods, posits a transformation into beasthood with the loss of virginity. The girl's red cape is here a polyvalent sexual symbol, for puberty and menstruation, for virginity and its loss with the breaking of the hymen (she throws off her cloak at the end):

> She stands and moves within the invisible pentacle of her own virginity. She is an unbroken egg; she is a sealed vessel; she has inside her a magic space the entrance to which is shut tight with a plug of membrane; she is a closed system; she does not know how to shiver. . . .
>
> She closed the window on the wolves' threnody and took off her scarlet shawl, the colour of poppies, the colour of sacrifices, the colour of her menses, and, since fear did her no good, she ceased to be afraid.
>
> What shall I do with my shawl?
>
> Throw it on the fire, dear one. You won't need it again.
>
> (Carter 1996: 215–19)

In spite of her firm and entirely deserved place in a canon of modern women's writing, Carter's status as a *feminist* writer is highly debatable. Her interest in and consequent adoption of pornography as a form liberating for women have proved controversial, and her transformations *do* come disturbingly close to rape fantasies, in which, overpowered and deflowered by beastly, phallic men, women themselves attain a kind of beastly transcendence:

> And each stroke of his tongue ripped off skin after successive skin, all the skins of a life in the world, and left behind a nascent patina of shiny hairs. My earrings turned back to water and trickled down my shoulders; I shrugged the drops off my beautiful fur.
>
> (Carter 1996: 169)

Written on the body

Since the late 1970s, the cinematic foregrounding of lycanthropic and other transformations, often as the *raison d'être* for entire films, has been a feature of the horror movie – sometimes controversially, as these developments in the technology of representation (what could or could not realistically be shown) were contemporaneous with, and contributed to, the video nasties debate of the early 1980s (what could or could not legally be shown). Together with the rather more cerebral *Wolfen*, *An American Werewolf in London* and *The Howling* formed an impressive trio of werewolf movies all released in 1981 (to which might be added a fourth, Paul Schrader's oversexed 1982 remake of *Cat People*); the last two showcased transformation scenes by Rick Baker and Rob Bottin respectively which were major contributions to the rise of 1980s' 'body horror', in which the human body is radically figured and disfigured as a site of horror. Even more significant here is Bottin's visceral work on Carpenter's *The Thing*, an ultra-paranoid reworking of the 1950s' original, with its vision of the flesh as a *corporation*, a relatively loose agglomeration of discrete units, each capable of acting autonomously, and thus capable of multiple combinations. In other words, Carpenter and Bottin's Thing has no intrinsic form, but is capable of assuming *any* form you or they can imagine, and many that you can't.

Clive Barker, a prolific and distinguished contributor to modern horror across a number of media (fiction, theatre, film, visual art), who also came to prominence in the 1980s, shares this vision of the body as the true site of horror, in its transformation, mutilation, and pain, but also its beauty, for Barker's characters achieve what he clearly sees as a kind of transcendence, an escape from selfhood, through their pain: 'for some of us,' Barker has written, 'monsters are welcome opportunities to be different, to act in anti-normal ways, hideous and beautiful at the same time' (1997: 198). Thus, Barker's work is full of hideous/beautiful monsters, grotesque arrangements of flesh presented as aesthetic artefacts: the fantastic communities of creatures in 'The Skins of the Fathers', or *Cabal* (1988) and its film-version, *Nightbreed*, or Pinhead and the other Cenobites from the *Hellraiser* series. Barker's best work is in the short stories collected as *Clive Barker's Books of Blood*, whose six volumes include 'In the Hills, the Cities', yet another view of corporate flesh, in which the populations of two Yugoslavian cities form themselves into two gigantic warring figures. Like Frankenstein's Monster or Hobbes's Leviathan, this is a literalized Body Politic, the one man made of many men – 'He was talking metaphor – ... It was some Trotskyist tripe' (Barker 1994: 1: 143), one of the characters insists when confronted with the story of the battling giants. The *Books of Blood* are prefaced by a lame pun ('Every body is a book of blood; Wherever we're opened, we're red') and a rather more effective introductory story in which the dead inscribe their histories in scars on the body of a young medium:

these are the stories which form the *Books of Blood*, written on the body. One of them, 'Jacqueline Ess: Her Will and Testament', tells of a woman literally able to reshape flesh at will. This is body horror's version of the beast-man transformation:

> The pain was terrible. It stopped even a voice coming out from him. Or was that her again, changing his throat, his palate, his very head? She was unlocking the plates of his skull, and reorganizing him. ... The man crouched down and stared under the table at the disgusting beast that was squatting there, bloody from its transformation, but alive. She had killed his nerves. He felt no pain. He just survived, his hands knotted into paws, his legs scooped up around his back, knees broken so he had the look of a four-legged crab, his brain exposed, his eyes lidless, lower jaw broken and swept up over his top jaw like a bulldog, ears torn off, spine snapped, humanity bewitched into another state.
>   'You are an animal,' she'd said. It wasn't a bad facsimile of beasthood.
>
> (Barker 1994: 2: 83)

The provenance of body horror lies in three distinct but interlinked areas, which we might call technological, ideological, and philosophical. The technological here encompasses the technology of representation – the ability, through improvements in make-up and special effects, and then through the use of Computer Generated Imagery, to present an audience with images not only technically impossible but probably literally unimaginable to previous generations of moviegoers (the real watershed here may be 1977, the year of the release of *Star Wars*, and thus of the rise of Industrial Light and Magic, creators of the cinematic present which we now inhabit). It also, however, encompasses a specific view of the human body as unstable, adaptable not only through prosthetics but through mechanics – the flesh machines of William Burroughs, J.G. Ballard, or David Cronenberg, and of cyberpunk; the cyborgs or computer-people of *Robocop* or *Strange Days*; the bleak vision of a mechanized humanity, complete with terrifying drill-bit phallus, in *Tetsuo: The Iron Man*.

Technology and ideology are indistinguishable here, as many of these works anticipate, caricature, or simply reflect the *actual* condition of the human body after 1980. It is no accident, in other words, that the era of body horror is also the great era of what Naomi Wolf famously called the 'beauty myth', in which the advertising, entertainment and sex industries have colluded to present an idealized, aspirational vision of the human body literally unobtainable without technological intervention though plastic surgery, liposuction, chemical injections, in a way which recalls nothing so much as the vivisectionist tendencies of cinematic mad science, 'irresponsible medical experiments [writes

Wolf], using desperate women as laboratory animals' – as, for example, did Dyanne Thorne and her team of Mengele-like scientists in the totally disreputable *Ilsa, She Wolf of the SS*. Wolf continues: 'in the first stabs at liposuction, powerful hoses tore out of women, along with massive globules of living tissue, entire nerve networks, dendrites and ganglia. Undaunted, the experimenters kept at it. Nine French women died' (1991: 236–7).

Thus, the human body is variously pushed, pulled, shrunk, inflated, sucked dry, discoloured, frozen, invaded, or mechanized to produce such varieties as the current incarnation of Michael Jackson (looking far more disturbing than he did as a zombie or a werewolf in John Landis's *Thriller* video), or images of desirable womanhood from, say, Pamela Anderson to Jordan, which posit vast, solid, dirigible breasts, the narrow waist of an adolescent, and the effectively hairless genitalia of an 11-year-old. These are grotesque, an impossible combination of infantilism and fecundity, and they are also, strictly, cyborgs.

Philosophically, the 1980s also saw the development of the academic study of the body as a signifier, a site of contested meanings. Heavily influenced by the work of Michel Foucault on sexuality, madness, and power, the period witnessed a reinvigoration within the humanities of, for example, the study of the history of medicine. In 1985, Elaine Scarry's influential book *The Body in Pain* analysed the relationship between bodily pain, political power, and verbal representation, in its studies of the creation of a theatrical *spectacle* of pain through institutions and instruments of torture, and its hypothesis that bodily pain lies beyond the limits of language, signifying that which is inexpressible, which has no linguistic object:

> Physical pain, then, is an intentional state without an intentional object; imagining is an intentional object without an experienceable intentional state. Thus, it may be that in some peculiar way it is appropriate to think of pain as the imagination's intentional state, and to identify the imagination as pain's intentional object.
>
> (Scarry 1985: 162–4)

'Long live the new flesh!'

The artist whose work best exemplifies all of these trends is David Cronenberg, perhaps the foremost practitioner of body horror. Cronenberg began his academic career as a scientist, and many of his films are inventive variants on the mad science tradition (with some equally inventive nomenclature). In his big-screen debut, *Shivers* – which Cronenberg originally wanted to call 'Orgy of the Blood Parasites' (and I wish he had) – Dr Emil Hobbes creates a parasite with the ostensible aim of replacing failed organs, but which actually transforms its hosts into insatiable nymphomaniacs. In *Rabid*, Dr Dan Keloid (Howard Ryshpan) performs experimental plastic surgery on Rose (played by porn-star Marilyn Chambers), leaving her with a phallic growth in her armpit with which to penetrate her victims, thus satisfying her craving for human blood, the only food she can now digest. *The Brood* has radical psychotherapist Dr Hal Raglan (Oliver Reed), founder of the school of 'psychoplasmics', whose patients are encouraged to externalize their neuroses as wounds on the body rather than scars in the mind, causing Nola Conleth (Samantha Eggar) to expel from her body a host of killer children (they grow in sacs like giant blisters on her body, which she then bites off), the corporeal products of her repressed rage. This in turn was followed by *Scanners*, where 'psychopharmacist' Dr Paul Ruth creates Ephemerol, a tranquillizer for pregnant women with the unfortunate side-effect of turning the unborn children into destructive telepaths (as in the Thalidomide case a drug given to pregnant women to alleviate morning sickness led to the births of limbless children). In *Videodrome*, Professor Brian O'Blivion (Jack Creley) develops a TV signal which causes brain tumours in viewers, while *The Fly*'s Dr Seth Brundle develops a matter-transfer device, and *Dead Ringers*'s Doctors Elliot and Beverly Mantle are crazy gynaecologists, inventors of 'the Mantle Retractor, which is now a standard of the industry', and also – in an echo of Scarry's ideas about the spectacle of torture – the creators of 'Gynaecological Instruments for Working on Mutant Women', which are simultaneously technological devices (variants on the 'Mantle Retractor') and an *avant garde,* sadomasochistic art installation which the Mantles commission from a metal-working artist.[5]

Also standard in Cronenberg's work is a consistent anti-corporatism, a recurring interest in the ways in which the products of science are manipulated and perverted by corporate interests – as for example the dubious research on the 'weapons capability' of the telepaths in *Scanners*, carried out by ConSec and its subsidiary, Biocarbon Amalgamate, which manufactures Ephemerol; or, in *Videodrome*, the shadowy work of Spectacular Optical ('Keeping an Eye on the World'), run by Barry Convex (!), which manufactures spectacles and weapons systems. For Cronenberg, the corporation is, as its etymology suggests, the human body writ large: 'An institution is really like an organism, a multi-celled animal in which the people are the cells. The very word "corporation" means body. An incorporation of people into one body' (Rodley 1997: 29).

If the corporation is a metaphorical version of the human body, then the human body is itself in turn a corporate product, a technological device:

> you can actually change what it means to be a human being in
> a physical way. ... We are physically different from our
> forefathers, partly because of what we take into our bodies,
> and partly because of things like glasses and surgery. But there

is a further step which could happen, which would be that you could grow another arm, that you could actually physically change the way you look – mutate.

(ibid.: 80–2)

Cronenberg has described his work as Cartesian, insistent on the duality of mind and body, and most concerned with giving the flesh – traditionally the less privileged half of this binary – its due. This is the Body Politic:

> I don't think the flesh is necessarily treacherous, evil, bad. It is cantankerous, and it is independent. The idea of independence is the key. It really is like colonialism ... I think to myself: 'That's what it is: the independence of the body, relative to the mind, and the difficulty of the mind accepting what that revolution might entail.'

(ibid.: 80)

Thus, Cronenberg's films are suffused with images of the mutation of the flesh (tumours a speciality), and particularly of its fusion with machines, from *Videodrome* (with squirmy effects by Rick Baker) and *The Fly* (which closes with Brundle fusing with his own teleporter pod) to *The Naked Lunch*, *Crash* (whose scientist-visionary-psychopath, Vaughan, dreams of a sexual fusion of man and machine), and *eXistenZ* (fusions of organic matter and computers, flesh guns which shoot bullets made of teeth). In *Videodrome*, Professor O'Blivion, who exists only on videotape, expounds his philosophy that 'The television screen has become the retina of the mind's eye', and runs the Cathode Ray Mission, where the homeless are given doses of television. O'Blivion's TV show, *Videodrome*, conceals a signal which causes brain-tumours in its viewers, leading to hallucinations: conceived of as 'the next phase in the evolution of man into a technological animal', the show creates 'a new organ' in the brain, to influence reality. The film repeatedly conflates and combines mechanical and organic matter: a pulsating video cassette, apparently made of flesh; televisions which breathe and writhe, which grow veins and mouths, which spill out bloody entrails. Max Renn (James Woods) grows a vaginal slit in his abdomen, into which he inserts a gun, penetrating himself (a powerful image of sex, violence and the screen, produced at the time of the video nasty debates: *Videodrome* can, in fact, best be understood as Cronenberg's own contribution to these debates); later, Barry Convex inserts a videotape into Max's slit, which turns him into a corporate assassin, and Max's gun is fused to his flesh by cables and wires; when corporate technocrat Harlan inserts his hand into the slit, it is chewed off, and the stump fused with a bomb. Yet another hand/gun comes out of a flesh television, shooting Max, who is reborn as a new species: 'I am the video word made flesh. ... Death to Videodrome! Long live the new flesh!'

Notes

1. Warren Zevon, 'Werewolves of London', *Excitable Boy*, Asylum Records (1978).
2. For an account of the influence of these 'Black Dog' legends on *The Hound of the Baskervilles*, see Frayling (1996: 169). Frayling also recounts the influence of Sabine Baring-Gould's *A Book of Dartmoor* (1900) on Doyle's novel.
3. Butler (1996: 308). For a full account of the history of the Wild Boy of Aveyron, see Newton (2002: 98–127).
4. See Auerbach (1995: 90–2), who draws parallels between Merrick and Count Dracula.
5. These were based on a sculpture which Cronenberg had made himself some years previously, 'Surgical Instrument for Operating on Mutants' (Rodley 1997: 34).

|8|

Hail Satan!

Diabolism, the occult and demonic possession

In his prophetic work, 'The Marriage of Heaven and Hell', William Blake makes this celebrated observation based on his reading of John Milton's *Paradise Lost*: 'Note: The reason Milton wrote in fetters when he wrote of Angels & God, and at liberty when of Devils & Hell, is because he was a true poet, and of the devil's party without knowing it' (Blake 1975: 182). True poets are of the devil's party – for the revolutionary strain of Romanticism, this amounted to, if not an article of faith, then certainly a central statement of principle. Here, in the aftermath of the French Revolution, the poet is figured as by definition revolutionary, a believer in Enlightenment ideas of liberty and justice, committed to rebelling against a tyrannical and unjust order, Old Corruption. By this reading, Milton's Satan, as the archetypal rebel or revolutionary (against a dictatorial order), was also, by definition, the archetypal poet. This idea is developed in Percy Shelley's long dramatic poem 'Prometheus Unbound', where Prometheus is clearly himself figured as a type of Satan, a rebel against tyranny, stealing fire from the gods to create mankind, and in one of the great political novels of its time, Mary Shelley's *Frankenstein*, subtitled 'The Modern Prometheus'.

This association of the devil with *popular* causes has a long history. Indeed, he is, as his 'biographer' Peter Stanford notes, 'a popular figure, not a dogmatic abstraction, and has come alive not in learned tomes or seminary debates, but in the minds of the faithful, terrifying, omnipresent and grotesque, evil incarnate' (1996: 93). Satan has a complex, evolving history in canonical scripture, from the prosecuting counsel of the *Book of Job* to the tempter of Jesus in the wilderness of the Gospels, to the Great Beast of the *Book of Revelation*, but his place within church doctrine has traditionally been rather shadowy and downplayed. That the church declines to give the devil his due is perhaps not surprising: any conception of Satan as a genuinely powerful force at work in the universe, an active agent in the affairs of humanity, is potentially destabilizing to Christianity's fundamentally monist view of the creation – that is to say, its belief that it was created by God in its entirety, and remains always under his complete control. Having a Satan whose influence on the course of history is too great potentially leads to heretical dualist or even Manichean views of creation – a belief, that is, in the coexistence of good and evil as equal forces. In 1975, the Catholic Church in England published a pamphlet, *The Devil*, summing up the position of the modern church: 'Let us therefore repeat that by underlining today the existence of demonic reality the Church intends neither to take us back to the dualistic and Manichean speculations of former times, nor to propose some rationally acceptable substitute for them.' The power of Satan, it concluded, 'cannot go beyond the limits set by God' (Catholic Church 1975: 19, 21). This position was reiterated in 1993 in Article 395 of the *Cathechism of the Catholic Church* (Stanford 1996: 210).

Apocalypticism, in which Satan has a major role to play, has always been most particularly the province of the disenfranchised or dispossessed, promising the overturning of an old, unjust order and the establishment of a new, empowering one. Thus, in the world of popular culture, and particularly in the world of horror, the devil has wielded rather more power than he has traditionally been allowed by the establishment.

From the Prague Ghetto to the Home Counties

The subject of this chapter is potentially a huge one, and giving even a basic history of Satanic representations is well beyond the aims and scope of this book, and the abilities of its author. All I want to do here is concentrate on some instances of the diabolic in cinema, and even to do that selectively.

As Nikolas Schreck has shown in his study *The Satanic Cinema*, the devil has been on the big screen from the very beginning. In 1896, the great cinematic pioneer Georges Méliès, who had a background in stage magic, directed himself as Mephistopheles in *La Manoir du Diable* (*The Devil's Manor*), which he followed with *Le Cabinet de Méphistophélès*, *Faust et Marguerite*, *Damnation de Faust*, *Le Diable au Couvent* (*The Devil in a Convent*), *Les Filles du Diable*, *Cake-Walk Infernal* (a Satanic dance movie!), *Damnation du Docteur Faust*, *Quatre Cent Farces du Diable* (*Four Hundred Pranks of the Devil*), and many others. As Schreck writes, 'Méliès turned to Satanic subjects more times than can be listed in the over 500 short films he made for his Star Films company' (2001: 19).

One of the great works of German expressionist cinema, *The Golem* was Paul Wegener's third film based on the legend of the Golem, the man of clay animated by Rabbi Loew to liberate the Prague ghetto – this legend also underlies Gustav Meyrink's (1914) novel of the same title, though Meyrink's Modernist study of urban alienation differs drastically from Wegener's film. What does, however, link Meyrink and Wegener quite clearly is the anti-Semitism underlying their choice of the Golem legend, an ideological motivation which was to mar several of the artistic products of

First World War and Weimar Germany including, as we have seen, Murnau's *Nosferatu*. As S.S. Prawer writes:

> The use made of grotesque Jewish figures in the consciously uncanny works of such writers as Meyrink, Ewers, Panizza, and Strobl should have given the wise food for thought. The same might be said of the use of actors with pronounced Jewish features, or made up to simulate such features, in German films made during the Weimar Republic.
>
> (1980: 132)

Wegener's film takes place against the background of a Pogrom against the Jews of Prague – one of the accusations against them is that 'they practise black magic'. Which is precisely what Rabbi Loew *does*. With his wizard's pointed hat and magic wand, Loew is nothing if not a black magician, summoning up 'the dread spirit of Astaroth' from within a circle of fire in his house/cave/laboratory (which looks like an inner ear!) full of astrological and alchemical symbols and other occult arcana. The Devil appears to Loew, giving him the word of power, Emeth ('Truth'), with which to give life to the clay.

The Devil is also conjured up on the silent screen in the Satanic rituals of *Häxan* (*Witchcraft Through the Ages*), which combines scholarly didacticism and bacchanalian eroticism in an absolutely unique way. The director himself, Benjamin Christensen, plays Satan, cheerily presiding over the corruption of a rather fleshy monk, and a good deal of orgiastic revelling. Understandably, the film proved controversial, both because of its frequent nudity and what Schreck calls its 'deliberately blasphemous, frankly anti-Christian tone' (2001: 34).

There are very few classic Hollywood horror movies that deal with Satanism, though one, *The Seventh Victim*, is particularly noteworthy, not least because it features modern-day Satanic cults, its New York setting anticipating *Rosemary's Baby*, as a group of Satanists, the Palladists, pursue their former member Jacqueline Gibson (Jean Brooks) across a nightmarish Greenwich Village to her eventual suicide in a police cell. Jacqueline's psychiatrist is none other than Dr Louis Judd (Tom Conway) – not, apparently, killed in his fateful encounter with Irena in the previous year's *Cat People* after all. Like Mark Robson, *Cat People*'s Jacques Tourneur was one of Val Lewton's directors at RKO, and his *Night of the Demon*, which we looked at in Chapter 5, is also an account of Satanism in a modern, domestic context, and makes great capital of juxtaposing the terrifying practices of the Satanic occult and the prosaic, even suburban contexts in which those practices are carried out.

Similar to *Night of the Demon* in its clash of intransigently rational modern science with ancient superstition, and often grouped together with it, is *Night of the Eagle*, a tale of witchcraft set among the ambitious, backbiting academics of Hempnell Medical College's sociology department.

Professor Norman Taylor (Peter Wyngarde), working on a study of 'Neurosis and the Modern Man' is, like *Night of the Demon*'s Holden, professionally dedicated to seeking out materialist explanations behind occult phenomena, and opens a lecture by writing 'I DO NOT BELIEVE' on the board, followed by a list of the things with which rational science should have no truck: the supernatural, witchcraft, superstition, psychic phenomena, all of which he describes as 'misguided, unobjective science, devoid of all empirical values – science completely based on *a priori* evaluations'. Norman seems, in the eyes of his bridge-playing colleagues, to have everything – a beautiful house and wife, a brilliant career: 'Have you sold your soul to the devil?' he is asked by a colleague's husband, 'You certainly seem to lead a charmed life, I must say?' And, of course, he does – unbeknown to Norman, his wife Tansy (Janet Blair) is a voodoo witch, practising propitiatory magic to save him from the Devil, conjured up in the form of a gigantic eagle by Norman's colleague Flora Carr (Margaret Johnston, giving a tremendous performance), who is animated by professional and sexual jealousy. Tansy says to Norman, 'You're so blind, so blind! What does it take to convince you?' The answer comes when the eagle (much more effective than Tourneur's demon) pursues Norman into his lecture-theatre, where he sprawls terrified against the blackboard, his body obscuring the word NOT in I DO NOT BELIEVE.

The undisputed master of Home Counties Satanism was Dennis Wheatley, who in a series of novels from the 1930s to the 1970s – including *The Devil Rides Out* (1934), *The Haunting of Toby Jugg* (1948), *To the Devil a Daughter* (1953), *The Ka of Gifford Hillary* (1956), *The Satanist* (1960), and *They Used Dark Forces* (1964) – explored the dark beliefs underlying an apparently stable, traditional Englishness. Indeed, many of Wheatley's novels strongly imply that this stockbroker-belt conservatism actually creates the conditions under which Satanism can flourish. Hammer studios filmed three of Wheatley's novels, and the best of these films is *The Devil Rides Out*, in which Christopher Lee's occult investigator the Duc de Richleau crosses swords with Charles Gray's deadly Satanic *ipsissimus* (wizard) Mocata. Wheatley was acquainted with Aleister Crowley, who provided him with information on Satanic rites, and on whom, at least in part, he based the character of Mocata. However, where Wheatley's Mocata was an untrustworthy foreign type, Gray's unforgettably purring performance turns him into an English establishment, public-school figure who, when he isn't summoning up 'The Goat of Mendes! The Devil himself!' sounds as though he should be commentating on the cricket.[1] Considerably less distinguished are *The Lost Continent* and *To the Devil a Daughter*. As we've already seen, the latter film has the dubious honour of being the last film from the Hammer studios. By 1975, Wheatley's gentlemanly, Tory-voting Devil had taken to vomiting green bile, masturbating with a crucifix, and turning his (or, rather, her) head through 360 degrees. *The Exorcist* had arrived.

Satan triumphant: *Rosemary's Baby, The Exorcist, The Omen*

The Exorcist is one of the most extraordinary movies ever made, and one of the great aesthetic documents of the twentieth century. Historically, though, it's worth remembering that the film was, in fact, the middle leg of the great trilogy of Satan movies, flanked by *Rosemary's Baby* and *The Omen*, which were themselves simultaneously the products and the causes of a veritable outbreak of Satanism on the screen during the period 1968–76, in forms ranging from the Satanic road movie of *Race with the Devil*, in which Peter Fonda and Warren Oates are pursued by a group of redneck Satanists, to the hardcore porn of *The Devil in Miss Jones*, in which Satan resurrects suicidal frump Georgina Spelvin as an insatiable nymphomaniac, to the strangely effective *The Car*, in which Lucifer's Long Black Limousine menaces a small American town.

It was largely the success of *Rosemary's Baby* that was responsible, in the first instance, for this wave of films. Roman Polanski's brilliant film of Ira Levin's novel has a young married couple, Rosemary and Guy Woodhouse (Mia Farrow and John Cassevetes), moving into the mock-Gothic Bramford Building (actually the Dakota on Central Park West – famously John Lennon's home in New York, and thus rather too upscale for Rosemary and Guy), a building which supposedly has an evil reputation as the former home of a number of Satanists and occultists, including the cannibalistic Trench sisters and the *ipsissimus* Adrian Marcato, who 'conjured up the living Devil'. On moving into the apartment, the Woodhouses' lovemaking is twice interrupted by noises (including strange chanting) coming from next door, the apartment of the gregarious Minnie Castevet (Ruth Gordon) and her courtly, much-travelled 'hubby' Roman (Sidney Blackmer), literally neighbours from Hell ('Roman Castevet' is an anagram of 'Steven Marcato': he is Adrian's son). Guy is an actor in TV commercials, and Polanski's coup is to set the film's Satanist milieu in the instantly recognizable world of American television of the 1950s and 1960s, a world in which the Satanists wear hideous synthetic leisure-wear, sew samplers, read the *Reader's Digest*, and drink Lipton's tea when they are not performing ritual sacrifices. It is, in other words, like an episode of the occult sitcom *Bewitched* played for real. Thus, one of a series of comic-grotesque Satanic Tupperware-parties round at the Castevets' (which come complete with Japanese Satanists taking snapshots, and chants of 'Hail Satan!') turns suddenly terrifying when the Devil himself materializes in beastly form to rape and impregnate the drugged Rosemary. 'This is no dream!' she screams. 'This is really happening!'

Satanism notwithstanding, *Rosemary's Baby* has a disturbingly materialist subtext. It is a film about men controlling women's bodies. Cassevetes's symbolically named Guy is intensely dislikable, just the kind of sleazy character who *would* give over his wife's body to bear Satan's child in order to further his career: watching the Pope's visit to Yankee Stadium, he says, 'That's a great spot for my Yamaha commercial!' Guy colludes with the eminent obstetrician Dr Sapirstein (Ralph Bellamy), also a Satanist, to prolong the extreme pains Rosemary feels through most of her pregnancy, where, in spite of eating raw meat and offal, she continues to lose weight. Rosemary's increasing sense of alienation and isolation breaks out into full-blown paranoia in a remarkable sequence of scenes in Dr Sapirstein's office, a phone box, and climaxing at the offices of Dr Hill, another obstetrician. Most disturbingly, the entirely secular Dr Hill placates the terrified Rosemary and willingly hands her back to her tormentors, Guy and Sapirstein. Hill is no Satanist, just as the conspiracy to control Rosemary's body is not entirely Satanic.

In September 2000, news broke that Pope John Paul II had attempted (and failed) to exorcize a demon who had taken possession of a teenage girl, 'screaming in a cavernous voice ... uttering disconnected phrases, and speaking in unknown tongues'.[2] It was the third exorcism of his Papacy. If this sounds uncomfortably medieval to modern, rational sensibilities (and it does), then it should be pointed out that the Pope here is only doing his job. As Stanford notes, exorcism has been a significant feature of Christianity since its very beginnings: 'In his three-year public ministry, Jesus's principal weapon in fighting the Devil is exorcism' (1996: 61). Mark's Gospel, generally believed to be the oldest of the Gospels, has the celebrated account of the exorcism of the demons cast out into the Gaderene swine:

> For [Jesus] said unto him, Come out of the man, *thou* unclean spirit.
>
> And he asked him, What *is* thy name? And answered, saying, My name is Legion, for we are many. ...
>
> And all the devils besought him, saying, Send us to the swine, that we may enter into them.
>
> And forthwith Jesus gave them leave. And the unclean spirits went out, and entered into the swine: and the herd ran violently down a steep place into the sea.
>
> (Mark, 5: 8–13)

Thus, as we saw in the Introduction, when William Friedkin directed William Peter Blatty's novel *The Exorcist* in 1973, the film was made with the blessing and assistance of the Catholic Church, and featured the Jesuit priests Father William O'Malley and Father Thomas Bermingham (the film's 'technical adviser' on matters pertaining to Catholicism) in prominent roles, as Father Dyer, Father Karras's friend and confidant, and as the President of Georgetown University. In spite of the film's controversial history with, for example, the British Board of Film Classification and the American religious right, the Catholic Church has continued firm in its support of *The Exorcist*.

Blatty, himself an alumnus of the Jesuit Georgetown University, based his novel on the 1949 exorcism of 'Robbie Mannheim' (his real name was concealed), a fourteen-year-old Maryland boy apparently possessed by the

Devil: like *The Exorcist*'s Regan MacNeil (who shares his initials), young Robbie grew violent, obscene and convulsive; writing and images appeared on his body, the words 'Hell', 'Spite', 'X' and 'Go', and an image of the Devil. 'Robbie' was exorcised over the course of two months, first at Georgetown Hospital by Father Albert Hughes, and then at home by Fathers Raymond Bishop, William Bowdern, and Walter Halloran. Finally, on 18 April, 'Robbie' exclaimed 'Satan! Satan! I am St Michael and I command you, Satan, and the other evil spirits, to leave this body in the name of *Dominus*. Immediately! Now! *Now! Now!*' – and recovered. An enquiry, commissioned by Archbishop Joseph Ritter, who had ordered the exorcisms in the first place, offered a secular, medical conclusion: 'a psychosomatic disorder with some kinesis action' (Kermode 1998: 11–16).

The Exorcist permits no such ambiguities, doubts, or materialist interpretations. Indeed, although Father Damien Karras (Jason Miller) is a distinguished psychiatrist – Georgetown University's foremost practitioner, who trained at Harvard, Johns Hopkins, and Bellevue, and is the author of a study of witchcraft 'from the psychiatric end' – the scholar-mystic Father Lankester Merrin (Max von Sydow) imperiously refuses, twice, to countenance or even to hear Karras's psychoanalytic diagnosis: a demon is a demon is a demon. And it is: in the film's lengthy opening sequence, on an archaeological dig at Nineveh in northern Iraq, Merrin uncovers a tiny stone head of the demon Pazuzu; the sequence closes with a celebrated shot of Merrin and the demon's full-size statue facing each other, twin monoliths, while below them two dogs fight, one black, the other white. However, the ostensibly straightforward clash of good versus evil emblematized in this tableau proves, in the practice of the film itself, to be rather more complex.

Like *Rosemary's Baby*, what may ultimately be most disturbing about *The Exorcist* is the way in which a young girl's body becomes a site of contested possession and control for *all* the film's competing interests: the Devil, obviously, but also the various clinicians who attempt to treat Regan, and the exorcists themselves. Regan MacNeil (Linda Blair) is twelve going on thirteen: she is, in other words, on the cusp of adolescence; her body, undergoing puberty, is about halfway between childhood and adulthood. Regan's mother, Chris (Ellen Burstyn), a famous movie star, sees a picture of the pair of them on the cover of *Photoplay* magazine: 'It's not even a good picture,' she tells her daughter. 'You look so *mature*.' What the film does, in part, then, is to allegorize the changing of the body and the (frequently terrifying) coming of adult sexuality in puberty – not for nothing does the film show Regan inserting a crucifix into her bleeding vagina, nor the Devil describe Regan to Chris as 'your cunting daughter' – and to do so in a way which is, unsurprisingly, consonant with traditional Christian thinking on the flesh. Consistent in Christianity at least as far back as St Augustine in the fourth century has been a dualistic conception of a humanity split into body and soul. When Adam and Eve fell after tasting the forbidden fruit of the Tree of the Knowledge of Good and Evil, the flesh fell with them and is now rightly the property of Satan; that in us which is exalted, the soul, belongs to God. Thus, it is ingrained into Christian orthodoxy to deny or even mortify the flesh, which is sinful or evil, particularly as it is manifested in sexuality and sexual desire. Consequently, once Regan's body becomes sexual, it becomes evil: the Devil, taking possession of her flesh, contorts, disfigures and scars it. But if the Devil is in an invasive relationship to Regan's body, so too are the exorcists, who tie her to the bed in another version of the type of ecclesiastical gang-rape we've seen elsewhere in this study, and, when they bless her body with holy water, leave bleeding gashes in her flesh. (This is even more disturbing given recent insights into the monstrous record of the Catholic priesthood on the issue of child sexual abuse: in Ireland, for example, serial paedophiles such as Father Brendan Smyth and Father Seán Fortune were protected by the Catholic hierarchy, which was fully aware of their activities over many years but nevertheless allowed them to continue their ministries, covering up for fear of scandal, and choosing instead to tyrannize the priests' victims.) If anything, the wholly secular practices of the doctors are more invasive still, as they perform a series of *incredibly* gruesome tests on Regan, hoping to diagnose a lesion on the brain – including an arteriogram which, famously, had audiences fainting in the cinema, and which even Blatty describes as 'the scene in the film at which I never look' (Kermode 1998: 53). While all this is happening to her, Regan, understandably terrified, writes 'help me' on her own body, from the inside. What is more, in order to achieve more 'authentic' performances, Friedkin – 'a maniac' according to Burstyn – conspired physically to abuse his cast during the making of the film – including Blair herself, who was strapped into a hydraulic device to mimic Regan's demonic convulsions. When, in the film, she screams, 'Make it stop! Make it stop!' she is not acting: this is a terrified young girl being tortured.[3]

The film has a fascinating, if potentially highly conservative, thematic interest in family politics, which comes close to suggesting that Regan's problems stem from the fact that she is the product of a broken home. The film is full of failed father-figures. Her parents are separated, and her father doesn't bother to call on her birthday – she overhears her mother scream 'He doesn't give a shit!' shortly prior to her possession. Regan asks whether Chris is going to marry the director Burke Dennings (Jack MacGowran), who will then become her new father: 'You don't like him like Daddy?' she asks; later, the possessed Regan breaks Dennings's neck and throws him out of the window. Father Karras is losing his faith because of his guilt over his mother's death: she dies alone in her shabby New York apartment, after having been committed to a public mental hospital – and as Karras's uncle rightly points out, were he a secular psychiatrist he would, with his talents, have a Park Avenue office and be able to house his mother in a luxurious penthouse apartment. Karras has a nightmare which intercuts images of his mother descending into a subway station with other images, including – so brief that it's almost subliminal – the demon's face. Lieutenant Kinderman

(Lee J. Cobb), a film-buff, asks Chris for her autograph for his daughter, though he immediately reveals that he doesn't have a daughter: 'It's for me.' Kinderman's very name means 'child-man'. Furthermore, and revealingly, since the majority of the film's action takes place among the Jesuits at Georgetown, virtually *all* of the men in the film are called Father.

The Omen is *The Exorcist* for Protestants. However, this realization of the prophecies of Revelation, dramatizing the coming of the Antichrist into the modern world, is a far more conservative piece than Friedkin's film, both formally and ideologically. Indeed, Schreck even considers the movie to be, quite deliberately, a work of Christian fundamentalist propaganda:

> its central paranoid idea – that the imminent birth of the Antichrist will rise from the world political landscape and signal the end of times – comes directly from a branch of the conservative fundamentalist movement at the centre of the American religious right.
>
> (2001: 181)

While this is probably an over-statement, it remains the case that, at the very least, *The Omen* propounds a covert ideological agenda that is in tune with the apocalypticism of the religious right. It is also, in radical opposition to *The Exorcist*, markedly anti-Catholic. When Cathy Thorn (Lee Remick), wife of the American ambassador to Rome, loses her baby in childbirth, a Catholic priest suggests to her husband Robert (Gregory Peck) that they secretly switch the dead child with another born at the same time, whose mother has died. What Thorn has not been told however, is that the baby who is to become young Damien Thorn was born of a jackal ... The implication is obvious: that the Vatican, which not only nurtures and protects the Antichrist but places him where he is in a position to do the greatest harm, as the son of 'the future President of the United States', is in league with the Devil.

The Second Coming: horror around the millennium

Satan had a quiet time of it in the cinema during the 1980s, perhaps because he was too busy elsewhere, directing political and economic policy-making in London and Washington. At the end of *The Omen*, Robert Thorn is shot while trying to kill his diabolic son with a set of ceremonial daggers, and by *Damien: Omen II*, the adolescent Damien is under the care of his plutocrat uncle, Richard Thorn (William Holden), and studying at an exclusive military academy – nicely set up for world domination. Unfortunately, the political career of Damien Thorn came to a crashing end in 1981, when at the end of *Omen III: The Final Conflict*, Sam Neill's ambitions are thwarted by the Second Coming of 'the Nazarene'. As an exception, the year 1987 *did* prove to be a lively one for the Devil, with the release of *Prince of Darkness*, *Angel Heart*, and *The Witches of Eastwick*. *Prince of Darkness*, probably John Carpenter's last unambiguously good film, has Father Donald Pleasance discovering Satan's son, imprisoned by the Catholic Church in a tube of green liquid in the vaults of St Godard's church, Los Angeles, alongside some ancient scriptures, predating the Bible, which foretell the apocalypse. Far more localized are *Angel Heart*, in which the sinister Louis Cyphre (Robert de Niro) engages sleazy detective Harry Angel (Mickey Rourke) in a job which turns into a metaphysical hunt for Angel's own soul, and *The Witches of Eastwick*, where Jack Nicholson's Daryl Van Horne, 'just your average horny little devil', has sex with Cher, Michelle Pfeiffer, and Susan Sarandon.

With the approach of the millennium, the 1990s understandably saw a revival of interest in apocalypticism, producing a series of works concerned with Satan and/or Catholicism. Christian cosmology, ever ingenious, posits a timespan of 6,000 years for history, with each thousand years symbolically representing one of the six days that it took God to create the universe, to be followed by the glorious 'millennium', the thousand-year reign of Christ upon the earth ending in the last apocalyptic battle in which the forces of Satan are finally defeated for good (Revelation 20: 1–10). Traditionally, the creation was reckoned to have taken place around 4000 BC, a figure arrived at by counting the ages of the Old Testament patriarchs and adding them together – the most celebrated of these calculations was that of Archbishop James Ussher, the Anglican Primate of All Ireland, in his *Annales verites testamenti a prima mundi origine deducti* (*The Annals of the Old Testament, Deduced from the First Origin of the World*, 1650), who calculated that the creation took place at noon on 23 October 4004 BC![4] What this meant was that the arrival upon earth of the Antichrist, whose initial defeat signalled the glorious millennium of Christ's reign before the Last Battle, was due any time between 1996 and 2000, with symbolic numerology obviously favouring 2000. Thus, it was foretold that the 1990s was to be Satan's Big Decade, and it was.

At the beginning and end of the decade there were two notable examples of Satan as a serial killer, the eponymous Jeff Goldblum in *Mr. Frost*, and the best-selling *Hannibal*, where Thomas Harris seems to have decided that his cannibalistic psychiatrist, always vaguely supernatural, was in fact the Devil after all. In a similar vein, *Fallen* has detective Denzel Washington on the trail of the demon Azazel, shifting from host to host and given to singing the Rolling Stones' *Time Is On My Side* (less inventively, the closing credits play out over the Stones' *Sympathy for the Devil*). Satan also appeared as the charismatic figure of John Milton (Al Pacino), head of a prestigious firm of New York attorneys in *The Devil's Advocate*. Here, the Prince of Darkness is out to convince his son, hotshot lawyer Kevin Lomax (Keanu Reeves again) to impregnate his sister (Connie Nielson), who will then give birth to the Antichrist. As Milton, Pacino gives a performance which is barnstorming and shouty even by his own exalted standards, and offers Kevin a spectacular, entirely convincing self-justification: God, he says, is 'an absentee landlord', whereas

I'm here on the ground with my nose in it since the whole thing began. I've nurtured every sensation man has been inspired to have. I cared about what he wanted and I never judged him. Why? Because I never rejected him, in spite of his imperfections. *I'm a fan of man!* I'm a humanist. Maybe the last humanist. Who in their right mind, Kevin, could possibly deny the twentieth century was entirely mine? *All of it, Kevin!* All of it! Mine! I'm peaking, Kevin. It's *my* time now! It's *our* time!

Doomed as usual to idiocy, Keanu blows his brains out rather than accept Satan's offer. In 1999, Gabriel Byrne featured both as Father Andrew Kiernan, investigating the wounds on the body of Frankie Paige (Patricia Arquette) and exposing a conspiracy which threatens to destabilize the Catholic Church in *Stigmata*, and also as the Devil himself, out to impregnate Christine Bethlehem (Robin Tunney) but no match for Arnold Schwarzenegger's vodka-swilling guardian angel, Jericho Cane, in the meat-headed *End of Days*. 'Everyone's very aware about the millennium, and this is the only movie coming out now that explores all the themes: Will the world come to an end? Will Satan return? It's a story of Biblical proportions' (Schreck 2001: 231), the theologically minded Arnie said of *End of Days*. He could not have been more wrong, either about the film's proportions or its uniqueness: as we can see, many films dealt with the same issues, and most of them did so far more interestingly.

Easily the best of the bunch, unless one accepts as literally Satanic the liminal figure of Keyser Soze (Kevin Spacey – or possibly even Gabriel Byrne once again!) in the brilliant *The Usual Suspects*, was *The Ninth Gate*, Polanski's triumphant return to the Satanic arena over 30 years after *Rosemary's Baby*. Based on Arturo Pérez-Reverte's novel *The Dumas Club*, *The Ninth Gate* stars Johnny Depp as Dean Corso, a disreputable, dishonest book-detective (called Lucas Corso in Pérez-Reverte's novel, and named, no doubt, in honour of the poet Gregory Corso, notorious for stealing valuable books from bookshops – he even stole his own manuscripts from Lawrence Ferlinghetti's City Lights bookstore in San Francisco and then tried to sell them back at a profit!) on the trail of a *grimoire* with engravings by the Devil himself (signed LCF, for Lucifer), who comes to discover that *he* is the one chosen as Satan's minister on earth.

Johnny Depp's entire film career, which began with *A Nightmare on Elm Street* in 1984, might profitably be viewed as an attempt at a modern *rapprochement* with the horror movie's illustrious history. *The Ninth Gate* was distinguished by a supporting cast which included Frank Langella (Count Dracula himself in John Badham's 1979 film of the Balderston—Deane *Dracula* of the 1920s), former Hammer queen Barbara Jefford (last seen in *Lust for a Vampire*), and Jack Taylor, a Jess Franco alumnus and thus the star of innumerable sleazy European horrors of the 1960s and 1970s. Two films Depp made with Tim Burton at the beginning and the end of the 90s also exemplify this process: *Edward Scissorhands* gave Vincent Price his last great role as 'The Inventor', a kindly mad scientist who creates the eponymous artificial man-child; while *Sleepy Hollow* is a self-conscious attempt at an updated Hammer, complete with fruity cameos from Hammer regulars Christopher Lee and Michael Gough. Also self-consciously in the Hammer mould, the Ripper gorefest *From Hell* showcases a supporting cast which, 30 years ago, would have graced any British horror movie: Ian Holm, Robbie Coltrane, Ian Richardson, Susan Lynch.

There is, finally, one more important instance of the Satanic cinema of the 1990s to be discussed. The year 1998 saw the British cinematic re-release, in time for its twenty-fifth birthday, of *The Exorcist* – which also, for the first time since the video nasty scandals of the early 1980s, got a video release. Its success on the big and small screen testifies to the film's enduring power to capture, horrify, and fascinate an audience which now spans at least two generations.

The relationship between horror and censorship has been a recurring theme throughout this study, and the last few years have seen a distinct and very welcome relaxation in British (and consequently Irish) censorship laws. Also in 1998, I went on a (funded!) research trip to the ABC Cinema in London's Shaftesbury Avenue: in what was then a radical step, the London Borough of Camden had given a licence for *The Texas Chain Saw Massacre* to be shown in this one cinema. I was as delighted, disturbed, and awestruck then as I had been when I first saw it in 1979. Now, the film is on general video release, and is even available in my own tiny local village video store, there on the shelves alongside *Night of the Living Dead* and, unbelievably, an admittedly edited but perfectly legitimate copy of *Cannibal Holocaust*, advertised as 'The Film They Did Not Want You To See'. And they didn't! So what are you waiting for?

Notes

1. Schreck helpfully elucidates this mystifying reference to 'The Goat of Mendes': 'the ancient Egyptian cult of Mendes ... venerated a lascivious goat-god said to copulate with favoured mortal females. Many of the Judaeo-Christian Devil's traditional attributes seem to have been borrowed from this pagan deity' (2001: 128).
2. 'Devil defeats the Pope', *Daily Telegraph*, 11 September 2000, p. 11.
3. See the 1998 BBC TV documentary *The Fear of God: 25 Years of the Exorcist*, for this. Friedkin's sadism led to both Blair and Burstyn suffering back injuries; he also hit Father William O'Malley to get him sufficiently agitated for the scene in which Father Dyer administers the Last Rites to Father Karras.
4. For Ussher and the dating of Christian cosmology, see Gould (1997b: 62–98).

Bibliography

Anderson, Benedict 1991: *Imagined Communities: Reflections on the Origin and Spread of Nationalism*, 2nd edn. London and New York: Verso.

Anon. *c.*1810: *The History of Sawney Beane and His Family, Robbers and Murderers*. Birmingham: S. & T. Martin.

Anon. 1824: Rome in the First and Nineteenth Centuries, *New Monthly Magazine and Literary Journal*, X.

Arata, Stephen D. 1997: The occidental tourist: Dracula and the anxiety of reverse colonization. In Stoker, Bram, *Dracula*, ed. Nina Auerbach and David J. Skal. New York and London: W.W. Norton, pp. 462–70.

Arnold, Matthew 1972: *Selected Criticism of Matthew Arnold*. Ed. Christopher Ricks. New York: Signet.

Auerbach, Nina 1995: *Our Vampires, Ourselves*. Chicago and London: University of Chicago Press.

Austen, Jane 1972: *Northanger Abbey*. Ed. Anne Ehrenpreis. Harmondsworth: Penguin.

Baldick, Chris 1987: *In Frankenstein's Shadow: Myth, Monstrosity and Nineteenth-Century Writing*. Oxford: Clarendon Press.

Barber, Paul 1988: *Vampires, Burial and Death: Folklore and Reality*. New Haven, CT: Yale University Press.

Baring-Gould, Sabine 1995: *The Book of Werewolves*. London: Senate.

Barker, Clive 1994: *Clive Barker's Books of Blood*, volumes 1–3. London: Warner Books.

Barker, Clive 1997: *Clive Barker's A–Z of Horror*, compiled by Stephen Jones. New York: HarperCollins.

Barker, Martin 1984: 'Nasties': a problem of identification. In Barker, Martin (ed.), *The Video Nasties: Freedom and Censorship in the Media*. London: Pluto, pp. 104–18.

Barker, Martin 2001a: Introduction. In Barker, Martin and Petley, Julian (eds), *Ill Effects: The Media/Violence Debate*, 2nd edn. London: Routledge, pp. 1–26.

Barker, Martin 2001b: The Newson Report: a case study in 'common sense'. In Barker, Martin and Petley, Julian (eds), *Ill Effects: The Media/Violence Debate*, 2nd edn. London: Routledge, pp. 27–46.

Bettelheim, Bruno 1978: *The Uses of Enchantment: The Meaning and Importance of Fairy Tales*. Harmondsworth: Penguin.

Bianchi, Tony 1995: Aztecs in Troedrhiwgwair. In Bell, Ian A. (ed.), *Peripheral Visions: Images of Nationhood in Contemporary British Fiction*. Cardiff, University of Wales Press, pp. 44–76.

Blake, William 1975: *Poetry and Prose of William Blake*. Ed. Geoffrey Keynes. London: Nonesuch.

Borges, Jorge Luis 1970: *Labyrinths: Selected Stories and Other Writings*. Ed. Donald A. Yates and James E. Irby. Harmondsworth: Penguin.

Borges, Jorge Luis 1998: *Collected Fictions*. Trans. Andrew Hurley. Harmondsworth: Penguin.

Botting, Fred 1991: *Making Monstrous: Frankenstein, Criticism, Theory*. Manchester: Manchester University Press.

Boucicault, Dion 1856: *The Phantom*. London: Dicks.

Bracegirdle, Cyril 1997: *Dr William Price: Saint or Sinner?* Llanrwst: Carreg Gwalch.

Broadie, Alexander (ed.) 1997: *The Scottish Enlightenment*. Edinburgh: Canongate.

Brontë, Emily 1991: *Wuthering Heights*. London: Everyman.

Brottman, Mikita 1998: *Meat is Murder: An Illustrated Guide to Cannibal Culture*. London: Creation.

Brown, Allan 2000: *The Wicker Man: The Morbid Ingenuities*. Basingstoke and Oxford: Sidgwick and Jackson.

Brown, Terence 1996: Cultural nationalism, Celticism and the occult. In Brown, Terence (ed.), *Celticism*. Amsterdam and Atlanta: Rodopi, pp. 221–30.

Brown, Terence 1999: *The Life of W.B. Yeats: A Critical Biography*. Dublin: Gill and Macmillan.

Bunson, Matthew 1993: *Vampire: The Encyclopedia*. London: Thames and Hudson.

Burman, Edward 1984: *The Inquisition: The Hammer of Heresy*. Wellingborough: Aquarian Press.

Burroughs, William 1986: *The Naked Lunch*. London: Paladin.

Burton, Jeffrey Russell 1977: *The Devil: Perceptions of Evil from Antiquity to Primitive Christianity*. Ithaca, NY: Cornell University Press.

Burton, Jeffrey Russell 1981: *Satan: The Early Christian Tradition*. Ithaca, NY: Cornell University Press.

Burton, Jeffrey Russell 1984: *Lucifer: The Devil in the Middle Ages*. Ithaca, NY: Cornell University Press.

Burton, Jeffrey Russell 1986: *Mephistopheles: The Devil in the Modern World*. Ithaca, NY: Cornell University Press.

Burton, Jeffrey Russell 1988: *The Prince of Darkness*. Ithaca, NY: Cornell University Press.

Butler, Marilyn 1996: Frankenstein and radical science. In Shelley, Mary, *Frankenstein*, ed. J. Paul Hunter. New York and London: W.W. Norton.

Byron, George Gordon, Lord 1997: *Selected Poetry*. Ed. Jerome J. McGann. Oxford: Oxford University Press.

Calmet, Augustine 1850: *The Phantom World: or, The Philosophy of Spirits, Apparitions, &c.*, 2 volumes. Ed. Henry Christmas. London: Richard Bentley.

Campbell, Thomas 1840: *The Poetical Works of Thomas Campbell*. London: Edward Moxon.

Caraher, Brian 2000: Edgeworth, Wilde and Joyce: reading Irish regionalism through 'the cracked lookingglass' of a servant's art. In Hooper, Glenn and Litvack, Leon (eds), *Ireland in the Nineteenth Century: Regional Identity*. Dublin: Four Courts, pp. 123–39.

Carey, John 1992: *The Intellectuals and the Masses: Pride and Prejudice among the Literary Intelligentsia, 1880–1939*. London: Faber and Faber.

Carter, Angela 1996: *Burning Your Boats: Collected Short Stories*. London: Vintage.

Catholic Church 1975: *The Devil*. London: Catholic Truth Society.

Chesney, George and Saki 1997: *'The Battle of Dorking' and 'When William Came'*. Ed. I.F. Clarke. Oxford: Oxford University Press.

Clarens, Carlos 1997: *An Illustrated History of Horror and Science Fiction Films*. New York: Da Capo.

Clarke, I.F. 1966: *Voices Prophesying War 1763–1984*. Oxford: Oxford University Press.

Clarke, Kenneth 1969: *Civilization*. London: BBC.

Clover, Carol J. 1992: *Men, Women and Chain Saws*. Princeton, NJ: Princeton University Press.

Coleridge, Samuel Taylor 1797: Review of *The Monk*, *The Critical Review*, XIX, February, pp. 194–200.

Colley, Linda 1992: *Britons: Forging the Nation 1707–1837*. New Haven and London: Yale University Press.

Craft, Christopher 1997: 'Kiss me with those red lips': gender and inversion in Bram Stoker's 'Dracula'. In Stoker, Bram, *Dracula*, ed. Nina Auerbach and David J. Skal. New York and London: W.W. Norton, pp. 444–59.

Creed, Barbara 1993: *The Monstrous-Feminine: Film, Feminism, Psychoanalysis*. London: Routledge.

Crockett, S.R. 1896: *The Grey Man*. London: T. Fisher Unwin.

Curtis, James 1998: *James Whale: A New World of Gods and Monsters*. London: Faber and Faber.

Daly, Nicholas 1999: *Modernism, Romance and the Fin-de-Siècle*. Cambridge: CUP.

Danielewski, Mark Z. 2000: *House of Leaves*. London: Anchor.

Davenport-Hines, Richard 1990: *Sex, Death and Punishment: Attitudes to Sex and Sexuality in Britain since the Renaissance*. London: Futura.

Davies, Paul 1993: *The Mind of God: Science and the Search for Ultimate Meaning*. Harmondsworth: Penguin.

Davies, R.R. 1997: *The Revolt of Owain Glyn Dŵr*. Oxford: Oxford University Press.

Dendle, Peter 2001: *The Zombie Movie Encyclopedia*. Jefferson, NC, and London: McFarland.

Dika, Vera 1987: The stalker film, 1979–81. In Waller, Gregory A. (ed.), *American Horrors: Essays on the Modern American Horror Film*. Urbana and Chicago: University of Illinois Press, pp. 86–101.

Douglas, Mary 1984: *Purity and Danger: An Analysis of the Concepts of Pollution and Taboo*. London: Routledge and Kegan Paul.

Douglas, Mary 1999: *Implicit Meanings: Selected Essays in Anthopology*, 2nd edn. London: Routledge.

Eagleton, Terry 1995: *Heathcliff and the Great Hunger: Studies in Irish Culture*. London: Verso.

Edwards, Hywel Teifi 1996: Celtophobia: an Arnold to the rescue?, *New Welsh Review*, 34, Autumn, pp. 18–20.

Eliot, George 1964: *Daniel Deronda*, 2 volumes. Ed. Emrys Jones. London: Dent.

Eliot, T.S. 1963: *Collected Poems 1909–1962*. London: Faber and Faber.

Empire: The Greatest Horror Movies Ever, The Definitive Guide c.2000. London.

Fenton, Harvey, Grainger, Julian and Castoldi, Gian Luca 1999: *'Cannibal Holocaust' and the Savage Cinema of Ruggero Deodato*. Guildford: FAB Press.

Fiedler, Leslie A. 1952: 'Come back to the raft ag'in, Huck honey!' In Fiedler, L.A., *An End to Innocence: Essays on Culture and Politics*. Boston: Beacon, pp. 142–51.

Flaubert, Gustave 1977: *Salammbô*. Trans. A.J. Krailsheimer. Harmondsworth: Penguin.

Florescu, Radu 1996: *In Search of Frankenstein*. London: Robson.

Foucault, Michel 1967: *Madness and Civilization: A History of Insanity in the Age of Reason*. Trans. Richard Howard. London: Tavistock.

Frayling, Christopher (ed.) 1992: *Vampyres: Lord Byron to Count Dracula*. London: Faber and Faber.

Frayling, Christopher 1996: *Nightmare: The Birth of Horror*. London: BBC.

Freud, Sigmund 1979: *Case Histories II: The 'Rat Man', Schreber, The 'Wolf Man', A Case of Female Homosexuality* (*The Penguin Freud Library*, volume 9). Trans. James Strachey *et al.*, ed. Angela Richards. Harmondsworth: Penguin.

Freud, Sigmund 1990: The uncanny. In Sage, Victor (ed.), *The Gothick Novel: A Casebook*. Basingstoke: Macmillan.

Garrett, Laurie 1994: *The Coming Plague: Newly Emerging Diseases in a World out of Balance*. Harmondsworth: Penguin.

Gelder, Ken 1994: *Reading the Vampire*. London: Routledge.

Gifford, Denis 1977: *Monsters of the Movies*. London: Carousel.

Gifford, Douglas 1976: *James Hogg*. Edinburgh: Ramsay Head.

Godwin, William 1820: *Of Population*. London: Longman, Hurst, Rees, Orme and Brown.

Godwin, William 1834: *Lives of the Necromancers*. London: Frederick J. Mason.

Godwin, William 1985: *Enquiry Concerning Political Justice*. Ed. Isaac Kramnick. Harmondsworth: Penguin.

Gould, Stephen Jay 1991: *Wonderful Life: The Burgess Shale and the Nature of History*. Harmondsworth: Penguin.

Gould, Stephen Jay 1992: *The Mismeasure of Man*, revised and expanded edn. Harmondsworth: Penguin.

Gould, Stephen Jay 1997a: *Dinosaur in a Haystack: Reflections in Natural History*. Harmondsworth: Penguin.

Gould, Stephen Jay 1997b: *Questioning the Millennium: A Rationalist's Guide to a Precisely Arbitrary Countdown*. London: Jonathan Cape.

Grainville, Jean Baptiste François Cousin de 1806: *The Last Man; or Omegarus and Syderia. A Romance in Futurity*. London: R. Dutton.

Haggard, H. Rider 1991: *She*. Ed. Daniel Karlin. Oxford: Oxford University Press.

Haining, Peter 1994: *The Flesh Eaters: True Stories of Cannibals and Blood Drinkers*. London: Boxtree.

Haining, Peter (ed.) 1999: *Great Irish Tales of Horror*. London: Souvenir.

Haining, Peter (ed.) 2000: *Great Welsh Fantasy Stories*. Llanrwst: Carreg Gwalch.

Hanna, Ralph (ed.) 1974: *The Awntyrs off Arthure at the Terne Wathelyn*. Manchester: Manchester University Press.

Hare, Augustus J.C. (ed.) 1894: *Life and Letters of Maria Edgeworth*, volume 2. London: Edward Arnold.

Harris, Thomas 1991: *'The Silence of the Lambs' and 'Red Dragon'*. London: Peerage.

Harvey, David 1989: *The Condition of Postmodernity: An Enquiry into the Origins of Cultural Change*. Oxford: Blackwell.

Hawking, Stephen 1988: *A Brief History of Time: From the Big Bang to Black Holes*. London: Bantam.

Herbert, James 1999: *The Rats*. London: Pan.

Herdman, John 1991: *The Double in Nineteenth-Century Fiction: The Shadow Life*. New York: St Martin's Press.

Higham, Charles 1986: *Orson Welles: The Rise and Fall of an American Genius*. London: New English Library.

Hogg, James 1981: *The Private Memoirs and Confessions of a Justified Sinner*. Ed. John Carey. Oxford: Oxford University Press (1st edn 1824).

Hoggart, Richard 1958: *The Uses of Literacy*. Harmondsworth: Penguin (1st edn 1957).

Jackson, Rosemary 1988: *Fantasy: The Literature of Subversion*. London and New York: Routledge.

James, Henry 1966: *The Bostonians*. Harmondsworth: Penguin.

James, Louis 1963: *Fiction for the Working Man 1830–1850: A Study of the Literature Produced for the Working Classes in Early Victorian Urban England*. Oxford: Oxford University Press.

James, M.R. 1992: *Collected Ghost Stories*. Ware: Wordsworth.

Jones, Ernest 1949: *On the Nightmare*. London: Hogarth Press / Institute of Psychoanalysis.

Jones, Stephen 1999: *The Essential Monster Movie Guide*. London: Titan.

Jouve, Nicole Ward 1986: *'The Streetcleaner': The Yorkshire Ripper Case on Trial*. London: Marion Boyars.

Kerekes, David and Slater, David 1995: *Killing for Culture: An Illustrated History of Death Film from Mondo to Snuff*. London: Creation.

Kerekes, David and Slater, David 2000: *See No Evil: Banned Films and Video Controversy*. Manchester: Headpress.

Kermode, Mark 1998: *The Exorcist*, 2nd edn. London: BFI.

Kiberd, Declan 1995: *Inventing Ireland*. London: Jonathan Cape.

King, Stephen 1976: *'Salem's Lot*. London: New English Library.

King, Stephen 1982: *Danse Macabre: The Anatomy of Horror*. London: Futura.

King, Stephen 1989: *The Dark Half*. London: Hodder and Stoughton.

King, Stephen 1992a: *Different Seasons*. London: Warner.

King, Stephen 1992b: *'The Shining', 'Carrie', 'Misery'*. London: Chancellor.

King, Stephen 2000: *On Writing*. London: Hodder & Stoughton.

Kracauer, Siegfried 1947: *From Caligari to Hitler: A Psychological History of the German Film*. London: Dennis Dobson.

Kristeva, Julia 1986: *The Kristeva Reader*. Ed. Toril Moi. Oxford: Blackwell.

Lamb, Lady Caroline 1995: *Glenarvon*. Ed. Frances Wilson. London: Dent.

Leatherdale, Clive (ed.) 1987: *The Origins of Dracula*. London: William Kimber.

Leavis, F.R. (1930) *Mass Civilization and Minority Culture*. Cambridge: Minority Press.

Leavis, Q.D. (1932) *Fiction and the Reading Public*. London: Chatto and Windus.

Leerssen, Joep 1996: Celticism. In Brown, Terence (ed.), *Celticism*. Amsterdam and Atlanta: Rodopi, pp. 1–20.

Le Fanu, Sheridan 1880: *The Purcell Papers*, 3 volumes. London: Richard Bentley.

Le Fanu, Sheridan 1993: *In a Glass Darkly*. Ed. Robert Tracy. Oxford: Oxford University Press.

Le Fanu, Sheridan 2000: *Uncle Silas*. Ed. Victor Sage. Harmondsworth: Penguin.

Lévi-Strauss, Claude 1970: *The Raw and the Cooked*. Trans. John and Doreen Weightman. London: Cape.

Lewis, Matthew 1973: *The Monk*. Ed. Howard Anderson. Oxford: Oxford University Press.

Lovecraft, H.P. 1992: *Crawling Chaos: Selected Works 1920–1935*. London: Creation.

Lovecraft, H.P. 1993: *Omnibus 1: 'At the Mountains of Madness' and Other Novels of Terror*. London: HarperCollins.

Lovecraft, H.P. 1994a: *Omnibus 2: 'Dagon' and Other Macabre Tales*. London: HarperCollins.

Lovecraft, H.P. 1994b: *Omnibus 3: 'The Haunter of the Dark' and Other Tales*. London: HarperCollins.

Machen, Arthur 1993: *The Great God Pan*. London: Creation.

Mackay, Charles 1932: *Extraordinary Popular Delusions and the Madness of Crowds*. New York: Farrar, Strauss and Giroux.

Marx, Karl 1973: *Grundrisse: Foundations of the Critique of Political Economy*. Trans. Martin Nicolaus. Harmondsworth: Penguin.

Marx, Karl 1976: *Capital*, vol. 1. Trans. Ben Fowkes. Harmondsworth: Penguin.

Marx, Karl 1983: *The Portable Karl Marx*. Ed. Eugene Kamenka. Harmondsworth: Penguin.

Matheson, Richard 1995: *I Am Legend*. New York: Orb.

Mathew, David n.d.: An interview with Phil Rickman, infinity plus, http://www.users.zetnet.co.uk/iplus/nonfiction/intrick.htm.

Maturin, Charles 1968: *Melmoth the Wanderer*. Ed. Chris Baldick. Oxford: Oxford University Press.

McCormack, W.J. 1997: *Sheridan Le Fanu*. Gloucester: Sutton.

McKeon, Michael 1988: *The Origins of the English Novel, 1600–1740*. London: Hutchinson Radius.

McMillan, Dorothy 1995: Constructed out of bewilderment: stories of Scotland. In Bell, Ian A. (ed.), *Peripheral Visions: Images of Nationhood in Contemporary British Fiction*. Cardiff, University of Wales Press, pp. 80–102.

McNally, Raymond T. and Florescu, Radu 1994: *In Search of Dracula*. Boston: Houghton Mifflin.

Miller, Elizabeth (ed.) 1998: *Dracula: The Shade and the Shadow*. Westcliff-on-Sea: Desert Island Books.

Miller, Karl 1985: *Doubles: Studies in Literary History*. Oxford: Oxford University Press.

Moers, Ellen 1978: *Literary Women*. London: The Women's Press.

Moi, Toril 1986: Feminist literary criticism. In Jefferson, Ann and Robey, David (eds), *Modern Literary Theory: A Comparative Introduction*. London: Batsford, pp. 204–21.

Montaigne, Michel de 1958: *Essays*. Trans. J.M. Cohen. Harmondsworth: Penguin.

Morrison, Robert and Baldick, Chris (eds) 1995: *Tales of Terror from Blackwood's Magazine*. Oxford: Oxford University Press.

Morse, L.A. 1989: *Video Trash and Treasures*, 2 vols. Toronto: HarperCollins.

Mulvey, Laura 1975: Visual pleasure and narrative cinema, *Screen*, 16, pp. 6–18.

Murray, Nicholas 1996: *A Life of Matthew Arnold*. London: Hodder & Stoughton.

Newman, Kim 1992: *Anno Dracula*. New York: Avon Books.

Newman, Kim (ed.) 1996: *The BFI Companion to Horror*. London: BFI.

Newman, Kim 1999: *Millennium Movies: End of the World Cinema*. London: Titan.

Newton, Michael 2002: *Savage Girls and Wild Boys: A History of Feral Children*. London: Faber and Faber.

O'Brien, Daniel 2001: *The Hannibal Files: The Unauthorized Guide to the Hannibal Lecter Trilogy*. London: Reynolds and Hearn.

Paley, Morton D. 1993: 'The Last Man': Apocalypse without Millennium. In Audrey A. Fisch, Esther H. Schor and Anne K. Mellor (eds), *The Other Mary Shelley: Beyond Frankenstein*. New York: Oxford University Press, pp. 107–23.

Parreaux, André 1960: *The Publication of 'The Monk': A Literary Event 1796–1798*. Paris: Librairie Marcel Didier.

Pérez-Reverte, Arturo 1999: *The Dumas Club*. Trans. Sonia Soto. London: Harvill.

Petley, Julian 2001: 'Us and them'. In Barker, Martin and Petley, Julian (eds), *Ill Effects: The Media/Violence Debate*, 2nd edn. London: Routledge, pp. 170–85.

Piric, David 1973: *A Heritage of Horror: The English Gothic Cinema 1946–1972*. London: Gordon Frazer.

Planché, J.R. 1820: *The Vampyre; or, The Bride of the Isles: A Romantic Melo-drama, in Two Acts*. London: John Cumberland.

Poe, Edgar Allan 1977a: *Poems and Essays*. London: Everyman.

Poe, Edgar Allan 1977b: *Tales of Mystery and Imagination*. Introduction by Padraic Colum. London: Dent.

Popper, Karl 1972: *The Logic of Scientific Discovery*. London: Hutchinson.

Prawer, S.S. 1980: *Caligari's Children: The Film as Tale of Terror*. New York: Da Capo.

Prest, Thomas Preskett (James Malcolm Rymer) 1998: *Varney the Vampire; or, The Feast of Blood*, 3 vols. North Stratford, NH: Ayer.

Punter, David 1996: Problems of recollection and construction: Stephen King. In Sage, Victor and Smith, Allan Lloyd (eds), *Modern Gothic: A Reader*. Manchester: Manchester University Press, pp. 121–40.

Radcliffe, Ann 1968: *The Italian; or, The Confessional of the Black Penitants. A Romance*. Ed. Frederick Garber. Oxford: Oxford University Press.

Rank, Otto 1979: *The Double*. Ed. and trans. Harry Tucker, Jr. New York: New American Library.

Rawson, Claude 1992: 'Indians' and Irish: Montaigne, Swift and the cannibal question, *Modern Language Quarterly*, 53, 3, pp. 299–363.

Renan, Ernest 1970: *The Poetry of the Celtic Races, and Other Studies*. Trans. William G. Hutchinson. London: Kennikat Press.

Rice, Anne 1976: *Interview with the Vampire*. London: Futura.

Rice, Anne 1994: *The Vampire Lestat*. London: Warner.

Rickels. Laurence A. (1999) *The Vampire Lectures*. Minneapolis: University of Minnesota Press.

Rickman, Phil 1993: *Candlenight*. London: Pan.

Rigby, Jonathan 2000: *English Gothic: A Century of Horror Cinema*. London: Reynolds and Hearn.

Roberts, Marie 1990: *Gothic Immortals: The Fiction of the Brotherhood of the Rosy Cross*. London: Routledge.

Robinson, Charles E. 1975: Mary Shelley and the Roger Dodsworth hoax, *Keats-Shelley Journal*, 24, pp. 20–8.

Robson, Margaret 1992: Animal magic: moral regeneration in 'Sir Gowther', *Yearbook of English Studies*, 22, pp. 140–53.

Robson, Margaret 2000: From beyond the grave: darkness at noon in 'The Awntyrs off Arthure'. In Putter, Ad and Gilbert, Jane (eds), *The Spirit of Medieval English Popular Romance*. Harlow: Longman, pp. 219–36.

Rodley, Chris (ed.) 1997: *Cronenberg on Cronenberg*. London: Faber and Faber.

Rousseau, G.S. c.2002, forthcoming: The Geriatric Enlightenment. In Cope, Kevin (ed.), *1650–1850: Ideas, Aesthetics and Inquiries in the Early Modern Era*. New York: AMS Press.

Ryan, Alan (ed.) 1991: *The Penguin Book of Vampire Stories*. London: Bloomsbury.

Sade, Donatien Alphonse, Marquis de 1990: From 'Idée sur les romans'. In Sage, Victor (ed.), *The Gothick Novel: A Casebook*. Basingstoke: Macmillan, pp. 48–9.

Sadleir, Michael 1927: *The Northanger Novels*, English Association Pamphlets, No. 68.

Sagan, Carl 1997: *The Demon-Haunted World: Science as a Candle in the Dark*. London: Headline.

Sage, Victor 1988: *Horror Fiction in the Protestant Tradition*. Basingstoke: Macmillan.

Sage, Victor (ed.) 1990: *The Gothick Novel: A Casebook*. Basingstoke: Macmillan.

Scarry, Elaine 1985: *The Body in Pain: Making and Unmaking the World*. Oxford: Oxford University Press.

Schreck, Nikolas 2001: *The Satanic Screen: An Illustrated Guide to the Devil in Cinema*. London: Creation.

Schwartz, Hillel 1996: *The Culture of the Copy: Striking Likenesses, Unreasonable Facsimiles*. New York: Zone.

Sedgwick, Eve Kosofsky 1985: *Between Men: English Literature and Male Homosocial Desire*. New York: Columbia University Press.

Shelley, Mary 1976: *Collected Tales and Stories*. Ed. Charles E. Robinson. Baltimore: Johns Hopkins Press.

Shelley, Mary 1996: *Frankenstein*. Ed. J. Paul Hunter. New York: W.W. Norton.

Simon (ed.) 1980: *Necronomicon*. New York: Avon Books.

Skal, David J. 1990: *Hollywood Gothic: The Tangled Web of 'Dracula' from Stage to Screen*. London: Deutsch.

Skal, David J. 1994: *The Monster Show: A Cultural History of Horror*. London: Plexus.

Skal, David J. 1996: *V is for Vampire: An A–Z Guide to Everything Undead*. London: Robson.

Skal, David J. 1998: *Screams of Reason: Mad Science and Modern Culture*. New York: Norton.

Smeed, J.W. 1975: *Faust in Literature*. Oxford: Oxford University Press.

Southey, Robert 1838: *The Poetical Works of Robert Southey, Collected by Himself. In Ten Volumes*. London: Longman, Orme, Brown, Green, and Longman's.

Stanford, Peter 1996: *The Devil: A Biography*. London: Heinemann.

Stein, Elliott 1970: 'The Night of the Living Dead', *Sight and Sound*, 38, Spring, p. 105.

Stevenson, Robert Louis 1994: *The Strange Case of Dr Jekyll and Mr Hyde*. Harmondsworth: Penguin.

Stoker, Bram 1997: *Dracula*. Ed. Nina Auerbach and David J. Skal. New York and London: W.W. Norton.

Stuart, Roxana 1992: The eroticism of evil: the vampire in nineteenth-century melodrama. In Redmond, James (ed.) *Themes in Drama 14: Melodrama*. Cambridge: Cambridge University Press, pp. 223–44.

Sullivan, C.W. 1987: A wizard behind every bush, *Planet*, 64, August/September, pp. 48–51.

Summers, Montague 1980: *The Vampire in Europe*. Wellingborough: Aquarian Press.

Sutherland, John 1976: *Victorian Novelists and Publishers*. London: Athlone Press.

Sutherland, John 2000: *The Literary Detective: 100 Puzzles in Classic Fiction*. Oxford: Oxford University Press.

Swift, Jonathan 1976: *'Gulliver's Travels' and Other Writings*. Ed. Louis A. Landa. Oxford: Oxford University Press.

Symons, John 1973: *The Great Beast: The Life and Magick of Aleister Crowley*. St. Albans: Mayflower.

Tennyson, Alfred 1987: *The Poems of Tennyson*, volume 3. Ed. Christopher Ricks. London: Longman.

Thompson, E.P. 1993: *Witness Against the Beast: William Blake and the Moral Law*. Cambridge: Cambridge University Press.

Thorne, Tony 1999: *Children of the Night: Of Vampires and Vampirism*. London: Victor Gollancz.

Tristram, Philippa 1976: *Figures of Life and Death in Medieval English Literature*. London: Paul Elek.

Tudor, Andrew 1989: *Monsters and Mad Scientists: A Cultural History of the Horror Movie*. Oxford: Blackwell.

Twitchell, James B. 1981: *The Living Dead: A Study of the Vampire in Romantic Literature*. Durham, NC: Duke University Press.

Twitchell, James B. 1985: *'Dreadful Pleasures': An Anatomy of Modern Horror*. New York: Oxford University Press.

Underwood, Tim and Miller, Chuck (eds) 1988: *Bare Bones: Conversations with Stephen King*. New York: Warner.

Walker, John (ed.) 2000: *Halliwell's Film Guide 2001*. London: HarperCollins.

Walpole, Horace 1968: 'The Castle of Otranto'. In *Three Gothic Novels*, ed. Peter Fairclough with an introduction by Mario Praz. Harmondsworth: Penguin, pp. 37–148.

Warner, Maria 1995: *From the Beast to the Blonde: On Fairy Tales and their Tellers*. London: Vintage.

Watt, Ian 1957: *The Rise of the Novel*. London: Chatto and Windus.

Wells, H.G. 1995a: *The Invisible Man*. London: Dent.

Wells, H.G. 1995b: *The Science Fiction*, volume 1. London: Phoenix.

Wolf, Naomi 1991: *The Beauty Myth: How Images of Beauty are Used Against Women*. New York: William Morrow.

Wollstonecraft, Mary 1976: *'Mary' and 'The Wrongs of Woman'*. Ed. Gary Kelly. Oxford: Oxford University Press.

Wood, Robin 1987: Returning the look: 'Eyes of a Stranger'. In Waller, Gregory A. (ed.), *American Horrors: Essays on the Modern American Horror Film*. Urbana and Chicago: University of Illinois Press, pp. 79–85.

Wordsworth, William 1977: *The Poems*, 2 volumes. Ed. John O. Hayden. Harmondsworth: Penguin.

Wordsworth, William and Coleridge, Samuel Taylor 1991: *Lyrical Ballads*. Ed. R.L. Brett and A.R. Jones. London: Routledge.

Yeats, W.B. 1982: *The Collected Poems of W.B. Yeats*. Basingstoke: Macmillan.

Filmography

Abbot and Costello Meet Frankenstein, dir. Charles Barton (1948)
Alligator, dir. Lewis Teague (1980)
American Nightmare, dir. Adam Simon (2000)
American Psycho, dir. Mary Harron (2000)
An American Werewolf in London, dir. John Landis (1981)
The Andromeda Strain, dir. Michael Crichton (1971)
Angel Heart, dir. Alan Parker (1987)
The Ape Man, dir. William Beaudine (1943)
Attack of the Crab Monsters, dir. Roger Corman (1957)
Bad Taste, dir. Peter Jackson (1987)
Basket Case, dir. Frank Henenlotter (1982)
The Beast with Five Fingers, dir. Robert Florey (1947)
The Black Cat, dir. Edgar G. Ulmer (1934)
Black Christmas, dir. Bob Clark (1973)
Blade, dir. Stephen Norrington (1998)
The Blair Witch Project, dir. Daniel Meyrick and Eduardo Sanchez (1999)
Body Snatchers, dir. Abel Ferrara (1994)
The Bogey Man, dir. Ulli Lommel (1980)
The Boys from Brazil, dir. Franklin J. Schaffner (1978)
Bram Stoker's Dracula, dir. Francis Ford Coppola (1992)
The Bride of Frankenstein, dir. James Whale (1935)
Brides of Dracula, dir. Terence Fisher (1960)
The Brood, dir. David Cronenberg (1979)
Bug, dir. Jeannot Szwarc (1975)
The Burning, dir. Tony Maylam (1980)
Le Cabinet de Méphistophélès, dir. Georges Méliès (1897)
The Cabinet of Dr Caligari, dir. Robert Wiene (1919)
Cake-Walk Infernal, dir. Georges Méliès (1903)
Candyman, dir. Bernard Rose (1992)
Cannibal Ferox, dir. Umberto Lenzi (1981)
Cannibal Holocaust, dir. Ruggero Deodato (1979)
Cannibal – The Musical, dir. Trey Parker (1995)
The Car, dir. Elliot Silverstein (1977)
Cat People, dir. Jacques Tourneur (1942)

Cat People, dir. Paul Schrader (1982)
Child's Play 3, dir. Jack Bender (1991)
Crash, dir. David Cronenberg (1996)
The Curse of Frankenstein, dir. Terence Fisher (1956)
Curse of the Werewolf, dir. Terence Fisher (1961)
Damien: Omen II, dir. Don Taylor (1978)
Damnation de Faust, dir. Georges Méliès (1898)
Damnation du Docteur Faust, dir. Georges Méliès (1904)
Dawn of the Dead, dir. George A. Romero (1979)
Day of the Dead, dir. George A. Romero (1979)
The Day the Earth Stood Still, dir. Robert Wise (1951)
Dead Ringers, dir. David Cronenberg (1988)
Death Trap, dir. Tobe Hooper (1976)
Deep River Savages, dir. Umberto Lenzi (1972)
Deliverance, dir. John Boorman (1972)
Demon Seed, dir. Donald Cammell (1975)
Deranged: The Confessions of a Necrophile, dir. Jeff Gillen and Alan
   Ormsby (1974)
The Devil in Miss Jones, dir. Gerard Damiano (1972)
The Devil Rides Out, dir. Terence Fisher (1967)
The Devil's Advocate, dir. Taylor Hackford (1997)
Le Diable au Couvent, dir. Georges Méliès (1898)
Dr Jekyll and Mr. Hyde, dir. Rouben Mamoulian (1932)
Dr Jekyll and Sister Hyde, dir. Roy Ward Baker (1971)
Dr Renault's Secret, dir. Harry Lachman (1942)
Dr Strangelove or: How I Learned to Stop Worrying and Love the Bomb,
   dir. Stanley Kubrick (1964)
Dr X, dir. Michael Curtiz (1932)
Dracula, dir. Tod Browning (1931)
Dracula, dir. Terence Fisher (1957)
Dracula, dir. John Badham (1979)
Dracula Has Risen From the Grave, dir. Freddie Francis (1968)
Dracula – Prince of Darkness, dir. Terence Fisher (1966)
Dreamscape, dir. Joseph Ruben (1984)
Dressed to Kill, dir. Brian de Palma (1980)
The Driller Killer, dir. Abel Ferrara (1979)
The Dunwich Horror, dir. Daniel Haller (1970)
Eaten Alive, dir. Umberto Lenzi (1980)
Ed Gein, dir. Chuck Parello (2000)
Edward Scissorhands, dir. Tim Burton (1990)
End of Days, dir. Peter Hyams (1999)
The Evil of Frankenstein, dir. Freddie Francis (1963)
eXistenZ, dir. David Cronenberg (1999)
The Exorcist, dir. William Friedkin (1973)
The Fall of the House of Usher, dir. Roger Corman (1960)

Fallen, dir. Gregory Hoblit (1998)
Faust et Marguerite, dir. Georges Méliès (1898)
Fight Club, dir. David Fincher (1999)
Les Filles du Diable, dir. Georges Méliès (1903)
The Fly, dir. Kurt Neumann (1958)
The Fly, dir. David Cronenberg (1986)
The Fog, dir. John Carpenter (1980)
Food of the Gods, dir. Bert I. Gordon (1976)
Frankenstein, dir. J. Searle Dawney (1910)
Frankenstein, dir. James Whale (1931)
Frankenstein Created Woman, dir. Terence Fisher (1966)
Frankenstein Meets the Wolf Man, dir. Roy William Neill (1943)
Frankenstein and the Monster from Hell, dir. Terence Fisher (1972)
Frankenstein Must Be Destroyed, dir. Terence Fisher (1969)
Frankenstein: The True Story, dir. Jack Smight (1972)
Frenzy, dir. Alfred Hitchcock (1973)
Friday the 13th, dir. Sean S. Cunningham (1980)
Fright Night, dir. Tom Holland (1985)
From Dusk Till Dawn, dir. Robert Rodriguez (1996)
From Hell, dir. The Hughes Brothers (2001)
Gods and Monsters, dir. Bill Condon (1998)
Godzilla, King of the Monsters, dir. Inoshiro Honda (1955)
The Golem, dir. Paul Wegener (1920)
Halloween, dir. John Carpenter (1978)
Halloween II, dir. Rick Rosenthal (1981)
Halloween H20, dir. Steve Miner (1997)
Hannibal, dir. Ridley Scott (2001)
The Haunted Palace, dir. Roger Corman (1963)
Häxan, dir. Benjamin Christensen (1921)
Hellraiser, dir. Clive Barker (1987)
The Hills Have Eyes, dir. Wes Craven (1978)
The Horror of Frankenstein, dir. Jimmy Sangster (1970)
House of America, dir. Marc Evans (1997)
The Howling, dir. Joe Dante (1981)
The Hunger, dir. Tony Scott (1983)
I Aim at the Stars, dir. J. Lee Thompson (1959)
I Know What You Did Last Summer, dir. Jim Gillespie (1997)
I Spit on Your Grave, dir. Meir Zarchi (1978)
I Walked With a Zombie, dir. Jacques Tourneur (1943)
Ilsa, She Wolf of the SS, dir. Don Edmonds (1974)
The Incredible Shrinking Man, dir. Jack Arnold (1957)
Independence Day, dir. Roland Emmerich (1996)
Invaders From Mars, dir. William Cameron Menzies (1953)
Invasion of the Body Snatchers, dir. Don Siegel (1956)
Invasion of the Body Snatchers, dir. Philip Kaufman (1978)

The Island of Dr Moreau, dir. John Frankenheimer (1996)
The Island of Lost Souls, dir. Erle C. Kenton (1933)
Island of Terror, dir. Terence Fisher (1966)
It Came From Outer Space, dir. Jack Arnold (1953)
The Jungle Captive, dir. Harold Young (1945)
Jurassic Park, dir. Steven Spielberg (1993)
Killers From Space, dir. W. Lee Wilder (1954)
King Kong, dir. Merian C. Cooper and Ernest B. Schoedsack (1933)
The Last House on the Left, dir. Wes Craven (1972)
The Lost Boys, dir. Joel Schumacher (1987)
The Lost Continent, dir. Michael Carreras (1968)
Love at First Bite, dir. Stan Dragoti (1979)
Lust for a Vampire, dir. Jimmy Sangster (1970)
Mad Love, dir. Karl Freund (1935)
The Man from Planet X, dir. Edgar Ulmer (1951)
Manhunter, dir. Michael Mann (1986)
Man Made Monster, dir. George Waggner (1941)
Le Manoir du Diable, dir. Georges Méliès (1896)
Mark of the Vampire, dir. Tod Browning (1935)
Martin, dir. George A. Romero (1976)
Mary Shelley's Frankenstein, dir. Kenneth Branagh (1994)
The Masque of the Red Death, dir. Roger Corman (1964)
The Matrix, dir. the Wachowski Brothers (1999)
Metropolis, dir. Fritz Lang (1927)
Mimic, dir. Guillermo del Toro (1997)
Mr. Frost, dir. Phillip Setbon (1990)
Murders in the Rue Morgue, dir. Robert Florey (1932)
The Naked Lunch, dir. David Cronenberg (1991)
Near Dark, dir. Kathryn Bigelow (1987)
Necronomicon, dir. Brian Yuzna *et al.* (1994)
Night of the Demon, dir. Jacques Tourneur (1958)
Night of the Eagle, dir. Sidney Hayers (1961)
Night of the Lepus, dir. William F. Claxton (1972)
Night of the Living Dead, dir. George A. Romero (1968)
Night of the Living Dead, dir. Tom Savini (1990)
Nightbreed, dir. Clive Barker (1990)
Nightmare City, dir. Umberto Lenzi (1980)
A Nightmare on Elm Street, dir. Wes Craven (1984)
The Ninth Gate, dir. Roman Polanski (1999)
Nosferatu: Ein Symphonie Des Grauens, dir. F.W. Murnau (1922)
Nosferatu: Phantom der Nacht, dir. Werner Herzog (1979)
The Old Dark House, dir. James Whale (1932)
The Omega Man, dir. Boris Sagal (1971)
The Omen, dir. Richard Donner (1976)
Omen III: The Final Conflict, dir. Graham Baker (1981)

Outbreak, dir. Wolfgang Petersen (1995)
Peeping Tom, dir. Michael Powell (1960)
Phantasm, dir. Don Coscarelli (1979)
Phantom From Space, dir. W. Lee Wilder (1953)
Piranha, dir. Joe Dante (1978)
The Pit and the Pendulum, dir. Roger Corman (1961)
Plague of the Zombies, dir. John Gilling (1966)
Planet of the Apes, dir. Franklin J. Schaffner (1968)
Poltergeist, dir. Tobe Hooper (1982)
Prince of Darkness, dir. John Carpenter (1987)
Prisoner of the Cannibal God, dir. Sergio Martino (1979)
Prom Night, dir. Paul Lynch (1980)
Psycho, dir. Alfred Hitchcock (1960)
The Quatermass Experiment, dir. Val Guest (1955)
Quatre Cent Farces du Diable, dir. Georges Méliès (1906)
Rabid, dir. David Cronenberg (1976)
Race With the Devil, dir. Jack Starrett (1975)
Raising Cain, dir. Brian De Palma (1992)
The Raven, dir. Lew Landers (1935)
The Raven, dir. Roger Corman (1962)
Ravenous, dir. Antonia Bird (1999)
Re-Animator, dir. Stuart Gordon (1985)
Rear Window, dir. Alfred Hitchcock (1954)
Red Planet Mars, dir. Harry Horner (1952)
Return of the Vampire, dir. Lew Landers (1943)
The Revenge of Frankenstein, dir. Terence Fisher (1958)
Ring, dir. Nakada Hideo (1999)
Robocop, dir. Paul Verhoeven (1987)
The Rocky Horror Picture Show, dir. Jim Sharman (1977)
Rosemary's Baby, dir. Roman Polanski (1968)
'Salem's Lot, dir. Tobe Hooper (1979)
Scanners, dir. David Cronenberg (1980)
Scream, dir. Wes Craven (1996)
Scream 2, dir. Wes Craven (1997)
Scream 3, dir. Wes Craven (2000)
The Serpent and the Rainbow, dir. Wes Craven (1987)
Se7en, dir. David Fincher (1995)
The Seventh Victim, dir. Mark Robson (1943)
Shadow of the Vampire, dir. E. Elias Merhige (2000)
The Shining, dir. Stanley Kubrick (1980)
Shivers, dir. David Cronenberg (1975)
The Silence of the Lambs, dir. Jonathan Demme (1991)
Sisters, dir. Brian De Palma (1973)
Sleepy Hollow, dir. Tim Burton (1999)
Son of Frankenstein, dir. Rowland V. Lee (1939)

Southern Comfort, dir. Walter Hill (1981)
Soylent Green, dir. Richard Fleischer (1973)
Star Wars, dir. George Lucas (1977)
The Stepford Wives, dir. Bryan Forbes (1975)
Stigmata, dir. Rupert Wainwright (1999)
Strange Days, dir. Kathryn Bigelow (1995)
Tales of Terror, dir. Roger Corman (1961)
Tarantula, dir. Jack Arnold (1955)
Targets, dir. Peter Bogdanovich (1968)
Taste the Blood of Dracula, dir. Peter Sasdy (1969)
The Terminator, dir. James Cameron (1984)
Terminator 2: Judgement Day, dir. James Cameron (1991)
Terror Train, dir. Roger Spottiswoode (1980)
Tetsuo: The Iron Man, dir. Shinya Tsukamoto (1988)
The Texas Chain Saw Massacre, dir. Tobe Hooper (1974)
Them!, dir. Jack Arnold (1954)
The Thing, dir. Christian Nyby (1951)
The Thing, dir. John Carpenter (1982)
This Island Earth, dir. Joseph Newman (1955)
To the Devil a Daughter, dir. Peter Sykes (1975)
The Tomb of Ligeia, dir. Roger Corman (1964)
Twins of Evil, dir. John Hough (1971)
The Usual Suspects, dir. Bryan Singer (1995)
Vamp, dir. Richard Wenk (1986)
The Vampire Lovers, dir. Roy Ward Baker (1970)
Vampires, dir. John Carpenter (1997)
Vampyr, dir. Carl Dreyer (1932)
Videodrome, dir. David Cronenberg (1982)
Village of the Damned, dir. Wolf Rilla (1960)
War of the Worlds, dir. George Pal (1953)
The Werewolf of London, dir. Stuart Walker (1935)
Wes Craven's New Nightmare, dir. Wes Craven (1994)
White Zombie, dir. Victor Halperin (1932)
The Wicker Man, dir. Robin Hardy (1973)
The Witches of Eastwick, dir. George Miller (1987)
Witchfinder General, dir. Michael Reeves (1968)
Wolfen, dir. Michael Wadleigh (1981)
The Wolf Man, dir. George Waggner (1941)
Zombie Flesh Eaters, dir. Lucio Fulci (1979)

Index